LEADERSH!T

A Look at the Broken Leadership System in Corporate America That Accepts Leaders Who are Really Good at Being Bad

BY RANDE SOMMA

Published by BookLocker.com, Inc., St. Petersburg, Florida.

Printed on acid-free paper.

BookLocker.com, Inc.
2017

First Edition

DISCLAIMER

This book details the author's personal experiences with, and opinions about, today's executive leadership system and culture in America's businesses. The author is not a licensed financial consultant.

The author and publisher are providing this book and its contents on an "as is" basis and make no representations or warranties of any kind with respect to this book or its contents. The author and publisher disclaim all such representations and warranties, including for example warranties of merchantability and financial advice for a particular purpose. In addition, the author and publisher do not represent or warrant that the information accessible via this book is accurate, complete or current.

The statements made about products and services have not been evaluated by the U.S. government. Please consult with your own Certified Public Accountant or financial services professional regarding the suggestions and recommendations made in this book.

Except as specifically stated in this book, neither the author or publisher, nor any authors, contributors, or other representatives will be liable for damages arising out of or in connection with the use of this book. This is a comprehensive limitation of liability that applies to all damages of any kind, including (without limitation) compensatory; direct, indirect or consequential damages; loss of data, income or profit; loss of or damage to property and claims of third parties.

You understand that this book is not intended as a substitute for consultation with a licensed financial professional. Before you begin any financial program, or change your lifestyle in any way, you will consult a licensed financial professional to ensure that you are doing what's best for your financial condition.

This book provides content related to topics finances and economic living. As such, use of this book implies your acceptance of this disclaimer.

DEDICATION

To Georgia...loving wife, best friend, and trusted mentor. Lucky me.

To Scott and Adam... nothing you do will ever make me more proud of the quality people that you are.

ACKNOWLEDGEMENT

I would like to express appreciation to Mary O'Donnell Meldrum for her contribution. Only with her exceptional talent and personal support for the message did this book become a reality.

To my good friend, Nate; I am grateful for your contributions, support and encouragement. You've got a gift.

To my unsuspecting mentors in Pittsburgh, Pennsylvania, Reading, Pennsylvania, Winchester, Kentucky, Marysville, Ohio, and Detroit. Through your words and deeds, I observed and learned that the best of the best leaders have three things in common; character, compassion and humility. It was what I did my best to emulate when it was my turn to lead.

Thanks to Dr. Thomas Cappas and Dr. Mary Weatherston for helping me process, understand and move on with the unexpected emotional injuries from refusing to sell out.

"Talent and character emerge not when you decide what you are willing to do. They emerge when you decide what - under any circumstances - you are absolutely not willing to do."

-- Rande Somma

TABLE OF CONTENTS

FOREWORD

At first glance this book's title may lead you to believe it will be a comical look at the role of leadership, something I am sure we all have observed in our own careers, often with a mix of disbelief and resignation. The cover could also suggest a humorous poke at bad bosses and the messes they tend to leave behind. While some of what you find here will seem almost like a corporate version of Keystone Cops, under it all lays a narrative about a serious and disturbing truth that is unfolding in companies both large and small; a truth that is rarely discussed openly or with any real objectivity. This book springs from one man's collision with that truth.

I met Rande Somma in 1997, at the time automotive supplier Prince Corporation was being readied for sale after the untimely death of its namesake, Ed Prince. Mr. Prince was an amazing man with an uncanny ability to connect vision to the realities of everyday business. Even more impressive was his ability to lead with integrity while at the same time running a business within the challenging and often dark context of the automotive world. After Johnson Controls (JCI) acquired Prince Corporation, Rande was designated as the JCI executive in charge of the integration of the two companies. I was the Vice-President of the Design team at the time and as such was selected to show off our studios and help guide the JCI team through our word-class technical center in Holland, Michigan. From that first walk together, Rande and I began a vibrant relationship that is still active today.

Rande was to become President of Johnson Controls' North American Automotive Operations within the year. He became my boss, taking care to always push, temper and encourage my own ability to lead. His entire team benefited from Rande's unflinching commitment to absolute integrity, authenticity and performance.

In 2000, I left JCI to start my own company; Rande left three years later. After that both of us would go through some very dark days as professionals, times that were shaped as a result of one word…. *Leadershit*. So rather than simply evoking humor, the cover of this book surrounds lessons from Rande's journey. In the years since his leadership of the JCI team, many of us have encouraged (begged) Rande to write his story for the benefit of us all. Although the book chronicles his own coming to terms with the realities of leadership at the highest levels, in frank and blunt terms, it is designed to encourage the reader to take up his challenge; to lead out of a place of selflessness and soul. Rande's words implore us all to emerge as leaders worthy of following.

Nate Young
Senior Vice President
Design and Innovation
Newell Brands
NewellRubbermaid Inc

INTRODUCTION

I grew up in a small home in Pittsburgh; a very average student; the son of a waiter and waitress -- two high school dropouts -- with a certain viewpoint that this personal history affords me. But I am a guy who has been to both ends of a spectrum.

Going from a young boy in the Burgh to running a $20 billion global operation, being a Corporate Officer of a Fortune 100 company, Chairman of a Corporate Board, Vice Chair of a Corporate Board, and a Director on three other boards – for profit and nonprofit, big ones and not so big ones – I have seen some things that deeply trouble me and I have something that I feel needs to be said.

Although I did not directly work for an automaker, as President of Johnson Controls Automotive Worldwide, I had a front row ringside seat as a Tier 1 supplier to the U.S. and international automakers at a pivotal time in the industry's history. Sometimes all that was missing was the bag of popcorn.

I have witnessed fraud, greed, corruption and choosing convenience over obligations even when lives were literally at stake. I observed a disgusting disregard for commitments made and not fulfilled, and it affected the livelihoods of innocent hard-working people who depended on those commitments.

I first thought that the auto industry was the problem. But when I got a wider view and more experience outside of that industry, I realized that they are simply an example of a bigger problem. It wasn't just these auto guys having a bad day or a bad week or year. I saw it repeated in other companies, other industries, other leadership situations. I realized that they were all following a system that doesn't serve us anymore, and therefore, it is the system that is the problem.

Understanding the impact of this insane system is difficult, but we have all in some way been stung by it either directly or indirectly. Big business in America is the engine at the top of the food chain of the economy, and leaders of these big corporations determine its course. Some of these people are screwing up the economy and taking huge profits from it. The vast majority of that money, their so-called compensation, or what I would call legalized larceny, belongs to the business. That money is supposed to be reinvested in the people and the necessary resources that generate legitimate short term, and more importantly, sustainable long term success. And, as a result, the communities that the businesses operate in will thrive.

Part of the impetus for writing this book comes directly from a conversation that I had with a student named Patrick some years ago about integrity. He knew my story, my views on the state of corporate leadership, which you will read about in these pages, and he wondered, "Do you ever feel lonely?"

That question has been percolating in my mind ever since. It means something deeply personal, from which this book has grown and taken shape.

Although I remember all too well the names of the companies and leaders that go with these stories, they are not all germane to the point of this book and have mostly been redacted. This work reflects my considered opinions about systemic problems, and only my opinions, but they are based on a long history as a corporate insider. And outsider.

This book is about a leadership system that is broken. I believe we have all seen evidence of this broken system. It can't be fixed with a tweak or a law or another regulation. Anything less than a complete intervention and reinvention will only amount to roasting marshmallows on the Hindenburg as it goes down in flames. This will seriously take a huge transformational change.

CHAPTER 1
THAT AIN'T THE WAY I SEE IT
ASSAULT ON THE DICTIONARY

JCI and Me-

I went to work for Johnson Controls in 1988 as the manager heading up the sales team that called on Chrysler Group. Johnson Controls Automotive was then one of the largest automotive interior companies in the world. We were selling to all the car manufacturers around the globe. Our primary product was the seat systems, but in addition to that, there were interior systems, electronic products, instrument panels, and overhead systems.

I was happy to be employed by this global player and engaged in doing a good job for them, and for myself and my family.

I was eventually promoted to run the sales teams for Chrysler, GM and Ford, and then promoted to Director of Sales of North America. From there, I was made Vice President of Sales and Marketing and Strategic Planning Worldwide. In 1998, I was once again promoted to President of North American Operations and then elected to a Corporate Officer position, which meant there were a whole lot more ways that I could go to prison.

I was moving right along on the corporate ladder, and what came along with that upward mobility were some weighty, serious responsibilities and the need for more diligence and intense scrutiny of our automotive operations.

Do Something Special

When I took on the title of North American Operations, Automotive in 1997, management asked me and my team to consider if our performance objectives were too conservative. Our assignment was to determine if it was legitimate to expect more from ourselves.

At the time, we were coming off of a very good year, but we were asked whether or not we set our ceiling too low. Were we capable of doing much more? If so, what action(s) could be implemented to achieve it?

We were working with a consulting company at the time, and JCI was a level three company in terms of performance (which was good). The consultant was showing us indicators of a few level one companies (which was better) and what they were achieving (which was all financial). It was all about the numbers. They could see that we had a lot of level one capability already in place, but showed us that, in order to make level one a real possibility for our company, some things would have to change. They asked if we wanted to make the effort and take the risk.

My team and I said yes, because we believed that we had the real potential of moving from good to something far better. We just had to figure out how to reinvent our operating model.

I wanted our initial meeting about taking on this challenge to involve something different and impactful for my team, so I asked my Director of Communications, "Give me something that we can take back after this meeting. Don't spend a lot of money, but make it something you don't stick into a drawer." I wanted this to be a small gift that would be a constant presence and a reminder for each team member as we cut a new path for the company.

The result was a colorful glass globe paperweight with the inscription, *"Do Something Special."*

Later at the meeting, I looked at the white board, and was faced with the enormity of the challenge, but also the enormity of possibilities. It represented freedom to create the "thing" that was going to catapult us into a great company.

I didn't say what everyone expected me to say. Typically, in brainstorming sessions, we would list out what needs to happen for us to move from here to there. For reasons I cannot explain, my first question to the team was **not** "*what do we need to do to meet that new level of performance?*" My first question was, "What **WON'T** we do?" It was counter-intuitive. Who knew that it would be the spark that launched us forward in the most unexpected way?

That day, we discussed setting boundaries and came up with a list of things that we, as leaders in this endeavor, would ***not do*** in our efforts to reach our goals. My team adhered to the new standard through some very difficult times. What we would ***not do*** included:

1. Lay off people in order to hit financial targets
2. Redirect strategic plan investments to the immediate bottom line
3. Increase dependency on creative accounting
4. Treat employee expectations as subordinate to those of customers and shareholders
5. Behave as if "living our values" is discretionary
6. Motivate with intimidation
7. Rationalize that the ends justifies the means
8. Manipulate and misrepresent actual performance data
9. Act entitled to unearned support, loyalty and compliance
10. Disregard the company's code of ethics to suit our convenience

In today's leadershit system, this list represents things that are routinely done in order to achieve short term goals. In far too many cases, these tactics are in direct violation of the organization's published core values, and often erode long term gains for the company in favor of short term fixes that masquerade as progress.

When I had the glass paperweights made, I thought our *"something special"* would be attaining the financial goal, the numbers that would move us to level one status. That was the original focus and the purpose of the entire challenge. I had no idea at the time that the *"something special"* would result in far exceeding our financial goals and producing extraordinary outcomes on every business front that we touched: customers, revenue, earnings, vendors, our own people, and industry-wide recognition, to name a few.

"Talent and character emerge not when you decide what you are willing to do. They emerge when you decide what – under any circumstances – you are absolutely not willing to do." – Rande Somma

Defining What is Really Important

When I took over North American Operations at Johnson Controls Automotive, I quickly learned -- and I still believe to this day – that there was so much more importance in *how* things were accomplished than the accomplishment itself. That may be a difficult concept to grasp. I am not saying that the results are not important. I am saying that the method of *how* you achieve them is also important. Actually, more important.

At certain times in my career, I was surprised to discover leaders who did not believe this, and that, for some, it didn't matter at all. To them, results measured by numbers alone were the only thing that mattered and the ends justified the means. And the means were sometimes very, very ugly.

Leaders in History – The Good, the Bad and the Unicorns

A leader is a person commissioned by a number of people and charged with the duty to serve and better the circumstances for the whole of a group. They are supposed to work for the *people* who have directly or indirectly put them in power. A leader's job is to lead *people*. History has delivered us many people who carved out a strong definition of leadership. We have seen our share of bad leaders and authentic leaders, and everything in between. For the sake of clarity, I would like to offer some of the personal definitions that I apply to these categories of leaders.

I think we can all agree that a bad leader is someone who lacks the character, integrity, or competencies needed to engage followers and master the position; someone who might be lazy or under-qualified and who doesn't plan ahead to avoid pitfalls or to create growth and opportunities. They might be someone who has hit their Peter's Principle ceiling and doesn't realize or want to admit that they are no longer qualified for the leadership position that has outgrown them. I call bad leaders knockoffs.

Knockoff leaders might be in it for the money, celebrity or power rather than to advance the people/company that hired or elected them. They get fired or pull the pin and make sure they are sipping mint juleps under a palm tree hundreds of miles away before the grenade detonates on Wall Street. Yeah, we've seen this guy more than a few times.

Authentic leaders, on the other hand, have qualities such as perseverance, insight, vision and a passion for getting it right. While we all possess many of these qualities in varying degrees, authentic leaders acquire them in quantities beyond what is found in most men and women, through experience and/or academia, and know how to apply them in difficult situations. Sometimes they have the ability to humbly surround themselves with the right people who can supplement their skill sets. They can be counted on to be successful in the execution of their duties with a laser focus on both long and short term results.

Although I am coming at this subject from a different angle, I don't stand alone in my observations. Characteristics of great leaders have been researched and authored by many journalists and scholars, such as Joseph

C. Santora, School of Business and Management, Thomas Edison State College, Trenton, New Jersey and James C. Sarros, professor of Management, Monash University, Victoria, Australia.[1]

Their study findings in the Ivey Business Journal in an article called The Character of Leadership are in alignment with my front line experience. Those characteristics that have proven to have strategic advantage for leaders include integrity, respectfulness, passion, self-discipline, fairness, cooperation, loyalty, communication, compassion and humility. These, combined with unwavering ambition, solid core competencies, and the ability to learn from mistakes, season a leader into a great and authentic leader.

Authentic leaders are gifted with character qualities beyond their resumes. These are not learned in a textbook. They are internalized hardwired traits. They include empathy, sincerity, charisma, integrity, and a blind commitment to the assigned mission and values that does not allow self-interest to trump obligation. They add value to the group/company that they are leading. They are not unicorns. They exist.

This is exactly the leadership that all companies need, and unfortunately, what many companies today are really *not* looking for. They all say that they are, but most of them are full of shit.

The bottom line: for many leaders today, there is often a difference between what they say and what they mean or do, hence, the difference between the knockoffs who "talk the talk" and the authentic leaders who "walk the talk."

---

[1] http://iveybusinessjournal.com/publication/the-character-of-leadership/

Drilling Down on the Meanings

Traditional meanings of right and wrong:

RIGHT

[rahyt] adjective

1. in accordance with what is good, proper, or just: *right conduct.*
2. in conformity with fact, reason, truth, or some standard or principle; correct: *the right solution; the right answer.*
3. correct in judgment, opinion, or action.

WRONG

[rong] [rawng] adjective

1. not in accordance with what is morally right or good: *a wrong deed.*
2. deviating from truth or fact; erroneous: *a wrong answer.*
3. not correct in action, judgment, opinion, method, etc., as a person; in error: *You are wrong to blame him.*

Non-traditional meanings of right and wrong:

There used to be just two options – right or wrong. Now there are three. Now you can be:

1. Right or
2. Wrong or
3. Wrong, but acceptable and convenient. Let's do lunch.

JAGOFF

[jag-off] noun

1. A term that originated in Pittsburgh meaning an asshole-like person.
2. An asshole.

KENNYWOOD'S OPEN

1. A term that originated in Pittsburgh meaning your fly is open.

CAN A CORN

1. A term that originated in Pittsburgh meaning something is easy.

CULTURE

[kul-cher]

There is no one apparent popular definition of culture, but most definitions talk about values. I believe culture is more about actions than values or beliefs or philosophies. Culture is formed by consistent reinforcement of what is appropriate and expected behavior in a designated environment or community. That behavior can be consistent or inconsistent with the stated values and beliefs of that same community.

LEADER

[lee-der] noun

1. A person or thing that leads.

2. A guiding or directing head, as of an army, movement, or political group.

AUTHENTIC LEADER

[aw-then-tik]

1. Personally worthy
2. Professionally qualified

KNOCKOFF LEADER

[nok-off]

1. *Cheap or inferior copy of something*

2. *Opposite of authentic (see above)*

BUSINESS REALITY

Business reality is a description of the reality of today's business environment. Unfortunately, this is where an enormous discrepancy happens in corporate settings. The discrepancy between the way things should be, and the way they really are. Let's apply this definition to some other business concepts:

INNOVATION
[in-*uh*-vey-sh*uh* n] noun
1. Something new or different introduced.
2. The act of innovating; introduction of new things or methods.

The Business Reality – While innovation is a critical aspect of a truly successful company, it is also hollow vernacular frequently used on company websites and marketing materials to describe the mission, vision and core values. Often there is little to no innovation going on at all. The word is there because it sounds good and it would be conspicuous if it were absent. In other words, it's bullshit.

STRATEGIC PLAN

[str*uh*-tee-jik] [plan]

1. An organization's process of defining its strategy or direction, and making decisions on allocating its resources to pursue it. May

include control mechanisms for guiding the implementation of the strategy.

2. A systematic process envisioning a desired future, and translating this vision into broadly defined goals or objectives and a sequence of steps to achieve them.

Strategic planning is an essential responsibility of any CEO. It is represented on most websites, in annual reports and in all PR collateral. It is a predominant factor in the hiring of and performance review criteria for virtually every CEO.

The strategic plan typically begins with a vision and aspirations of where the company wants to be longer term – typically a 5-year horizon. Based on those aspirations, it is an actionable and measureable plan that establishes a detailed roadmap for the essential changes to be generated. Progression of the plan is a critical responsibility owned almost exclusively by the CEO and the board of directors.

The Business Reality - As high profile as the strategic planning leadership function is, too often it is all talk and no walk. Having a strategic plan props up a glowing image of the company, and if it was missing, someone might notice. Since this is a future-focused item, it is frequently a low priority for leadershit, who are focused on their short term gains and personal goals.

I have experienced some tough conversations with CEOs who, it appeared, would rather have diseased coyotes eat off their limbs than establish the strategic vision, an associated plan, and be held accountable for managing its progress. Even when a CEO takes the time to pen a strategic plan and hand it in like homework, many times it is only "box-checking," and there is no real energy dedicated to implementation or to preservation of investment in the future. At the same time, when it became the board's turn to insist on compliance, what you pretty much hear is the sound of crickets. If a board member persists in challenging the CEO, it is only a matter of time before he/she gets their shiny plaque on their way out the door. It is not just the CEO who participates in leadershit.

One thing to note is that both innovation and strategic plans are long term propositions that require short term investment. They both have some associated risk and a long term return on investment. With the average tenure of a CEO being three to five years, this flies right in the face of the compensation model that pays out only on short term results. More on that to come.

CORE VALUES

[kawr, kohr] [val-yoos]

1. Principles that guide an organization's internal conduct as well as its relationship with the external world. Core values are usually summarized in the mission statement or in a statement of core values.
2. Principles or standards of behavior; judgment of what is important in life.

Core values are published by organizations, often right up on their websites for all to see. They establish what an organization believes and is committed to as it conducts its business. They define what is appropriate and acceptable. They also define what is unacceptable and will not be tolerated.

Core values act to firewall decision making from available but unacceptable options and therefore, toward better, more legitimate answers.

The Business Reality – Psychologically pleasing concept *implying* that because these things are listed and appear to have value, they will not be violated in the process of decision making, conducting business and managing the organization. In fact, core values will be violated if they stand in the way of making easier decisions in the interest of convenience, comfort, personal gain and short term benefit.

So as to mitigate any feelings of the disgraceful irresponsibility of such decisions, the following phrases were invented:

- "If you are not cheating, you are not trying"
- "You gotta do what you gotta do"
- "It's just business"
- "The ends justify the means"
- "I'm not here to make friends, I'm here to make money"

Many companies include integrity as one of their core values. How in the world can they value integrity if what they advertise as their values is a bunch of bullshit?

SUCCESS

[*suh* k-ses] noun

1. Achievement of something desired, planned or attempted.
2. The favorable or prosperous termination of attempts or endeavors; the accomplishment of one's goals.

The *Ideal Business Reality* – True success in business is marked by:

- Consistently meeting all stakeholders' expectations
- Authentic leadership
- Quality people, a healthy culture
- Effective systems & processes
- Extraordinary execution
- Guided by the core values
- Long and short term objectives legitimately achieved
- Credible and sustainable results

This definition of success includes the "how," therefore establishing credibility and sustainability. It represents the vitality of the business fundamentals and not the proficiency of manipulating the numbers and the audience, which is what happens in so many organizations today.

Business Reality – success means that it meets stakeholders' expectations by generating results benefitting the short term objectives at the expense of credible, sustainable corporate health.

The stakeholders that I am referring to, in the order of *Ideal Priority*:

1. People
2. Customers
3. Shareholders
4. Suppliers/partners   Really this is often a five-way tie for second
5. Community   place.
6. Environment

That same stakeholders list in order of priority for success under today's *Business Reality*:

1. Shareholders (Financials and primary metric for calculating executive bonuses)
2. Customers
3. People
4. Suppliers/partners   Really another five-way tie for second place.
5. Community
6. Environment

So while they all say "People are the organization's most important asset and therefore its #1 core value," here is a list of the low hanging fruit most CEOs go to when there are profit concerns, in no particular order:

1. Cut pay
2. Reduce benefits
3. Freeze earned merit/performance increases
4. Freeze or discount earned bonus payments

5. Layoffs
6. Freeze necessary hiring, placing a strain on existing personnel
7. Cut budgets for resources necessary for employees to meet management expectations
8. Cut/eliminate budgets for people training and development

ETHICAL CONDUCT

[eth-i-k*uh* l] [kon-duhkt]

1. Acting in ways consistent with what society and individuals typically think are good values. Ethical conduct tends to be good for business and involves demonstrating respect for key moral principles that include honesty, fairness, equality, dignity, diversity and individual rights.

2. Being in accordance with right and wrong.

The Business Reality – Businesses desire to be ethical at all times, unless of course it is necessary to take liberties with the definitions of right and wrong in order to optimize financial results, advance personal interests, or if it is just more convenient. Hence, the introduction of "wrong, but acceptable."

CHAPTER 2
LEADERSH!T
A LEADERSHIP SYSTEM THAT JUST PLAIN STINKS!

Lead-er-ship:

Definition:

Noun

1. The position or function of a leader. A person who guides or directs a group.

2. Ability to lead.

3. An act or instance of leading; guidance; direction.

4. The leaders of a group.

Nowhere in the dictionary definition will you find the list of rich characteristics and core competencies of an effective leader, or a description of how to engage in effective leadership. There is no mention of the influence, command and clout of a person with leadership ability to successfully manage and steer a group of individuals toward a common goal.

What is at the crux of that definition of leadership and who can we point to as stalwart examples of sound leadership? In truth, good leaders can be found almost anywhere. They might be among the rank and file – which is a great place to find a leader because they have humble beginnings and they know all the inner workings of a company from the inside out and from the bottom up. Their insight and empathy for the everyday worker can unite a workforce quickly. Good leaders can rise from the sales force. Great sales men and women have a natural affinity for reading people and contagious energy and charisma that can translate very well into leadership.

Understanding the impact of this insane leadershit system is difficult, but we have all in some way been stung by this either directly or indirectly. Big business in America is the engine at the top of the food chain of the economy, and leaders of these big corporations determine its course. Some of these people are screwing up the economy and taking huge profits from it. The vast majority of that money, their so-called compensation or what I would call legalized larceny belongs to the business. That money is supposed to be reinvested in the people and the necessary resources that generate legitimate short term, and more importantly, long term success. And, as a result, the communities that the businesses operate in will thrive.

Who holds our leaders to task on their responsibilities once they are in a position of power? Great question.

Kennywood's Open

It was revealed by the press in early October of 2014 that Alex Molinaroli, the CEO of Johnson Controls, Inc., was having an extramarital affair with Kristin Ihle, a psychologist employed by a consulting firm that had been working for Johnson Controls for many years. The affair was discovered by Molinaroli's wife, who then threatened Ihle with bodily harm, causing Ihle to file a restraining order against the CEO's wife, bringing the affair into public view.

This is where things get interesting from a leadership perspective.

Johnson Controls spokesman, Fraser Engerman, offered this official statement to the press: "The Board reviewed the referenced relationship and determined that no conflicts of interest occurred."

Oh really?

They want us to believe that the personal relationship had absolutely nothing to do with the business relationship. Even if this were true, that conclusion stretches one's imagination.

He went on to add this: "To avoid any perception of potential future conflicts, management elected to terminate the consulting firm. Mr. Molinaroli continues in his role with the full support of the board, and the company considers this matter to be closed."

Great. That's done. Let's do lunch.

The JCI Board's downplay of the "referenced relationship" is interesting in light of the fact that the canned consulting company specializes in assisting businesses with leadership development and succession planning services. Seriously, you can't make this stuff up.

With that firing and the JCI Board voicing their "full support" of Molinaroli as CEO, they pointed the finger of blame at the consulting company for the transgression instead of holding its own leadership accountable.

Values When They're Convenient

I'm not entirely sure how to digest this turd of information in light of the company's published (possibly somewhat irrelevant) core values:

"We act with honesty, fairness, respect and safety, furthering a culture of unquestioned integrity. This strengthens relationships across businesses and functions."

What I watched with interest was the stock. It took a little dip when the affair was revealed in the press, which could have been incidental and not necessarily associated with the news of the affair. Then it started a steady climb back up. The announcement of the CEO's gross misconduct might have been nothing but a short-lived hiccup on the ticker tape for the company stock, with no lasting effect on its value.

This gets back to the perception of the quality of the company. When you discuss the quality of a company, does it even matter versus the immediate financial results at the end of the day? It doesn't appear to when you look at the daily news. But let me assure you, it matters. It matters a great deal.

It's not nice when someone cheats on their spouse in an extramarital affair, but typically you don't fire them for that indiscretion. In the case of Johnson Controls – regardless of what the Board says – it is now out there that the CEO has clearly violated the code of ethics. Having an affair with someone is one thing. Having an affair with a paid consultant is entirely different.

Unfortunately, it is just another minor scandal that is almost daily fodder in business news these days. Like a soap opera or reality TV, it is scintillating and many of us have all but come to expect this type of misbehavior with leadership figures as "white noise." An affair might not be a dismissible offense in and of itself, but when it is between a company leader and a hired consultant whose firm's service *directly impacts the leadership* of Johnson Controls – hello – this is clearly a conflict of interest. In my opinion, this should have resulted in a deeper look at the CEO's performance and possibly his termination.

The real news would be coming from the employees, if anyone cared to ask them. Would they trust this leader? Does he "walk the talk?" I would guess that the obvious answer would be a resounding NO! And the board's reaction to that would be "so what?"

By the way, Johnson Controls, Inc. has a governance committee. They have a long list of duties and functions, including: *"Oversee the Company's ethics policy and review any potential violations of the ethics policy referred to the Committee,"* and *"[R]eview potential conflicts of interest referred to the Committee involving the Company, directors or executive officers."* And yet, while the Board of Directors quickly and publicly absolved Molinaroli's participation in the "referenced relationship" and cleared him of any wrongdoing in October, they changed their tune just a few weeks later. In early December – when the stock had sufficiently recovered following the Board's suggestion that all was okay, we could all move on, nothing to look at here; – they claimed that Molinaroli "failed to inform the corporation's audit committee about the _potential_ conflict of interest in his extra-marital affair." So much for the "full support of the Board" they had declared just weeks earlier.

$1 Million Public Flogging

So the Board charged Molinaroli $1 million for not proactively disclosing an extra-marital affair that may possibly be considered a conflict of interest. Seriously?

Let's put that in perspective. The $1 million was charged against his 2014 performance payout (bonus), so instead of receiving a total of $20 million in 2014 in stock options, salaries, bonuses, etc., he would only receive $19 million. (That'll show him!) Hmmm, $19 million doesn't really seem to be as much a punishment as it is a reward for a man who put his own wants and desires ahead of his responsibilities. With so much at stake, shouldn't the depth of the punishment match the height of the responsibility? Wouldn't that help him keep his eye on the proverbial ball?

The whole thing seems to be a manipulation of the public image. By isolating and minimizing the incident, they are managing the perception to contain the market's concerns. It is damage control. I think we can all understand that.

Managing the response to the crisis and the release of official corporate information may have prevented a stock sell-off. Fair enough. I can understand that type of protection. But it does have me wondering if that is all that is going on. What else is this leader doing under the radar that has him distracted from his weighty duties as CEO? What other toxic information is the board buffering to buoy their stock? That may be unfair, but you know what they say, "First time shame on you, second time, shame on me."

Think about that. From a stopgap standpoint, it all comes out ok. No harm done to the short term stock value. We are being asked to just watch the numbers; don't pay attention to the leadership.

If the stock *had* dropped significantly and it was directly attributed to the CEO's misbehavior, you can bet that the board would have fired him and screamed from the highest mountain, "See? That's what happens when you violate our values."

The point is that the only things they want you to watch are the numbers . . . because in today's leadershit system, they are simply all that matters. As we continue to explore this system, you will see why that is not so good for corporate health in the big picture.

What is involved in running a company like Johnson Controls or any Fortune 500 company? How much focus, energy and time does it take? The future of the company, the trajectory of the company and the failure or success of the company all boils down to the tenacity, competence and leadership focus of the CEO. This is true for small, medium and large companies. Right down to the smallest business, the leader should be immersed in the company and aware of both the quality of the people and the quality of its results.

When you are the CEO of a large publicly traded corporate organization, your family and the company are your supreme responsibilities and focus every day…and not necessarily in that order. Significant time and energy should be consumed by the business in order to milk all the success out of it you can. Unfortunately, sometimes even your family is a lower priority. If there is anything that deserves a premium in compensation, it is the amount of time, energy and sacrifices an authentic leader devotes to the business to do it the right way. But we don't always distinguish "authentic" from "jagoff" or "knockoff," and premium compensation has grown to "ridiculous" in many cases.

Johnson Controls provided a juicy example of leadershit with their handling of the Molinaroli fiasco. There are many others from publicly traded corporations that reveal a system that accepts this kind of bullshit without even a "you've got to be shitting me!"

Look at ME!

Leadershit comes in all forms. Some leaders like to make sure that they are in the spotlight and gaining celebrity as a result of their corporate position. For some, there are benefits to milking success. There is a guy that just jumps into my head. He was the CEO of another large auto supply company. They built a big facility that you could see from the highway with their company name on a huge sign on the side of it. The only reason any company puts something like that up is to make sure everyone sees them. Look how big I am. Look at me. Big sign.

Back in the 1990s and early 2000s, the Detroit Three automakers' purchasing departments looked at supplier profitability as an indicator that their prices were too high. If they thought suppliers were doing well, they came at you with price cuts to suck you dry. Heaven forbid our successes as suppliers were due to cost efficiencies. Anything that indicated a supplier was profitable put the auto company buyers in attack mode. They routinely used their suppliers as ATM machines, so as soon as they knew you had money, they came to collect.

I'm pretty sure that plastering your name on a shiny high-rise building up next to an interstate highway was not intended to display profitability, but the Detroit Three saw it as just that, and so it wasn't a smart tactical move for that supplier! That particular supplier company wasn't doing that well, but so what? As far as I was concerned, it seemed like that shiny sign was designed to feed egos.

Rubber Chicken Dinners

This former CEO enjoyed the spotlight in other ways too. If there was a rubber chicken dinner somewhere and they needed somebody to speak, he was in. You could always count on him to show up and talk. It was a bit confounding to me because I was frequently invited to speak at these dinners and had to turn them down. I was extremely busy. Where do these guys find the time? In order to do a presentation, you have to write the presentation, create the PowerPoint presentation, practice the presentation, edit the presentation, and set aside several hours to go give the presentation.

You also have to have a deep understanding of your material, the facts and figures and circumstances that led up to your conclusions. It takes a lot of time. And you can't simply give the same presentation each time you're invited to a rubber chicken dinner. Facts, figures and circumstances change with time. When people catch on to your stale facts and repetition, you will stop being invited to speak for fear that you will bring the same old news and repeat yourself. Agreeing to speak at a rubber chicken dinner is agreeing to set other things aside and spend precious days preparing for that evening.

Maybe it's just me, but think about it. Something has got to come off the table in order to make time for this stuff. You have to wonder what it is that the rubber chicken dinner presenters are eliminating from their other obligations in order to appear at these events. And how often do they make the choice to replace those obligations with presentations and rubber chicken dinners?

I had the occasion to meet with this same CEO in his office for business once. There was nothing on his desk. Not a single note or even a pen on the desk. There was nothing there. Nothing.

Our job levels and duties were pretty similar, so I knew the volume of work he was responsible for. With the amount of responsibility this person had as a leader and the number of things that he had to juggle, I was puzzled. How could his desk be so clean? Where is the work? Where is the urgency? It is like driving past a construction site and you see the "Men at Work" sign, a lot of barrels neatly lined up, and a row of clean trucks, but no dirt, shovels, men, or sign of any actual work being done.

There are different approaches, different styles, and different personalities to running a company. It's not a one-size-fits-all thing, but I don't care how smart you are; there are only so many hours to anyone's day. If you are doing all that you should be doing as a leader, you will barely have time to come home and see your family, let alone give 10 speeches a month, and your desk will be a mess.

That auto supply company today is a mere shadow of its former self after emerging from Chapter 11.

We Are Great. Just Ask Us

What were once widely understood meanings of the words relevant to leadership are often now gutted to the point that their only relevance is that they would be conspicuous by their absence. These include words like "values," "ethics," "innovation," and "strategy." When a CEO uses these buzzwords, they appear to know what they mean and live by them. Frequently, though, they are simply giving lip service to the expected jargon. When uttered with authority and confidence, the words are useful shields for fending off critics and close inspection of work. On the other hand, ask a buzzword-loving CEO to create and act on a strategic vision or implement a business-wide innovation process, and they might rather shave their head with a cheese grater.

In the leadershit system, leaders know what you want to hear and they say that. Whether they are actually doing or living by the things they say, we have no idea. So we listen to leaders use these buzz words and some people even believe they have substance. But for me, it is like believing a beauty pageant contestant who says she is for world peace will actually then be responsible for pulling it off. It's just lip service.

Overblown marketing has amped up the corporate images of anyone willing to pay for the makeover. Sadly, Americans have become numb to the "spin" of words that mask a very different corporate reality. Honesty and culpability in leadership have been replaced with tactical image management. Shiny websites and brochures all offer similar catchy corporate tag lines and slogans that promise great products and service from yet another quality leader in the industry.

Where corporate leadership is concerned, it is becoming harder and harder for employees, stockholders and the American public in general to recognize genuinely great leaders or to trust the traditional words used to describe them. As a result of today's distorted standards of who is qualified to lead, it appears to me that new words associated with leadership are emerging; those include manipulative, deceptive, believable, and delusional. These are the words that have redefined leadership "skill sets."

I have grown cynical. I hear what everyone else hears, but I have been in those meetings and board rooms and I know what I know. So now when a leader presents their story, I start by not trusting it because I think it is likely that I am not getting all the facts, just the ones they want me to receive.

If you love a restaurant and want to keep eating there, you should probably avoid taking an unannounced tour of the kitchen.

The Beatings Will Continue Until Morale Improves

An executive from a huge cable network once revealed that when he interviews job applicants, his one favorite question is: "What is more important, effort or results?" He goes on to say that everyone says "effort," because it sounds like it should be the right answer. "Results is the right answer," he smiles. "I don't care if you have to kill baby bunnies to get me what I need, bring me the results."

Mmmmkay. A little violent, but that's solved and we can do lunch.

Can you detect the erosion of principles in that leadership model? His take-no-prisoners delivery model is probably a reflection of the pressure that is on him from his leaders, who also don't care how you get there, just deliver results. The threat of losing a bonus for failure to deliver results is probably being handed down. Under this terrorist model of leadership, the end results justify the means, and it will be messy as baby bunnies die.

In many corporate settings, results trump methods. These days, things that are typically the hard number measures of good leadership fall on the spreadsheets in the accounting department. Increased productivity, increased profits, lowered material costs, and benchmarks reached in a given timeline are all results. They don't care how you get them, just get them. The implied message is: I don't care about you. I just care about what you can do for me, and if you don't do it, I will get rid of you and replace you with someone who can. You are just a baby bunny to me.

What I call the "disposable employee" model has been around since the industrial age and spawned the advent of the unionized workforce. The constant threat of replacing someone – and essentially destroying their family's stability and livelihood – is an effective method of forcing short term financial results. If that is your end goal, then by all means, continue. To make that model really hum though, you will have to follow through on the threat and fire people, to make sure that your employees know you mean it and that the paper results are your first priority, not them.

A Box of Kleenex

My first experience with having to tell people they lost their job happened when I was only about 27 years old when I was the Manufacturing Manager for a large plant in Ohio. The corporate office had decided to shut down the plant as part of the overall manufacturing footprint realignment. The HR Manager was going to assist me in meeting individually with each member of my team as we set about informing them that they would be let go and what their separation package would be.

We set up a dedicated room for meeting with each of them. I pulled my chair in and sat at a table with chairs on the opposite side for employees before our first meeting. The HR Manager pulled his chair up to the table and set a box of Kleenex down in front of us on the table. I had no understanding of why that box was put there . . . until the first few emotional meetings were over.

That day is burned into my memory and was one of the worst days of my professional career. I made a commitment to myself then to never get into a position where screwing up people's lives was going to be my only solution.

Aside from the crushing heartbreak that layoffs and firings can bring, there are many sound business reasons why this kind of day should be avoided. Let's examine this a bit further. Under the "disposable employee" business model, the repetitious firing, hiring and training of new people that you can threaten is expensive and exhausting. True loyalty or trust will never be nurtured under those circumstances, and employees will always be ready to bolt for a new job to gain security and relief from the stress of your threats. Companies do not lose only poor employees under this model. They lose the productive and the valuable ones because everyone wants out. Those who stay are just going through the motions until they too can escape. Under these stressors, results can become even more difficult to achieve as workers are focused on survival rather than performance. To offset this deterioration, more "bunnies" may have to die. So what happens when you run out of bunnies?

Look Mom, No Hands!

In the feeder-frenzy world of corporate projections and shareholder demands, over-reaching to cover the spread on quarterly projections is not unheard of. Many millions and sometimes billions of dollars ride on pennies over and pennies under a quarterly estimate. Heads roll when numbers fall, and with the continuous ticker tape recording of stock prices, little attention is paid to whether company morale is high or low, or whether communication inside the corporation is effective, or whether the corporate culture is healthy. The focus is on the numerical results, and the pressure is on CEOs to produce those numbers.

Making the numbers work month after month is a high wire act that can leave some companies bleeding after a fall. The "Band-Aid" for more and more companies is defaulting leadership positions to finance experts who can balance the numbers and walk the high wire with grace, but who have little or no training and experience in leading people.

Look Mom, No Clue!

The gap in this strategy is not just a little flawed. There is a Grand Canyon of difference between getting a person to manage your numbers and getting a person to manage the business. It is — and it has always been -- through effective leadership of *people* that profitability increases. Legitimate sustainable performance in the corporate world is culture driven, and therefore, people driven. Those workers in that culture then translate to become systems and process driven. That is what makes for good performance. Not a bunch of accountants in a room huddled over a spreadsheet doing the math and getting a bunch of numbers to work. In other words, it is the people who drive the systems and processes, so ultimately good leadership of people is what makes for good corporate performance.

"Culture is not the most important thing -- it's the only thing" – Jim Sinegal, Co-Founder, Former CEO Costco

Often when leaders talk about culture, it comes across as blah, blah, blah. That's because they really have no damn idea what they are talking about, they are just reading a script. Many fail to realize that culture is an end result of holding to high standards and principles, not simply lofty rhetoric. There are lines in the sand demonstrating what is acceptable and what is not acceptable. When leaders don't demonstrate and delineate those high standards and hold everyone – including themselves – accountable to them, there is no culture. There's fear and confusion and misguided endeavors. Clear understanding of what is appropriate, what is inappropriate, what is tolerable and what is completely intolerable, is necessary for proper leadership. And this applies to everyone. Expect nothing from your team that you are not willing to expect from yourself.

Not surprisingly, this is the same approach that marks successful parenting. Success happens over time through delivery of consistent messaging, consistent oversight, consistent behavior, fair expectations, and timely and consistent responses.

Unfortunately, development of a solid corporate culture around corporate values is a long-term difficult acquisition. Like parenthood, it really never ends.

In this world of instant gratification where winning and short term results rule corporate behavior, there are very few opportunities for legitimate leaders to make that kind of long term impact on corporate culture. Taking time to change the course of a business model to create a successful culture seems to be considered an unnecessary long term proposition in corporate

America these days. The system will not wait for you to turn the Titanic around to avoid that fatal iceberg up ahead that nobody else can see yet.

Lee Iacocca wrote a book called *Where Have all the Leaders Gone?* (Iacocca, 2008) They are here. There's just no market for them anymore. They are either not included on the short list of candidates, or they have refused to get involved because they see that they don't fit and their leadership methods and efforts would be futile.

Creating an environment where every team member is aligned with a successful vision for the company and invested in the outcome takes a leader who understands *people*, not just numbers. Making employees deeply commit to their employer's outcome is a process that involves building trust and security, and ultimately ties their success with that of the company. That kind of environment empowers employees to make a difference for themselves and ultimately for the company. And that takes time.

And they don't teach that in accounting class.

Lead-er-shit:

Definition:

Noun

1. The position or function of an overpaid person who has been unjustly granted authority without truly earning it. Misdirection of a group by a person who lacks industry insight or skill, or who is lazy or greedy.
2. Inability to lead.
3. An act or instance of not leading; blaming others; selfish acquisition of fame, cash, and prizes.
4. A self-promoting, untrustworthy bastard.

CHAPTER 3
THE DUMBING DOWN OF VALUES
NEW NORMAL...NEW CRISIS

Didn't See That Comin'

A few years after I left JCI, I had a fair amount of interaction with other companies either as a board member or as a consultant. It was during this time, around 2007 and 2008, I began to notice that running a business with integrity and righteous moral compass seemed more like an exception than the norm.

Two friends who were authentic leaders and former teammates of mine at JCI had become victims of the leadershit system. They were both on a one-year severance and trying to figure out what they wanted to do with their lives.

We got together, as friends do, and collectively reflected on the incredible results generated at JCI back in 2000 to 2003, because it was driven by a system that managed the business rather than the numbers. We talked about how our team had been anchored to an unwavering commitment to our stated corporate values and the unprecedented returns we experienced.

The three of us felt sure that we could form a company whose purpose was to share that blueprint of success with other organizations. We were sure that there would be enthusiastic reception of such a plan. So we started to formulate the business.

During a related conference call between us, I reflected on our great results at JCI versus what I was learning about business standards and expectations now in 2007 and 2008 with the broader business community. Now there were lowered standards of qualified leaders and associated shifted priorities and lowered expectations of the businesses they were leading. They wanted to improve their businesses, but they were not willing to do the hard work and take the time and the risk to get to those improvements.

I just want to interject here to talk about the word results. Results is a word that is used in business circles to generally refer to many things in very basic terms. When someone determines that a certain business is "doing great" or "doing terribly", what are they looking at to make that determination? They are usually looking at revenue/sales to see if the company is growing. They are also looking at earnings -- which is typically the earnings before interest, taxes, depreciation and amortization (EBITDA). Some people are also talking about the balance sheet, which means they are looking to see if a company is in liquidity or in debt. But typically when someone is talking about a company with "great results", they are referring to the financial status of that company, specifically, their sales, revenue and earnings are going up. When someone talks about results in business, they are referring to quarterly and/or annual financial numbers of a company.

What results do NOT refer to is how a company gets to their financial status. I want to make the distinction that focusing on results is not necessarily bad, but it is important to understand how anyone achieved their results. Consider Lance Armstrong's results and how he achieved them.

I clearly remember standing in my yard as I was on the phone with my friends, and a realization swept over me.

I said, "Guys, what we have to share – not ideas or concepts, but a proven system – has tremendous value to virtually any organization." I went on, "With that said, from what I am seeing as a result of my broader business experiences post-JCI, is that this system has no market."

This was an "ah-ha" moment for me. We had a great business plan and passionate experts on board to execute it. We genuinely wanted to help businesses optimize their potential, and we knew exactly how to do it. But I was finally coming face to face with everything that I had seen, heard and experienced in corporate America in recent years that settled for outcomes that were just good enough. It was demonstrated to me over and over again that the standards had dropped below what my friends and I were trying to do. There seemed to be a different focus; different priorities; a new normal.

My friends and I had been launching our new business concept from the belief that every organization wanted to make their business better and do it in the best way possible. The way it is advertised on company websites and published in mission statements and core values; the way it is articulated in all corporate communications and identified in the job descriptions of teams, executives and their boards. But that is not really what every organization wants. That is just what they say.

When my friends, my team and I experienced great outcomes at JCI some years before, we blew the lid off of what previously had been determined to be the ceiling for "excellent performance." That performance was a protracted effort generated from the people, the culture and the systems that we put in place, not from the creativity of our accounting department. It was also not a result of reverting to gimmicks like selling off certain operations or moving to a foreign country for a one-time tax benefit.

Many leaders today do not want to work harder to achieve extraordinary outcomes. They do not want to invest in anything that detracts from short term gains. They don't want to try anything that could threaten their bonus.

And the system is such that they don't have to.

From that day when I hung up on that call right up until now, I have seen little to change my mind.

Lonely

One evening in 2012 after dinner and an ethics workshop I presented, we had our annual *Integrity First* scholarship awards at Robert Morris University. I gave a brief talk centered on leadership and ethics/morality. Afterwards, young people came up and introduced themselves and asked questions. I ended the evening talking to a student by the name of Patrick.

Patrick asked me a lot of questions. The conversation was basically about character and values. He recognized how hard it was to remain true to these things in business, and wasn't sure they would get him where he wanted to go in life. He wanted some assurance that it was possible to succeed without compromising his character and his values.

Patrick had been elected President of Society for the Advancement of Management on campus, which is an association of students. As President, Patrick thought the right thing to do was to go around and ask the members what they would like the association to do for them, what they would like to see implemented (pretty much the way leaders are supposed to operate).

"Rather than me just deciding for them what is best and telling them this is the way it's going to be, I thought I would ask them what they wanted. I wanted the association to provide value for them, not through my filter or idea of what that might be," he said. It turned out when he asked people what they think, or what they want from the association, they looked at him funny and said nobody has ever asked me that before. They were conditioned to believe it was normal that they don't get asked.

He said, "I talk to business students, and I do what I know I am supposed to do. I try very hard to do it the right way, and every time they ask me, "what are you doing?"

And then he asked me something I will never forget: "Did you ever feel lonely?"

That was a jarring question for me. It really hit. I told him yes.

Of all the words to choose – not alone; not odd; not weird; not confused – lonely. How did he know the exact right word to describe that feeling?

I try to live up to my responsibilities. My perception is that as a society, we have drifted to a place where that behavior sticks out, and you are left alone to wonder what is going on here? It is a place where you feel like an outcast and don't know what to do.

I personally have not been able to comply with the new "normal" exhibited in companies led by leadershit. I feel lonely because it seems to me that we have a system now that doesn't require leaders to do what they are supposed to do. Sometimes it actually encourages them *not* to perform their duties or live up to their obligations. And sometimes it punishes those leaders who insist on leading the right way.

This memory of talking with Patrick is vivid. It stands out as a defining moment in my life, one where I came to grips with a lot that has happened to me. It is one of the main reasons I am writing this book.

I told Patrick, "I do feel lonely, but now I know there is you, and you know there is me. And I bet there are a lot more Randes and Patricks out there."

Authentic Leaders – The Stuff

Historically, what defines successful authentic leadership is a set of human qualities in people who produced both great company cultures and great results. If we are only measuring, hiring and assessing leaders on the reported outcomes of their leadership, then rest assured, we will be "Enronned" again and again. Authentic CEOs and leaders are not solely defined by course completion in an MBA program. They are also not solely defined by how many widgets are sold in a quarter or the number of bullet-pointed achievements on a resume.

Authentic leaders are a rare breed of sharp, mission-focused, committed human beings who inspire people to freely and energetically follow them. They have more than the checklist of competencies seen in an MBA curriculum guide or resume. Many have mammoth ambition, uncanny business sense and a wisdom borne out of painful lessons. They are vigilant and wary to avoid business pitfalls. They create corporate pride. Authentic leaders actively engage and listen to all their employees – not just a few select members of their management staff. Their title and position at the top of the organizational chart does not feed a distorted need for power and celebrity. Rather, it is a reminder of their enormous obligations and responsibilities both as a professional and as a person. I have met some of these people, worked for them and with them. In the business, you can't help but hear about them.

Formally trained leaders in general are expected to possess many competencies that are the framework of their skill set. Some of these include mastering conflict resolution, enterprise communication, implementing change management, accountability, motivation, company morale, teamwork, relationship building, and employee empowerment. Again, this is just a checklist on an MBA curriculum guide or a candidate's resume. True utilization of these intangible qualities in a real life corporate setting is a difficult thing to identify, let alone quantify. And because these are traits that are elusive to calculation, even substantiating their existence to accurately identify who is indisputably "competent" is not an easy task.

While corporate success and leadership competency are intimately intertwined in corporate America, tendencies to "gray out" the ingredients that go into the recipe for an accomplished leader have become too common. Because in the current system, the only measureable – and therefore dominant -- outcome of corporate success is defined by hard numbers in the short term profit margin. All the other more subtle or intangible leadership criteria – including strong ethical values -- that do not have a line item on a spreadsheet have lost priority.

It can certainly be argued that to ensure a company has legitimate long-term sustainable success, delivery of the intangible competencies needs to happen, as well.

Pittsburgh Kid

I grew up in Pittsburgh's South Hills. Although it has been several decades since I have lived there, according to some folks, I still have a little accent and the same mannerisms and character. You can take the kid out of Pittsburgh, but you can't take Pittsburgh out of the kid.

Pittsburgh is a big city that feels like a small town. It is a melting pot city, and I think some other melting pot cities, especially in the Midwest, have that same feel. Classic blue collar Pittsburghers never allow you to get too full of yourself, folks who work hard to make a life for their families, and who recognize that other people have to work hard too.

My sons, Scott and Adam, both moved to Pittsburgh at different times. They agree, "Dad, people here judge you for _who_ you are, not _what_ you are or _what_ you have or _what_ you do."

Although I admit I am biased, I thought their assessment was spot-on. It always seemed to me that Pittsburgh folks decide whether they like you based on the quality of person you are. The ones I remember don't look at titles or credentials. They don't care what kind of car you are driving or what your salary is. That is all irrelevant in their view. I grew up in this culture, and so credentials, titles and the stuff you can buy are not all that relevant in my view, either, to the quality of person you are. Like most people I knew in Pittsburgh and much of the Midwest, I have a *"don't bullshit me with your excuses and pomp and circumstances"* attitude. I'm not saying that Pittsburgh doesn't have any jagoffs; I'm saying the tolerance for assholes is really low.

What Is It With You?

There are seminal moments that have been very compelling and meaningful to me. This is a story about one of those powerful and stunning moments.

I was an Executive in Residence and speaking to an Information Technology (IT) class at Oakland University in 2008 or 2009. This was an evening class for MBA students composed mostly of young adults who had been in the workforce for some years.

The idea behind the Executive in Residence program was that young people get their knowledge at the university, but there is a bridge they have to go over from knowledge to application of that knowledge in the working world. The program was designed to help them cross at least part of the way over that bridge, so they are more prepared to effectively integrate into corporate settings once they get there. It also gives them a glimpse of how to optimize their abilities and best deploy their knowledge. The program basically recognizes that a high GPA or IQ won't get you far in business unless you know how to use it.

So I developed presentations for the MBA students that covered MBA topics such as change management, global strategic planning, ethics and IT.

I spoke to one class about how we leveraged IT competencies to manage Johnson Controls Automotive Operations, a global business with 250 facilities and 75,000 people. We had tech centers around the world, and we needed to act like we were in the same room with each other even when we were on opposite sides of the planet. That's what IT did. We needed IT to facilitate important stuff. It was a big deal. IT was a core competency that enabled us to have the opportunity to truly operate as a global company.

By the way, I do not like IT. It takes me about ten seconds to feel a tumor growing in my head when anyone wants to talk to me about software. But I don't let that disqualify IT as something that is a core competency for us. Whether I like it or not is irrelevant.

The conversation in this IT class drifted off into a wider scoped Q and A, about other ways that JCI stayed successful through the economic downturn in the early 2000s. This included managing the "generators" of the company's results, most important of which were the people and their morale.

A young guy in the front row raised his hand and I called on him. He asked, "What is it with you?"

Holy crap. *"What is it with you?"* I thought, damn, I don't know what the hell that means, but it can't be good.

I said, "I'm sorry. I don't understand."

He turned his back to me and turned around to face the rest of the class and said, "I have a few friends who work at Johnson Controls, and they were there while *he* was president," pointing at me. I held my breath. I thought he was going to tell everyone that they hated working there or that I sucked. I thought that was the next thing coming out of his mouth. I started to think about my escape route.

"They really enjoyed working there," he said. And I exhaled. No pitchforks and no lynch mobs.

The student went on to say that what it really came down to was, "They trusted *him*," pointing at me again. "They didn't agree with him all the time, but they knew they could depend on whatever *he* said." What an unexpected and fantastic endorsement.

Trust is a big deal. Trust in your leader takes the confusion and the anxiety out of the equation for an employee who is trying to do a good job, and allows them to focus more on the task at hand. The focus on establishing trust and a culture of inclusion at JCI was not easy but was, in my opinion, the defining reason for our off-the-charts success during a time when all of our competitors were struggling.

The student turned back to face me and asked, *"How did you get like this?"* His exact words. They are etched in my memory.

"I'm sorry. I don't really understand that question either," I answered.

"Mr. Somma, any president, any CEO of any Fortune 500 company, any leader of any company would have said every word you have said here tonight," and then he paused. "But none of them do it," he clarified. "But I happen to know that you did. *Why did you do it?*"

So his question about how did I get like this was really about why didn't I just follow the herd. There is anonymity in the herd. You don't bring attention to yourself, let alone conflict, and you don't feel lonely when you follow the herd. People who work for corporations are so conditioned to management *mis*behavior as the herd mentality that any demonstration of doing things the right way is not seen as a relief. It is a red flag.

That's how it works. Bad behavior by leaders – like taking unsavory shortcuts such as laying off hundreds of people just to hit the earnings target – doesn't stick out because we have normalized it. While sometimes layoffs are necessary in order for an organization to survive and compete, leaders within the system are now simply doing these things because it is the way it is done. And even though there are other options, they require more work. Layoffs are an easy way to make the numbers on the spreadsheet work. It is seen as a legitimate option, even though there are others.

These leaders are inside a bad culture. When you do bad stuff inside of a bad culture, you just do it. It is not seen as bad behavior within that culture. It is not, "eh, who cares?" or "maybe I will feel bad about this." It is even more normal than that. They don't feel bad about it because *that is how it is done*. Bad has become our new routine.

I was really struggling to address this young man. I already knew all this, but I did not know that anyone else was aware of it. I said, "That is a fair question, and at the same time, it is a heck of an indictment on my generation of leaders, that simply by doing what you are supposed to do – no more and no less – that I am a freak." They realized that I stuck out. I shouldn't have stuck out. The guys who are not truly fulfilling their leadership roles – those are the guys who should have stuck out.

I answered the only way I knew how. "I had a job description outlining my responsibilities and obligations, and the company had values that established for me not what you are allowed to do, but what you are not allowed to do. Those set the boundaries. Core values are non-negotiable, mandatory commitments that are relentlessly honored no matter what the circumstances. I was given a map, and I just followed the map."

This was a pivotal moment for me. It rocked me. And it got me thinking.

I am not crazy and I am not special. And when I take a harder look at this, I am certainly not the one who is out of step and has changed. The system and its standards have changed.

The Greatest Influence

Leadership was defined at an early age for me by my father, who was in charge of food and beverage operations at the Pittsburgh Hilton. I spent a great deal of time with my dad as a young impressionable teenager. Because the Hilton hosted a number of sports-related banquets, I had the unique opportunity to meet a lot of star athletes and get autographs and sports paraphernalia – the things that really get a young boy's juices flowing. Additionally, I could order anything I wanted off the menu, which was a nice bonus for a hungry growing kid!

I still remember to this day the number of times he would walk from the ballroom to the kitchen. While the ballroom was plush and luxurious, the kitchen was messy, loud and lacked any of the grand appointments of the ballroom. I didn't realize then how any of this would be meaningful to me later in life in terms of leadership and business in general, but my dad's actions influenced me a great deal. He would walk through that kitchen – and it didn't matter if it was the captain of the wait staff, a chef, a cook, a waiter or a dishwasher, he would say hello to them and often stop to talk with them. The communication was consistently very informal, friendly and unassuming. It was the identical conversation and voice he had when he spoke to guests in the ballroom.

Sometimes I would be standing there after my dad had said hello and moved on, and many times that individual would say, "Your ole' man's a hell of a guy; he treats everybody here as equals." Obviously, the point was that he didn't have to, and I guess they didn't expect him to, because he was an executive and they were not. Yet he would relate to them just like he did with other executives, and just like he did with the guests. They recognized that and appreciated the respect that he showed them. I remember hearing more than once, "Y'know, I'd go through walls for him," or "I'd do anything for him."

I reflect on that today and think of the quiet power of that kind of humanization and connection. There was mutual respect because he didn't treat anyone as if they were less important than him, or as if the work they did had any more or less value than anyone else's work. I'm sure in my dad's mind – although he never said it to me – that was important from both a human standpoint and a business standpoint. They felt that what they did mattered. They mattered. These employees were valuable to the smooth operation of Hilton events, but they were motivated to perform at a high level because they *felt* valuable. My dad made sure of it.

At one point during my rise through the executive ranks, my dad somehow felt the need to tell me that "Two things that can't ever be taken from you are your honor and your integrity. Life will present you with many opportunities to give them away . . . don't ever do that!"

This was memorable, and it was my first exposure to a culture of an organization or group that wasn't driven by org charts or titles, but by their relationships with each other. My father set the example for how the employees treated each other, how they engaged with Hilton's visitors, and how they really tried their best to do good work, and I'm sure it had a lot to do with the success he had in his career. For a man who didn't finish high school and started at the Pittsburgh Hilton Hotel as a waiter, his character and work ethic made him a standout and a natural leader. His eventual rise to that executive level position taught me that everyone has value and that there is more than one kind of "smart."

Means > Results = Good Leader

Many years later, I learned some valuable lessons at Johnson Controls when I took over the North American Operations. One lesson was that there was so much more importance to *how* things were accomplished than the accomplishment itself. That might be difficult to grasp because it implies that the accomplishment – or the result – isn't really essential, but that is not true and not the point. They are essential, but it is critical that the results be achieved right way. The "how" speaks to the credibility, repeatability and sustainability of the accomplishment. Motivating the employees by treating them well, cultivating their success within the company, as my father so masterfully did, is a big part of that "*how.*" By cutting corners, or people, to achieve results, a company's own published values are frequently violated and a company's ability to authentically live up to its reputation is undermined. Under these circumstances, success is an illusion. Why does this matter?

Cost Reduction vs. Cost Efficiency

There is a difference between getting something done quickly in the short term that has a negative influence on the long term effect, and getting something done the right way regardless of how much time it takes. In business, cost reduction is a general term that can be accomplished in many ways, some of them very brutal and quick. Cost efficiency, on the other hand, is a more thoughtful approach that takes the future success of the business into consideration, and of course, time.

There are answers to problems that work short term, but they don't work long term. Let's say that you went to the doctor and the doctor told you that it was in your best interest to lose 20 pounds. You need to lose 20 pounds. That's what you need to do.

So you go home, and a few days pass, and then you call your doctor. And you tell your doctor, "Hey, doc, I lost 20 pounds!" And he replies, "That's great! How did you do that so quickly?" And you tell him, "I cut off my left leg." Well, you did it, you lost 20 pounds. Amputating your leg gets the job done. Just like in business, when you have to get to a certain goal by a certain deadline, as a leader, there are always short cuts available to you. But like the Bozo who cuts off his leg to lose weight, your overall health will be compromised, your mobility is compromised, and your ability to compete is compromised by taking the short cuts every time. And what happens when you run out of limbs to cut off to reach your goals?

Cost efficiency is about eliminating waste. Cost reduction is sometimes simply eliminating costs. It doesn't distinguish between costs that are waste and which ones are essential to the long term health of the company. Both make the numbers work, but it is the long term process that is clearly the best way.

If the goal is to lose weight, it is best to invest in exercise and diet, and over time get lighter and stronger. Cost efficiency, like a good diet and exercise plan, takes time and determination. Effective, healthy change takes time. Simply laying off 20 people, like chopping off a limb, is not a plan for long term health. Layoffs, closing plants, selling off parts of the company, or manipulating your spreadsheets to make the numbers look okay, become the paths of least resistance in business because they are quick. They get the job done for the short term but don't get to the root of whatever problem they are trying to solve. In fact, just like that Whack-a-Mole® game, the problem will poke its head up again.

Tom Stallkamp

Unfortunately, in my 15 years working with the Detroit Three and their leaders, I can only think of a handful of leaders that I respected and trusted. Leaders like Tom Stallkamp, Ron Majeske, Frank Zematis and Bob Socia were good examples of those trusted leaders.

Tom Stallkamp was in charge of purchasing at Chrysler in the mid '90s. He was promoted to Executive Vice President of Procurement and Supply and General Manager of the Minivan Operations for Chrysler Corporation in January of 1996. At this time in the industry's history, all three of the U.S. automakers were intently focused on cost reductions in order to push the price of their automobiles down. And they achieved their cost reductions by leaning hard on their suppliers. This was a huge problem both for the suppliers and for the car makers' futures.

Of all the people who I associated with at GM, Ford and Chrysler, Tom Stallkamp is the only one who really understood that cannibalizing suppliers in order to make the automaker's numbers work is not a good method for doing business.

While the other automaker purchasers were ripping and tearing at the prices from the suppliers, he was trying to build something that would last. All the suppliers knew that and respected him and respected his approach.

Simply taking money from suppliers is not dealing with the root cause of the problem that their cars were crappy and they were not making any long term adjustments to be competitive. This was the reason why U.S. automakers were losing market share to foreign automakers. Taking 5 percent from suppliers every year was putting Band-Aids on the symptoms of their much bigger problem of bleeding money. The only way the U.S. automakers were making any money in the late 90's was they were shoving inventory down the throats of their rental fleets and dealerships, and they were discounting their cars constantly because they couldn't sell them on their merit. Despite the lower quality, U.S. cars were more expensive than the better foreign cars.

Americans wanted to buy American made cars, but it comes down to dollars and sense. It was not about being anti-American. It was about getting a better value for less money; and actually, that is about as American as you can get. We believe in a competitive capitalistic market. U. S. automakers were not really competing effectively.

The underlying problem was that the operating models for GM, Chrysler and Ford were so old and broken that they were losing market share and losing money. But they were not trying to fix that.

The theory behind the price reductions that the U.S. automakers were taking from the suppliers was logical. When suppliers were awarded contracts by the automakers, those contracts were typically agreements that spanned three to four years since car models that go into production usually are produced for that time. The Detroit Three automakers felt it was appropriate to share in the year-over-year cost efficiencies since suppliers received supply agreements that had terms of three to four years. The market and the industry are very dynamic over that period of time and it is difficult, if not impossible, to predict every turn of event. So the automakers' cost-cutting was accepted in order to help adjust to changing markets and circumstances. Fair enough.

Then, somehow, 5 percent was picked by the automakers as the number for the annual reduction of costs they would take from their suppliers, *up front*. In other words, the U.S. automakers paid the suppliers 5 percent less each year under the agreement. The theory was that *after* the U.S. automakers (all three of them) took the 5 percent, the suppliers would go back to the drawing board and develop and bring the automakers proposed value analysis (VA) ideas that essentially reduced the cost of the part without negatively affecting the other critical product performance criteria. The VA ideas proposed by suppliers would be assessed by the automakers, then either approved or turned down. Once an idea was approved and accepted by the automaker(s), the supplier could *then* generate the 5 percent cost reduction to offset the 5 percent price reduction taken up front by the automakers and therefore, retain their profit margins.

In theory, it sounded good, but in practice, that is not the way it worked.

Since the automakers *already took the 5 percent price reduction*, they had no incentive to approve any of the changes proposed by the suppliers to recuperate their costs; no incentive to invest the resources and time to even evaluate the VA ideas. Also, the automakers had no upside to introducing a new design into their system.

It didn't take long for suppliers to realize that they would need to keep giving the annual 5 percent cost reduction to get or keep the business from the Detroit Three automakers, and had little reason to believe that the offset in cost would ever be realized. We felt bullied, but what could we do? These were huge contracts in a competitive industry that had a handful of customers for suppliers like JCI. We had designed our business around their business.

But Tom Stallkamp at Chrysler had the integrity and competence to do business the right way with his suppliers. He implemented the Supplier Cost Reduction Effort (SCORE) method. He got his price reductions and then some, and his suppliers' profits were preserved in the process simply because he chose to design a process that kept Chrysler's skin in the game.

He said that if Chrysler was going to be good, it needs healthy suppliers. It needs suppliers that were investing in their business, getting involved in innovation and technology and ultimately becoming a better resource for Chrysler, which will make the automaker better and more competitive in the industry.

He did not take the 5 percent up front. He still expected to achieve it, but in partnership with the suppliers and not by leveraging their business for it. He also expanded the scope of the SCORE program from parts to systems.

Tom urged suppliers to be creative and aggressive in bringing in cost efficiency ideas with the objective being to eliminate waste. He shared in the burden and risk of innovation with his suppliers, while the other automakers just took their cut and ran. The result of this seemingly minor difference in Tom Stallkamp's approach versus GM and Ford's was that Chrysler would get more for less and the other two got less for less, if they actually approved the ideas.

And were suppliers inspired to work harder at generating ideas for Chrysler's review? You bet your sweet ass we were. Here was a guy who was actually interested in our long term success. All the suppliers revered and admired Tom Stallkamp, when really all he did was the right thing. He had the integrity to follow the process as advertised. Imagine being a hero for simply doing what you said you were going to do.

And for that very reason, Tom Stallkamp stuck out like a sore thumb in the leadershit system.

After Daimler merged with Chrysler in 1998, Tom Stallkamp was made President of Daimler Chrysler North American Operations. There were big changes following the merger. Tom voiced his real concerns on how the integration of the two companies and cultures was creating more of a "we/they" environment rather than "us."

In my opinion, his commitment to doing business with integrity rendered him unable to adapt and conform to the decisions being made to the tune of that new culture, and eventually led to his separation from Chrysler in 1999. He was excused for doing what he was supposed to be doing . . . for doing what they _all_ should have been doing. He was rejected by a broken system that ultimately swept the American car industry to their demise.

Tom was an authentic leader who stood his ground with his beliefs. His vision of business was long term success for the entire industry as well as for Chrysler. His vision was the right one. If industry leaders had followed his lead, listened to Tom and done things his way, it is difficult to imagine Chrysler eventually ending up, as it did, a division of Fiat.

Five Percent Dinner

Every year, GM, Ford -- and now that Tom Stallkamp was gone -- Daimler Chrysler too continued to take 5 percent off of the price of parts from their suppliers up front. The reductions were "negotiated," but there was really no discussion about it anymore. It had become routine. The theory that the automakers used – that the 5 percent would force the suppliers to get more cost effective – had become a fairy tale by this time.

It was really all bullshit. It was the car companies treating suppliers like ATM machines because their own system was terminal and they needed money. Instead of reinventing a new system that would work more cost efficiently themselves, it was easier to take money out of the supplier end and tell them to get more efficient, while they continued on their merry way of doing business the same way they had since the 1960s.

Right after Daimler merged with Chrysler in 1998 (and if you are familiar with the details of this famous union, the word "merge" might not be what comes to your mind) Chrysler took *another* five percent from its suppliers. This was on top of the annual five percent that was already negotiated with GM, Ford and Chrysler.

The new Daimler Chrysler company unilaterally issued new purchase orders and took another five percent. No negotiation, no explanation. That's a lot of money and a huge burden to pass onto suppliers. And that second five percent came midway through the year, so now we only had six months to figure out how to offset another five percent off and still meet our full year earnings commitments to our investors.

Think about it. At JCI, we were doing about $1.5 billion in transactions with Chrysler alone. So the initial 5 percent price cut amounted to nearly $75 million that we had to trim. Do that twice and it is $150 million, for just Chrysler. We were halfway through our fiscal year when the second cut came, and I was already challenged to meet the projections and commitments I had made to our shareholders. Now with only six months left, I had to find another $75 million of cost efficiencies to meet those commitments.

There was an association that a lot of the top auto suppliers belonged to called the Original Equipment Manufacturers Association. A lot of suppliers belonged to that because we kind of needed to have a support group to deal with the abuse we were taking. Some suppliers wanted to use this association when the second five percent started to destroy Chrysler's ability to operate in the system because the five percent that was not negotiated clearly violated the contract law. Unfortunately, in my opinion, the bigger picture here was 'win the battle, lose the war.' Doing business with the Detroit Three was tough enough. This took it to a whole new level.

Suppliers were mad and there was talk about stopping shipments to Chrysler. So Dieter Zetche, the new Chairman of Daimler Chrysler, decided to throw a dinner for the angry suppliers to try to smooth things over. It was in the Chrysler museum, with apparently the top ten suppliers, who probably represented over 50 percent of Chrysler's North America purchases.

At the dinner, Dieter gets up in front of this group to say a few words, and he says something to the effect that "this is good for you too because if we go down, you are going to lose way more than five percent." No attempt to justify the money grab – just putting lipstick on their pig. But what was he going to say to a mob of angry suppliers who wished they were holding pitch forks instead of cocktails.

So Dieter finished up his little talk, and he asked if anyone had any questions. One guy raised his hand and asked the perfect question. I am not sure exactly who it was that posed the question, but it wasn't me and I really wish it had been, because it was epic!

He said, "Are you ever going to do this again?" Everyone was quiet trying to figure out what he meant by that, but a few of us got it. I got it.

Dieter answered, "What do you mean?"

And this guy said, "Look, there is one of two scenarios going on here. One is that for whatever reason, you guys got yourself in a bad spot, so you need a financial bridge while you do a root cause analysis and you are going to reinvent yourself on the fly and engineer out of your operating model all the shit that brought us to this dinner tonight. So what you need from us is that *one-time* financial bridge so you can go from where you are now to the new system. If that is so, then the answer to my question is 'no, we are not going to do this again.'"

And then he said this, "Or, the second scenario is you are just taking five percent now, kicking the can on any permanent correction, and we're going to be out here for dinner again in, oh, about another three years? Which one is it?"

I have no clue what the answer was, but I know what the answer *wasn't!* It was such a great question that should *never* have to be asked! But in a system where everyone is shirking responsibility and kicking the can down the road to the next guy, not only is it the best question, everyone in the room pretty much knew the answer, and it was *not the right one!*

Look, if it was simply that Daimler-Chrysler was bridging the gap to a new system, why wouldn't they just have that conversation up front? The five percent is bad enough, but what made it worse was that they obviously had no plan to fix anything. They were just using us and there was no end in sight.

Daimler sold its interest in Chrysler for roughly 20 percent of its investment in the merger. Not long after that, we all remember that Chrysler had to solicit the U.S. government to bail them out. Today, Chrysler is the U.S. subsidiary of their parent company, Fiat of Italy.

They should have put Tom Stallkamp at the helm of Chrysler. The history books would have a completely different story concerning Chrysler in the 1990s and 2000s.

After I was fired from JCI in 2003, I made it a point to catch up with Tom. I met with him quietly to tell him how much I respected him for his leadership. We reflected on how the leadership system had shifted to a place where the very people who are truly worthy and able to lead are rejected and labeled unfit.

And that, Mr. Iacocca, is where all the leaders have gone.

Humpty Dumpty Sat on a Wall Street

Enron became headline news at the end of 2001 when financial corruption and accounting fraud was revealed in their creative bookkeeping. Using loopholes and sketchy financial reporting, the leading Enron executives hid billions of dollars in debt from failed projects and deals, misleading their Board of Directors, auditors and stockholders with inflated revenue reports.

Enron was a company that claimed $101 billion in revenues in 2000 and was named "America's Most Innovative Company" by Fortune Magazine for six years running. Before the catastrophic scandal, Enron was a world player in several natural resource industries, including electricity, natural gas and paper.

Disclosure of the corruption precipitated a historic and complicated bankruptcy and liquidation of Enron assets. Enron's stock prices plunged from a high of $90.75 per share to less than $1 by late fall 2001.

The scope of the human tragedy precipitated by the Enron scandal is not directly evident in those numbers. Innocent people suffered the loss of reputations, careers, income, pensions and homes. It caused losses to hundreds of thousands of investors. The atrocity also led to the fall from grace of the once revered Arthur Andersen accounting firm – one of the top five auditing and accounting firms in the entire world at the time.

Enron was the largest corporate bankruptcy in U.S., history with $63.4 billion in assets, until WorldCom filed for bankruptcy in the summer of 2002 under a similar cloud of corruption.

What delivered Enron down the path to destruction was its leadership's deliberate deception of and disassociation from employees, shareholders and every defined measure of corporate success except profitability. The only viable reasoning behind their decision to inflate the bottom line of the company was selfish greed. Enron certainly was "America's Most Innovative Company," if you include innovative bookkeeping.

How Low Can You Go?

Unfortunately, Enron is not the only company whose leadershit covets profitability above all else. More recently Volkswagen was caught cheating emissions testing. And not too long ago, the CEO of United Airlines was caught in a Federal corruption investigation after he cut a back room steak dinner deal with the Port Authority. He took $10 million in taxpayer money in exchange for the airline's reinstatement of an unprofitable flight route to Columbia, SC where the then-chairman of the Port Authority (an equally illustrative example of corrupt leadershit) had a vacation home.

These are just a few examples. I believe there are many companies that have been commandeered by the executive officers for their own benefit and to meet projections. They are operating under these same low, and sometimes corrupt, standards. They just haven't been caught. This type of leadershit culture seems to be outgrowing our methods for detection, which can no longer keep up with the pace of deception. News cycles spit out incidents like these with alarming frequency. As a society we have been force-fed these stories so much, they don't even strike us as shocking anymore. Like cows chewing cud, now we just digest it all.

This brand of leadershit exemplifies a caving in of the value system that once distinguished right from wrong and bad from good. As a society and as a nation, we have been kind of giving up because we don't know how to stop it.

This type of acceptance has seeped into other areas of our life, as well. For instance, no matter your position on legalizing marijuana, you can't avoid recognizing that our political and media leaders used to say that marijuana was bad, and now say, well, we can't stop it so we are going to legalize it because we might as well benefit from the tax revenue of it. Then we, in turn, rationalize the shit out of that narrative to gain acceptance of the new lowered standard, to hush the opposition and to kid ourselves that it really is good.

If we spin it enough we can feel like we actually did something to benefit the greater good, even though the black market sales of marijuana in Colorado have never been better, because illegal dealers can easily beat the price point for the highly taxed and regulated stuff. Hell, I bet the "munchies" sales in Colorado have gone through the roof. So there's that.

In order to accommodate that new way of thinking and a fresh flow of revenue, there is a lot of back-pedaling and painting the target around the arrow that has to happen. So the focus shifts from what is bad about marijuana to shining the spotlight on what is "good" about it. News flash: marijuana is still bad. It hasn't changed. We have.

This same thought deterioration is happening around sports gambling. We can't stop it, so we are going to legalize it and profit from it, even though it is as bad as it has always been. It's like finding out that despite your "best efforts" your 15-year-old has been drinking alcohol and you have been unable to alter his continuing bad behavior, so you throw up your arms and say, well, what's the harm in letting him drink if he isn't driving?

This is a good place to introduce and discuss absolute versus relative morality. Absolute morality indicates that there is a set of moral rules which are absolute and universal. Relative morality indicates that morals are not absolute and depend upon a situation.

Since anyone can declare their particular moral beliefs are the absolute, and since nobody can clearly demonstrate the validity of those claims, the whole premise of absolute morality is arbitrary. In that system, anything can be declared absolute. In reality, different religions, communities and countries recognize different morals. Even different households in the same neighborhood can have different morals. There is no universal code of absolute morality.

Each society establishes its own set of morals, but they are treated as general guidelines, not one-size-fits-all. That is why when a police officer pulls over a driver, even though they were caught speeding or rolling through a stop sign, not every driver gets the same ticket. Plaintiffs found guilty in court of the same offenses can receive vastly different sentences. These are instances of relative morality, with punishment fitting that specific situation. What is strongly established is a system of values in which wrongdoing is recognized and punished, albeit with different levels of punishment.

In my opinion, in the corporate world, violation of morals are by far the worst violation of all, and yet we don't act like it even matters when we cover our tracks with excuses like "It's just business". When you, as a leader, have a decision to make that meets the criteria to satisfy shareholders, and maybe even customers, but you do something horribly wrong to somebody else in the process, the right leader won't do it. They won't go there. It is wrong.

In this time in history, we have become sloppy with the value systems used to define leadership under a corporate banner, and have allowed the lines of right and wrong to become too fuzzy in the name of the bottom line. This "permissive parenting" of the value system is seeping into everything we do. We need to take a focused, hard look at today's leadership performance standards which have dipped so pathetically low, bringing us all down to their level, and the fundamental impotence of the mechanisms in place that regulate those standards.

It has become painfully obvious to me that authentic leaders are being replaced with knockoffs in such a pervasive manner that we, in effect, are reduced to grading them on a curve.

I am the Great and Powerful OZ! Ignore that Person Behind the Resume!

It might have become more difficult to ascertain whether a leader is going to be authentic or not, but our definition of leadership has also become weak. Anyone who has tried applying for jobs in today's market recognizes that it is the keywords you use in the online application, not your actual qualities that determine whether you get a chance at being hired. This should bother you because that is a similar method by which our corporate leaders, your employers, in some cases, are also selected.

We look at the wrong markers for qualifications, letting paperwork take the place of personal inquest to determine whether or not someone is truly competent to lead a company. While there are background checks and references, it is also a sterile checklist of eligibility requirements that has replaced a more exhaustive and accurate personal assessment process. We might know whether or not a candidate has committed a felony, but that doesn't necessarily mean they are a good person. It might simply mean that they were never caught. We still hire people without really knowing their nature. And it is a person's nature that defines their depth of character and their ability to be an effective leader.

Authentic leaders are humble, compassionate and highly effective. The transformation any leader needs to make to be authentic is from the "I" to the "We." While you can learn this "leadership language" in most MBA courses, saying the words without living them is disingenuous. It is the sincere and consistent demonstration of the "we," and the shedding of the personal ego that marks the authentic leader worthy of following.

Author Jim Collins brings this to light in *Good to Great: Why Some Companies Make the Leap...and Others Don't* (Collins, 2001). In an effort to discover why some organizations go from good to great, Collins and his research team uncover the answer to the book's question in a leadership formula. What they discovered is that great companies sustain their greatness over time due to what Collins refers to as "Level 5 Leaders." These are leaders who possess a combination of two enigmatic qualities: colossal ambition and personal humility.

While Collins clearly lays out the importance of Level 5 leaders in his book, he does not offer a way to identify them or to guide future leaders in developing the essential "Level 5 Leader" qualities. I can certainly relate. I have some notions, but no clear path of how to do it either. But I think he is certainly onto something.

In every university in America you can find an MBA course that delivers the information needed to climb a corporate ladder. Becoming a COO, CFO or a CEO is a formulaic rite of passage outlined in countless textbooks. But knowing the right steps to take and making the correct career moves should not necessarily be a reason for anyone to be granted a corporate CEO position. Other less tangible credentials, like competence and character should play into the selection process that produces quality leaders and great companies.

It seems to me that boards of directors who hire CEOs are ignoring these intangibles when they vet candidates. (If you have heard differently, it is likely to be bullshit.) There is often a box-checking of tangible criteria and achievements that determines the consolidated vote of a board to hire or not hire a CEO. I wish that achievements were more synonymous with character.

Now we have big companies like Enron and WorldCom as part of our history. And you have people like Lance Armstrong, whose resume includes seven Tour de France race wins . . . and we all know the rest of that story. He was an international hero until we found out *how* he did it.

It's on the Internet So It Must Be True

Once upon a time, the fat, fine printed, snail-mailed and regulated annual prospectus was a corporation's main contact with the public. In the world of the internet, however, that public reach is unregulated and expanded.

A great deal of attention has been paid to website narrative. It is there where corporations get to tout their supposedly superior expertise in the latest and greatest marketing form and industry best-practice standards. They all sport the proper branding and messaging that will convince people to engage with that company. They all say the right things. They all say the same things. According to every company profile, they are all great. They are all the best. They all use the appropriate jargon and have the right answers as well as the right color, right font and right logo.

But the words are all suspect, and quite possibly hollow because there is no reveal about shortcomings. CEO applicants – just like websites – do not list their past mistakes and transgressions; what they learned from those mistakes and how it made them better people and better leaders. Similarly, resumes and websites talk about the person/company, the work and the results, but they do not always talk about the process and the quality of that process or the person.

We have all learned the value of image management. Report only the best. Do not show any chinks in the armor. Take credit for everything good that happens in your universe. Job applicants often do not share the limelight with co-workers who shared project successes with them, simply claiming it as their intellectual property. In fact, many times they take full credit for accomplishments that were actually completed as a part of a group or overall corporate effort. It is difficult to determine a person's character.

But if you haven't vetted the person's character to find out if they are trustworthy and truthful, why would you believe any of their stated accomplishments?

Gentlemen, Start Your Generators

The starting place in a company's search for its ship's captain, the controller of its corporate destiny, is to define what kind of leader it is looking for. Who are you hiring? You are hopefully hiring a leader who is fully committed to executing the business consistent with the values and mission set forth in the website and other official materials. You want to hire a leader who has profit and loss responsibility and good financial results. This can – and should – be dissected even further.

There are the results, and there are the generators of the results. The results comprise the performance, productivity and financial position of a company; the outcomes in numbers, spreadsheets, charts and graphs. The generators are the employees. Leaders are supposed to manage the generators of the results, which in turn indirectly impact the results/outcomes. Authentic leaders manage the business. Knockoffs manage the results.

In presentations to MBA students, I define management of generators. It means establishing a corporate culture that motivates employees to do their best and be invested in the outcome of their work. This means providing the necessary resources to achieve the expected performance, and communicating high expectations and accountability with clear and appropriate benchmarks for success and boundaries for behavior. And by the way, the boundaries apply to *everybody*. Leaders are not excluded in the formula.

I tell them that management of the generators is one of the centers of gravity of quality leadership in a company. Others include:

- Creating formulas for prevention versus reaction: The leadershit system is focused on – and rewards – controlled reaction to bad news rather than prevention of it. Quality leadership provides formulas for both.
- Understanding that organizations do not fail because of people. They fail because of people operating in a flawed design, a suboptimal culture and system. They fail because of leadershit.
- Ensuring good employee morale and a healthy corporate culture where employees are working for each other and not for paychecks. Employees feel valued and heard by leadership, they trust leadership and don't want to let them down.
- Focusing on the future, not the present. A CEO's time should be weighted mostly on the future trajectory of the company and the tactical application of getting to that goal. So a quality CEO is focused on the means, not the ends. Time is spent transforming the company for a better future, not trying to manage the public image of the company in the present.
- Hiring good operational people who can be trusted to hold up the day-to-day operations, allowing others to focus on the future path.
- Finding and hiring a talented team who work well together so that the whole is greater than the sum of their parts. Key talent traits include selflessness and humility. (Have you seen that on any recruiting requirements lately?)

Note that most of those bullet points involve people/employees, not numbers. This represents the ideal CEO management style. I believe it used to be more prevalent and that things seem to have changed in the past few decades. So when did it all turn around? When did the ends become more important than the means? When did long term investments in the future become subordinate to what is good for now?

Results > Means = Good Enough Leader

Do I think that there has been a radical shift in our center of gravity in terms of integrity and honesty? Yes.

When Hank Aaron broke Babe Ruth's record for homeruns in 1976, nobody thought for a minute that he cheated to achieve that. No. Fast forward to 2006 when Barry Bonds broke Hank Aaron's record, nobody on the planet believed that his achievement was legitimate. Bonds never got caught, but neither did a lot of CEOs that we haven't heard of yet.

A new normal has formulated. So what has changed? What do we really care about now?

What caused the shift where honesty and integrity went from the way business was done to getting in the way of doing business? Did it happen when the salaries and bonuses became so big? Is it a result of the "me" generation coming into power in the world of business? It is difficult to say what triggered the tipping point. Perhaps it was a multitude of factors in the perfect storm of circumstances. For whatever reason, in corporate America, in board rooms across the country, standards seem to have systematically dropped; a drift that led to a fundamental shift. And it took many of us by surprise.

With every exposure I had – running a large business, consultant, and board member – I kept thinking that my last two or three experiences with leadershit were anomalies. But what I have come to consistently see and eventually believe is that the exceptions have become the rule.

It seemed like everything flipped when near-term results became king. Building a strong future became less important than showing up every quarter with the right numbers. Instead of nurturing the people who drive the success and future of a company, spreadsheets became the CEO's focus. There is the question that stock analysts should ask, but do not ask on the earnings call: "It's good that you have met your quarterly numbers and that you are confirming your full year earnings commitment. Was that in addition to, or instead of, making appropriate financial investments in your five-year vision plan?" Yeah, right! Think what that answer might do to the market!

Performance reviews drill down on two aspects of a CEO's job duties. A strategic plan by a CEO – if it is done right – requires a transformational change from where your company is now to a new and better place in the future usually utilizing innovative methodologies. It looks for growth opportunities for the company, or maybe even reinvention or redefinition of it.

A succession plan (planning a blueprint for the future leaders) – if it is done right – is a process of identifying and *developing* internal people with the potential to fill key business leadership positions in the company seamlessly. That takes time and effort. You have to really evaluate people, train them, give them increasing responsibilities, and get to know them and their work ethic and production. It is a big investment.

Succession plans for corporations used to focus on developing good operations managers to get them ready for promotion. These folks have solid operational skills and are intimately familiar with the minutia of the business, the people, and what has to happen on a day-to-day basis to drive success for the company. They live day-in and day-out on the "means" side of the scale. Today, that focus has shifted. More and more corporate succession plans target candidates with financial skills rather than operational skills for CEO positions. And why not? With today's system placing a premium on managing the financial results, it makes sense to have a leader that can expertly manage a spreadsheet.

Succession planning is hard work, but keeps the company in a better position to react to change and adversity through seamless transitions in executive positions. And it is a big deal. Bringing someone up internally through the ranks, preparing them for the position, giving them the necessary exposure and experiences helps a company get the right person in place quickly who can do the work efficiently.

Fox Overseeing Hen House

Somebody sent me an email asking me what a governance committee does on a board. None of the boards that I had served on had a governance committee, but I had heard of them. So I looked it up.

The governance committee of a board of directors is elected to basically assure that the board is doing their job. The governance committee members are made up of members of the board. It's a subgroup of the board overseeing the board. They don't bring in a bunch of new people. It's the same people. So it is the fox guarding the hen house. When the dust settles, there probably is little oversight. It is mostly optics.

The idea behind governance committees is that the stakeholders and activists don't trust the board, or the board isn't behaving like the board should, so they set out to create a committee to oversee the board. It's like putting belts and suspenders on the whole thing to keep the pants from falling down to reveal the dysfunction of the core elements. From what I can tell, this might all be about the board appeasing activist groups who don't trust boards to do their jobs, so they put themselves in charge of oversight of themselves. We all can't be this stupid, can we?

There are shareholder activists that are getting pretty vocal and powerful regarding corporate boards. They are trying to create a critical mass to force the SEC to regulate boards and how they operate. Sometimes, what they are saying makes sense and is legitimate. However, in my opinion, sometimes they go a little too far to make their point. They get overinvested in their "solutions," which can be excessive in the face of limited budgets and shareholder expectations.

For instance, most boards are staggered boards. That means that if you have nine board members, only three of them are up for election on any given year. If all three are not re-elected, the most turnover you could have would be three out of nine – assuming the other six do not quit. You still have six held over from year to year and you have continuity. That makes sense if everyone is doing their job. The board's job is to remain objective and oversee management of the business to growth and profitability on behalf of the shareholders. They work for the shareholders, not the company. Business 101 stuff.

What often happens if you don't have a policy that requires the board to turn over regularly is an overall loss of objectivity. It's human nature. When board members are initially elected, they need to have zero emotional investment in the business, and certainly must be free of even the slightest conflict of interest. If they are on that board long enough, naturally they begin to cultivate familiarity and gravitate away from objectivity. This might not happen the first year, second year or the fifth year, but there are a lot of board members who have been on boards for decades. Common sense would tell you that they are no longer objective. Longstanding board members integrate into the team and become too familiar. Their obligations often shift from being beholden to the shareholders, to being beholden to the chairman. It couldn't be more upside down.

The Golden Mean

Shareholder activists are aware of this problem and some say that all board members should be up for re-election every year. I understand why they want that. They want to remove the opportunity for any board member to settle into a position. I doubt board members intend to get too comfortable with their work. It is the system that provides the opportunity for them to be on the board long enough to lose objectivity and forget their fiduciary duties. People naturally become more emotionally attached to things that are familiar. In addition to the compensation with lucrative fees, stock option grants, and celebrity, board members settle in and get comfortable with their work.

So shareholder activist groups support the idea of independent board members. Independent board members are members who don't work for the company; they are not a supplier; they don't sell to them and they have no commercial interest or investment in the company. Independent board members are part of a solution to the loss of objectivity on boards. A good concept, although they, too, can get too close if they stay too long, because they are human.

But these same activists overreach sometimes. They come up with unworkable propositions involving environmental and other causes that most companies cannot afford in these economic times. There are federal mandates and OSHA requirements serving the environment. Every company complies with them – or should – but activists sometimes want more than compliance. What they sometimes don't understand is that, for every step you want to take me beyond those compliance requirements, it can become very expensive to implement. You can't work in either extreme.

Aristotle's theory of the Golden Mean does not claim that there is a universal or mathematical middle that applies to every situation. Rather, the Golden Mean represents a fair balance between two extremes. The example often used is courage as the middle between cowardice and recklessness.

So let's say now I do try to accommodate activist desires relative to the environment. Now I've got a bunch of shareholders upset because I can't appreciate their stock because I'm too busy investing in the environmental agenda. Authentic leaders are constantly trying to find the Golden Mean between increasing revenues and profits, and being a responsible corporate citizen. On any given day, somebody will not be completely satisfied.

Diverse views are healthy as long as all involved — whether they agree or disagree — respect each other's positions. And as long as everyone understands that the only best answer is usually a healthy compromise.

The idea of environmental protection is a good one. We should all be aware of and careful with the environment, but there needs to be a reasonable balance struck that allows steady incremental changes that add up in everyone's win column over time.

The same thing with throwing out all nine board members every time there is an election. You have no continuity, but the good news is you can be pretty sure everybody is fairly objective near term.

When a board loses its objectivity and makes decisions that don't work toward that Golden Mean, but only works toward the board's own self-perpetuation, that is a red flag of a broken system. Putting another layer of governance by installing a governance committee is simply a Band-Aid attempt to shore up the broken system. It is probably not effective. It makes the whole thing top-heavy, when in reality, you could probably achieve better results if you talked to the people at the bottom; the workers.

So a governance committee over a board of directors is a way to project an *image* of control, an image of management to shareholders. So shareholders can check a box and elect the officials that are supposed to oversee their interests, and they feel good about that extra layer of management thinking that it means they have another layer of protection. But shareholders don't know what I know. If they did, they would be asking why is that box even there. If the board was doing their job, that should be sufficient; the governance committee would not be necessary.

The most fundamental point about all of this is who can you trust? I mean really . . . who?

What is the truth and what is deception and what is a spin on the truth? CEO and management presentations to a board of directors can be very interesting to watch. There are things that leaders do not want to say to the board. There are things that they do not want to reveal. They don't want to give the board any reason to question the methods used or the fuzzy math applied. Don't give them any more information than is necessary because it can become ammunition for them to question the leaders about things they don't want to defend or justify. They play the plausible deniability card. Sometimes it is best for the board to remain in the dark; wink, wink.

So some leaders present information to try to manage the perspective outside of their walls. They want to manage it, but not necessarily distort it. There is a fine line. The reason that this works is because board members, shareholders, the public and other stakeholders don't have the ability to call out leaders who are withholding pertinent information. They do not know what questions to ask. And better yet, if the numbers are what they are supposed to be, then great. Meeting over. Let's do lunch.

Not OK

There were many times in board meetings and corporate meetings where I needed to simply say one word with two letters, "OK," to agree to something that didn't align with who I was, or with what I agreed to be responsible for. And I was certainly not the only one who felt this pressure to surrender the standard and go along to get along. I am not giving myself credit for wanting to do the right thing rather than the easy thing. It's like I just didn't get the memo that the easy thing was even available. Many times I simply didn't know that there was an option and it took me by surprise.

Authentic leaders are still here. There are plenty of them, but most corporations that are looking for leaders are not interested in those guys or gals. They want the results guys; they want the guys who will stop at nothing to get them. Corporate America is fostering a new breed of so-called leaders who are not focused on leading people. They are focused on winning at all costs and/or they are focused on leading us down the primrose path.

I am talking about a *lowered standard* that has become a preferred method. For many corporate leadership positions, in order to be considered a good candidate as a leader now, your value system should fit this new substandard platform. It seems often that even the bad guys do not have to make much effort to blend in because the system accepts his/her behavior and does the work for them.

Company leaders are now being baited to get results and earn their big piles of money, at the expense of the leadership standards the company claims to value. Even the most moral among us would be tempted to ignore fundamental job requirements to hit the kind of jackpot many of today's CEOs get . . . even when they somehow get themselves fired. With severance packages.

I don't believe this is just ideological theory. Shit is going wrong. Big shit. When compensation and bonuses are the overwhelming motivating force behind performance for CEOs, and they are weighted heavily on the present, everything else is just in the way, including the future of the company and the people that they are supposed to be leading. I don't think that many CEOs have any portion of their bonus based on measuring their organization's morale or how they are viewed by their employees. And I also don't think their bonus is measured against *following up* to make appropriate improvements in company morale or a culture that generates legitimate outstanding results. I don't think that any portion of their bonus is based on positioning the company for growth and prosperity long after they are gone either. Why the hell not?

The Gift of Character

Americans have traditionally identified with the virtues of honor, dignity, justice, perseverance, ethics, humility, valor, modesty, morals, self-control, integrity, self-respect and trustworthiness. Belief in these foundational virtues was fixed and served to self-police every individual. There were internal (shame and guilt) as well as external consequences for violators.

In modern corporate America, however, there are few consequences for failing to adhere to such virtues, and so there is little to no self-policing for compliance. As a result, these virtues have been minimized and made nearly irrelevant in leadership in the toxic environment of corporate America. I believe we all need to give some serious thought to where our country is headed as it is being driven by a corporate leadership culture lacking those virtues. As human beings, certain things have to matter to us. When it comes to our future success as a society and as a nation, I believe our character really matters.

Why do some CEOs do the right thing and others chase the numbers? That line has to do with a system that values outcomes over character, but it also has to do with character. And character is something that starts long before that leader is in a position of power. It goes way back to a time in a person's life before employment, before school, before the MBA. It starts early. It goes back to who you are and how you became the person that you grew up to be. I believe that only people who acquired the gift of character should lead.

If you have known any authentic leaders, you recognize certain things about them. They are driven first and foremost by earning trust, and they do that by demonstrating their reliability, transparency, integrity and thoughtful follow-through. They have a belief system that carries everything, and it sweeps people up like a magnet, engaging them in working for the same goals. When these leaders talk about their work, they do it with fire, pride and belief in its importance. Authentic leaders are comfortable in their own skin, know their shortcomings, admit mistakes and know when to ask for help. They are sincere, frank, trustworthy, and they work hard.

This leader comes to the table with a gift of character of which they are sometimes completely unaware, but they gravitate toward utilizing it naturally.

Authentic leaders are not the ones who manage their companies by doing anything necessary to hit projections. If at all possible, they will avoid laying off employees to make the math work. They try to find ways to cut costs without reducing quality in products. They won't delay payment on accounts to manipulate the monthly numbers. They don't rely on fear or intimidation to motivate employees to perform at high levels and achieve things. They know what they will NOT do to achieve success.

Unfortunately, in this system, authentic leaders are undervalued and, instead, the leaders who WILL do anything, sacrifice anyone, to plug the right numbers and collect the bonus are controlling modern corporate America. The winners are "me" and "now." The losers are "we" and "future," and if that doesn't make you nervous, if that is not some kind of call to action, then you are probably part of the problem.

CHAPTER 4
LEADERSHIT
COMPENSATION
THE PRICE OF INCOMPETENCE

We Don't Print $ Here...Oh Wait. Evidently We Do

Anyone can do the research to find top salaries and compensation packages online. For the highest paid CEOs in America, these packages are worth hundreds of millions of dollars. There are cash, stock and stock options included with salaries, bonuses and other compensation. Personally, I really don't care what is represented in the compensation package; cut it in half. Cut it by two-thirds. Cut it by 90%. No corporate leader should be paid hundreds of millions of dollars even if they are doing a fantastic job.

"As corporate America engages in an unprecedented buyback binge, soaring CEO pay tied to short-term performance measures like EPS [earnings per share] is prompting criticism that executives are using stock repurchases to enrich themselves at the expense of long-term corporate health, capital investment and employment."

– Special report: Buybacks enrich the bosses even when business sags, By Karen Brettell, David Gaffen and David Rohde

12/12/2015 (Brettell, Gaffen, & Rohde, 2015)

Hand in the Candy Jar

A stock repurchase, or buyback, refers to publicly traded companies buying their stock back from shareholders. Buybacks reduce the amount of outstanding shares in the market, soothing shareholders. Based on market dynamics, they also cause a raise in the price per share of the stock. Companies have to come up with cash in order to repurchase stock. They frequently raid the coffers of the future infrastructure, innovation, and investment in human capital in order to "artificially" inflate stock prices, and unlock performance bonus payouts for senior leadershit.

Buybacks can be perfectly legitimate strategies if used correctly by organizations that have genuinely generated extra cash and don't have to strip away the long-term corporate potential of the corporation. Unfortunately, the pay-for-performance system in corporate America is structured around incentives that drive shortcuts and the WIFM (what's-in-it-for-me) mentality.

Which publicly traded companies include the impact of buybacks in their publicly available per-share metrics? Out of the S&P 500, fewer than 20 disclose that information in their proxies. The impact of buybacks on corporate value should be a separate WIFM graph on the very first page of the financial statements of every publicly traded organization. Shareholders would cease to be "soothed" if they knew the entire truth.

"...[S]hare buybacks by U.S. non-financial companies reached a record $520 billion in the most recent reporting year. A Reuters analysis of 3,300 non-financial companies found that together, buybacks and dividends have surpassed total capital expenditures and are more than double research and development spending." –

– Special report: Buybacks enrich the bosses even when business sags, By Karen Brettell, David Gaffen and David Rohde

12/12/2015 (Brettell, Gaffen, & Rohde, 2015)

In a nation where innovation and gritty competitiveness has always been our economic strength and salvation and the envy of all other nations, I see the colossal volume of buybacks in recent years as eroding away the very fiber of who we are as an economic powerhouse. Mammoth stock repurchases subsidize a growing reward/bonus system for those who least need it (the leadershits), and subvert the progress needed for U.S. companies to compete in global markets by undercapitalizing their innovation and infrastructure. Buybacks are frequently disassociated with, and have little relevance to, the company's true fundamental performance, and give shareholders a false sense of security.

This is *just one* example of the financial gymnastics by leaders to advance short term thinking to boost compensation. There are so many others. But Wall Street is mostly blind to it. Wall Street has its eye on metrics to determine a company's value, not on how well the business operations are being executed. In reality, there are frequently finance geeks on both ends of these transactions – corporate executives, board members and institutional investors – reaping huge profits while in many cases the company, its people and its future are merely cogs in the equation of their personal wealth formula.

Buybacks have become one of the – dare I say -- leadershit "schemes" that are helping to widen the income gap between high paid corporate executives and the rest of the people in America . . . you know, the people that those same leaders were hired to lead.

And no, greed is not good. Greed is evil. It is one of the seven deadly sins. Greed is not about capitalism. It is about human beings who have sold their soul.

"At those levels, CEOs last year were paid 303 times what workers in their industries earned, compared with a ratio of 59 times in 1989." –

The Economic Policy Institute, a Washington-based nonprofit – June 21, 2015.[2]

I don't think there is any question what is happening to America.

I think it is important to note that in some situations, corporations are afraid to invest their money. Uncertain corporate tax policies created through government leadershit have disincentivized corporations from doing much of anything with their money other than buybacks and hoarding it. Because hoarding too much cash can make a company vulnerable to hostile takeover, the buyback route becomes one of few viable options.

Corporations are sometimes afraid to invest because of ever-changing tax laws that can undermine investments. On the other hand, providing corporations with tax policies that make it safe and prudent to invest their money is no guarantee that they will. Leadershit might not invest corporate cash for the good of the company, but rather for their own personal good. In a free market system, government cannot control the way that corporations decide to spend their cash. Even if businesses are given the tax breaks and incentivized to grow their company and expand, they might choose to spend that money differently.

Let's Talk About Value

I was giving a talk at a business school class, and during the Q & A session, a student asked me what I thought of the general discrepancy between an hourly worker in a company making an average of $15 to $20 an hour and the CEO of that company making $10 or more million a year.

I first explained that there is a difference between the hourly rate that an employee makes and the "all-in" hourly rate, which is the total cost to an employer for an hourly worker, including health insurance, benefits, payroll

---

[2] http://www.epi.org/publication/top-ceos-make-300-times-more-than-workers-pay-growth-surpasses-market-gains-and-the-rest-of-the-0-1-percent/

taxes, etc. I said that I couldn't really comment on the $15 to $20 an hour job because I don't know the value that hourly wage work had with regard to the operation. She asked me to clarify.

I used an example that I was familiar with. At that time, around 2004, 2005 or 2006, the all-in rate at one of the three Detroit auto companies was $65 an hour. Now say the work is a forklift truck operator, and their job involves safely and efficiently moving parts around an assembly plant. This is necessary work, for sure, and has value for the company. But with all due respect, I don't see it as $65 an hour worth of value to the operation. Now if that same forklift truck driver was safely and efficiently moving boxes of nitroglycerin around a child care center, I'd say that worker should probably be paid maybe $1,000 an hour.

The point here is that the cost has to be proportionate to the value, not how much leverage you have to demand it.

I said, "Now, with respect to the CEO, in my opinion, no one – and I mean no one – that I know is worth $10 million a year." These leaders are not curing cancer. They are not solving world hunger. What they do has to be related to the value that they provide to the employer, the market, and the industry, both near and long term.

Value is about proper and reasonable alignment of compensation with duties, obligations and performance. In the case of CEOs, this is out of whack. Too often ridiculous salaries are being paid for short term results and image management by redeploying money that would otherwise be invested in the long term future and stability of the company.

Authentic leaders strive to leave an organization in a better position with a brighter future than when they arrived. Compensation for their efforts comes in more forms than money. In fact, while money does matter, it may not be the most compelling validation of an authentic leader's impact on the business both now and in the future. Other forms of validation or acknowledgement include things like pride and personal fulfillment in what the business and its people achieved. Legacy is another form of validation, when it is a legacy of good repute – not the Enron kind of legacy.

CEO = Honey Hole

Usually, when companies need a new leader, and haven't developed one internally, they are on the hunt for CEOs who are already sitting CEOs for another company. The reasoning behind this decision is that you can hire someone who is already a seasoned CEO, and you don't have to suffer through the learning curve. In my experience, while it makes theoretical sense, in reality it is bullshit. Boards do it because it is easier on them. When they can check the "sitting CEO" box, they have far less work to do to justify their decision. And the sitting CEO applicant has zero work to do to justify their desired compensation. That little check box did it all.

See, if you want a CEO that is on the job somewhere else and you want to hire them away to work for you, you have to make it worth their while to make that jump. You have to make the pot sweeter than what they have or they will just stay where they are because it is easier for them.

Part of sweetening the pot is buying them out of their existing contract. "I'm not walking away from $30 million salary. You want me, you gotta give me $30 million to start with." The contract often involves the "golden parachute" too. In order to minimize their risk in making the jump to a new company, a CEO wants money up front in the amount of his existing contract (the example of $30 million), a salary on top of that, bonuses, stocks, and also assurances in the form of an exit payment in the event things don't work out.

So to review, a contract to hire a sitting CEO away from a job that he/she already has might include the following:

1. A check for $30 million (or $5, $10, $50 million – whatever it is) to buy out their existing contract
2. Plus lump sum buyouts of any retention bonus arrangements, i.e., like unvested stock options.
3. Plus a new salary that is in excess of their old salary of $30 million (or whatever it is)
4. Plus bonuses
5. Plus stocks and stock options
6. Essentially unlimited expense accounts
7. Perks like company car, company phone, computer and use of the company aircraft and personal use of the company aircraft *after they leave*
8. And an exit clause that guarantees them $100 million (or $10, $50, $500 million – whatever it is) which they will receive when they leave, even if they are fired for doing a crappy job and running the company into the ground or bankruptcy.

Is that market? Yep, that is market. But the whole system is wrong because the unintended consequence of this model is that incentive to do a good job – even a decent job – has been taken out of the equation. If you have already given me $130 million, and then everything goes wrong, I still get $130 million. There is no downside to that for me.

Leaders are getting paid too much to care about things that should matter a lot, but are not being given any meaningful connection to the problem.

Passing the Big Buck

In 2001, the Sarbanes-Oxley Act was enacted specifically to try to avoid another Enron. So now, every quarter when public companies turn in their earnings reports, corporate leadership – specifically the CEO and CFO – have to sign a management letter certifying that the numbers being reported were accurate. The management letter holds corporate leadership specifically responsible for those numbers and prevents them from claiming that they didn't know what was going on.

In the case of Ken Lay and Jeffrey Stillings, the leadership at Enron, their defense was, hey, look, this is a huge company with thousands of people. I can't keep track of what every person books all the time. Apparently they missed the memo that that was exactly what they were being paid the big bucks to do. The Sarbanes-Oxley management letter established a method of accountability that changed that dismissive excuse. It basically says that if you sign this, and we find out later that your numbers are not real, you will be held personally liable. So now, if you are the leader, you had better go and make sure that the numbers you are receiving aren't a load of jumbo.

Much like Watergate was for political America, Enron may have been a tipping point in corporate America. This was a huge and public shift from a trust-based system to a deception-based system for keeping tabs on leaders. Enron's calamity was about leadershit greed, illegitimately leveraging compensation for the top leadershit.

Following Enron, America started to question leaders more, and rightly so. The media coverage and "perp walks" of leaders caught in the dragnet following Enron showed us how little we really knew about corporate leaders, and it shifted us to a place where we have built entire regulatory structures around anticipated deception. This came about because of the enormity of the problem with corporate entities like Enron and WorldCom and the massive tragedy left in their wake.

I see this as comparable to the rework stations in U.S. manufacturing plants. Rework stations are areas -- usually a bench with appropriate tools -- along the length of an assembly line used to pull faulty, noncompliant parts off of the line and fix them. Reasons for rework stations are poor quality of product due to faulty assembly, faulty components, upgrades and engineering changes. In America, there is an entire industry of businesses built around assisting companies with reworking their products.

As I recall, rework stations don't even exist in Japanese manufacturing plants. In America, we expect non-compliance and facilitate reaction while the Japanese do everything humanly possible to prevent non-compliance. We accept non-compliance and deal with the consequences – which are very costly – when we should/could establish a culture where non-compliance is not allowed to exist and not an option.

Now there are so many leaders doing the wrong thing for the wrong reasons, we seem to use all our resources reacting to the ones we catch, instead of preventing the problem in the first place. That ship sailed. Now the problem is huge.

The situation is comparable to things happening in other areas where leadership is constantly reacting to problems instead of preventing them. There was a time when we didn't test baseball players for steroids. We found baseball players taking advantage of an unprotected system and misbehaving in their own interests. And the reaction is testing. Possibly a deterrent, but not a preventative measure, given the many new ways of cheating that are outpacing the testing technology.

I was speaking to an MBA ethics class at Oakland University when I was asked about the effectiveness of having reformed white collar criminals speak to management meetings. They would tell the story of their corporate indiscretions and how "this could be you." My response was that those are fine for reminding people to walk the straight and narrow, but again, I question whether it is effective to fix the system that allows and even encourages such criminal excesses.

Sarbanes-Oxley was about putting something in place to minimize the economic disruption and pain corporate leaders can cause. It is a tactic to try to catch the greedy bastards who are gaming the system in their favor. This is about money. Loads and loads of money.

Leadership compensation is so out of control, even very good leaders get tempted to cheat. When leaders get fired they frequently get tens of millions of dollars to leave. When you suck at your job, you should not get tens of millions of dollars to *leave*! Something is very broken in a system where there is a substantial reward for a job poorly done. Or maybe it just wasn't done at all. It doesn't matter. The outcome would be the same for that leader: tens of millions of dollars. What the hell are we doing?

Where is the incentive to do good work? Where is the incentive to work hard? Where is the incentive to work at all? Without such incentive, what could we possibly expect from our leaders but apathetic performance leading to substandard outcomes? It may seem like it sometimes, but companies do not run on autopilot. They must be vigilantly steered and guided or they will eventually run aground.

"There has never been higher compensation for leadership positions, while the standards for who is worthy for those positions have never been so low."
- Rande Somma –

Low Risk/Big Reward

Excessive executive compensation introduces opportunity for incompetent leaders to invent multiple and exotic tactics to represent good results through unethical, illegal, or immoral behavior. The risk that the behavior will be detected, however, is low - despite Enron-inspired systematic changes and legislation.

Institutional investors – banks and other large entities who buy up large blocks of stocks – generally either don't know or don't care (or both) that good financial results may have absolutely nothing to do with the fundamental vitality of the organization and its people.

If you are in the market for a home and you see one that aesthetically looks great; right size, right location, etc. Is that the limit of your assessment before you decide its value and whether to purchase it? No. You take steps to assess the structural integrity, the things you cannot immediately see. It would be reckless not to inspect it thoroughly.

But Wall Street's (institutional investors) scorecard often stops at the aesthetics, the results, and I suppose that they assume those results are an accurate representation of the structural integrity of the business. Reckless? You bet.

Misbehavior on the part of leaders has become so rampant that they are typically one step ahead of detection. Oversight of corporate leadership is inadequate, more of a hindsight forensics event than a prevention or detection protocol. It was never designed to handle the volume and spectrum of deception being practiced by leadershit. Consequences for leadershit fall short, and whistle-blowing is too dangerous. As a result, the risk for leadershit deception has become very low relative to the extreme reward they get for either doing or not doing their jobs.

When laying off a bunch of people in order to make the quarterly numbers work is routine, you know we have gone off the road into the rut. But then when the leader who laid those folks off is rewarded with a monetary bonus for making those numbers work, we are doubling down on a seriously bad system. But this *is also routine*. This is normal in corporate America.

This bears repeating: layoffs actually support bonuses for leaders. This needs to be reformed. The way it is set up now, a leader's merit increases by slashing spending to meet expectations. Layoffs are used as the necessary reason to meet those expectations, and then the same leaders receive huge bonuses for the bigger bottom line created by those layoffs. In essence, the leader's bonus is the laid off employees' salary. You only need to rub together two brain cells to know that isn't right.

In the words of the great Vince Lombardi, "What the hell is going on out here?"

Come on. We can do better. We have to do better.

Pull the Rip Cord on the Golden Parachute

The origins of the golden parachute in corporate culture are rooted in moral intentions. They used to have a valuable place in the corporate setting. Let's say that you worked for my company, and you were a valued employee of mine. Let's say I was now planning to sell the company to somebody else. When sold, I will no longer have control over whether they keep you on or fire you. But because you mattered to me, I am going to give you a golden parachute. This is a contract that essentially says, if the company is sold, and the new owners choose not to keep you, then as part of their acquisition they are required to pay you a significant severance – what I would call a soft landing. It was typically a year's compensation – way more than the typical severance. It makes sense when employees are victimized by decisions that have nothing to do with their performance or talent.

That was the original intent of the golden parachute. It somehow got expanded and abused in the acquisition process of a CEO, and now implies that even if you screw up this amazing leadership opportunity and we fire you, you are going to get a butt load of money. This makes no sense, but if you up the ante enough, you pass through the threshold of reason. These huge amounts of money in leadership contracts disincentivize anyone from doing a great job because the worst-case scenario is now it doesn't matter what I do as a leader because the reward is the same, and it is ridiculously huge, so why would I even try?

Think of it this way. Unqualified leaders are like unqualified pilots flying your airplane. They are given a butt load of money and a parachute. They know they cannot really fly a plane, so they keep it aloft for as long as it makes sense to them, maybe till after lunch is served, then they bail out with their bags of cash. They were never really invested in flying that airplane very far because, well, they didn't know how.

This is your captain speaking. If you look out the left side of the plane, down in the water you will see a dingy. I parachuted out of the plane and I'm speaking to you from that dingy. Can you see me with my bags of money? I did the best I could. I kept you up for as long as I could, but I had to go. Have a nice flight.

They are bailing before the plane even starts to descend. They are not even sure when exactly that's going to be, but they are not sticking around to try to figure it out. Like selling a stock that is about to crash, too soon is much better than too late.

And when they go to look for another pilot's position, they get hired again because the people selecting the new pilot for the new company are only interested in whether you flew a plane before. They don't look to see if you are truly qualified or if you actually landed the damn thing.

Oh, By the Way, Gas Up My Jet, Please

Sometimes it seems that people are enamored with the celebrity of some leaders. They don't even begin to understand the true history or credentials of a person, or whether or not they are really bringing anything of value to the table. Hiring leaders is sometimes little more than a junior high popularity contest.

While I was a senior advisor to a company board, the company wanted to go public. It was an auto supplier, but wanted to diversify into other industries, so they decided to bring in an independent chairman (separate from the CEO position) who, based on past experience, could also help the company achieve some product and market diversity.

There was a guy on their radar for the chairman position who had just retired as chairman/CEO of a large public company which was a significant player in a targeted non-automotive industry sector. Because his company was a major player in that sector, they somehow got it scrambled in their heads that, as their new chairman, he would certainly use his prestige to shower the company with a bunch of new business. But really, they were just so intoxicated by the celebrity of this person and where he was coming from, that they fell in love with the idea of it.

So they brought him on board. One of the positives to acquiring this new chairman was that Wall Street knows him and his reputation was good. That's ok, but the only real value that his good reputation on Wall Street added to the business was the fact that he didn't have a *bad* reputation. Period.

But this new chairman wanted $600,000 a year *plus* annual stock option grants, *and* because he owned a jet, he wanted to be compensated for the plane's operating expenses when he flies in for board meetings. Really? This individual has a good reputation and chairman's experience. I'm not taking anything away from his credentials, but he's not running the company.

He is going to attend and lead four meetings a year that last maybe a half a day each. If there is really serious stuff going on, maybe a whole day. You have to read some stuff ahead of time. So let's say that over a year's time, the four meetings and all the collateral preparation and follow up – it's probably like a month, but maybe its two months' work out of a year. Maybe.

Doing the math, that $600,000 plus jet expenses works out to more than $10,000 a day. Come on, man! I'm sorry, that's just not right. Reason got blinded by the twinkling star and theory trumped reality here.

When I heard this multimillionaire wanted over half a million dollars a year to run a handful of board meetings *and* gas money for his personal jet, I thought no way. Then when his requirements were met and he was hired, I thought holy shit, the system is so screwed up that this deal actually appeared to make sense.

These are not bad people, they just somehow fell under the spell of this dysfunctional system, in which paying someone over half a million dollars a year to run a handful of meetings seemed reasonable to them. It could be considered reasonable if in the course of those meetings they cured cancer or eliminated world hunger.

So I spoke to my contact at this company and I told him, if this new chairman assured you that he would go back to his former company and bring back a lot of their business – which is the idea that they all fell in love with – he would have to probably break several clauses in previously signed contracts to do it. He is probably not going to do that. What he can get you is one thing – an opportunity to meet somebody. That's it. He is not going to rig it so you get a bunch of business. Number one, he does not have that influence or clout there anymore. He just doesn't. Number two, if he tries to do that, if his former company has any ethical standards, they are going to tell him to go to hell.

So, apart from being star-struck, one of the main reasons this company wooed this guy with over $600,000 a year (conservatively, $10K a day) to be the chairman of their board is because they believed he could bring in business from his previous job, and it's not going to happen.

Oh, and one other thing. That would not really even be his job as a board member. That job is oversight, not sales.

Stars in Their Eyes

Not long after this candidate was hired to be the Chairman, the company acquired another small company with capabilities that would allow them to compete for business in non-automotive industry. That same company was sold just a couple of years later. Why? No new business; no new profits.

I have had many opportunities to see what I know to be pretty smart people get sucked in by some pretty naïve ideas. This was a bad acquisition that was made for all the wrong reasons. I tried to talk them out of the acquisition, but once they make up their minds, people tend to shut down to discussion or opinions.

I don't know what became of the employees who worked for that smaller company that was bought based on a theory, and then sold when realities made it impossible to achieve the goals. I would guess that they and their families were at least rattled by the whole thing.

They have had to hustle to find work and reinvent themselves to reclaim their lives that were turned upside down from circumstances beyond their control. They have been bumped from their jobs because somebody decided that it was a good idea to hire someone with a jet for $600,000 plus a year. How many people get hurt in the fallout from these decisions? A lot . . . but not the board or the millionaire with the jet.

No Discounts at this Market

I have been using examples drawn from real life leaders in corporate America. At the same time, regular Joe's are getting up at 6:00 a.m. every morning, going to work and most of them are busting their asses to earn a tiny fraction of what these leaders are making *not doing their jobs!* Most people in the world do not make a fraction of these annual executive salaries over the course of their lifetime, and they have families to support; most are honest and hardworking and trying their best to be good people.

This bears repeating. Many top executives make more in one year than almost everyone else earns over the course of their lives, and many of these leaders are not *earning* these millions. *They are being handed the money and being asked to leave.* This is what we are tolerating.

Additionally, the perversion of the system establishes the incentive for leaders to hit the numbers. Successful completion of that short term task, regardless of the long term consequences, doles out more money to leaders.

I don't want anyone to think that all executives are overpaid slackers. Certainly there are some really great ones in the bunch who deserve healthy compensation, but the point is that they don't have to be good or hard working in order to be considered successful and in order to become very wealthy. The leadershit system is rigged to pay out huge returns regardless of performance. Reaching the pinnacle of your executive career – the CEO title -- is all you have to do. The system will carry you from there, and so there is very little incentive to really try hard once you arrive in the C suite. You can coast and probably nobody will notice or care. Nobody except workers whose livelihoods have become so vulnerable.

Leadership positions hold enormous responsibility. The fate of thousands of individuals and families are held in the palms of these leaders' hands. Shouldn't the accountability and consequences match the income level?

This is not a problem that is prevalent only in the business world. Sports figures are experiencing the same kind of treatment – which, by the way, is why we are seeing so much cheating. The payout for landing a position with a professional sports team is huge. Jim Harbaugh was recently offered $8 million to come and coach at the University of Michigan. That just rolls off our back. As a matter of fact, there are many who would happily stand behind U of M if they were to offer him twice that. We are desensitized to it.

But just stop and think about that. If we get our heads on straight for just a minute and get off of the precedent shit, the only person on the planet that I think is worth $8 million a year is somebody who cures cancer. That's the level of value and accomplishment that I think you would have to rise to in order to be worth $8 million a year.

Remember the CEO who received over $20 million for failing? He didn't cure cancer or world hunger. He ran a multi-billion company with very poor results, was fired and walked away a multi-millionaire.

And remember that the CEO of Johnson Controls received a $1 million hand slap for violating the ethics of his position when he slept with the company's leadership consultant? He gets to keep his job, and the rest of the $19 million annual compensation, but how is anyone going to respect or trust him? How can you create a culture if you are not holding yourself to the most obvious and important standards? And was that just a one-time 'oops' or are you an 'oops' kind of guy? When you behave like that your entire leadership is undermined. But at the end of the day, the stock is going up and the board is satisfied with his work and they are protecting him. The only way any of this would have mattered to the board, which is not keeping its eyes on the ball, only on how many times it bounces, is if the stock crashed in sync with his actions, because that is all that we are conditioned to look at or care about anymore.

Why Everyone Should Care –

Understanding the impact of this insane leadershit system is difficult, but we have all in some way been stung by this either directly or indirectly. Big business in America is the engine at the top of the food chain of the economy, and leaders of these big corporations determine its course. Many of these leaders are screwing up the economy and taking huge profits from their organizations. The vast majority of that money, their so-called compensation or what I would call legalized larceny belongs to the business. That money is supposed to be reinvested in the people and the necessary resources that generate legitimate short term, and more importantly sustainable long term success. And, as a result, the communities that the businesses operate in will thrive.

Lee Ioccoca wrote the book *Where Have All the Leaders Gone?* (Iacocca, 2008) He is not very approving of our modern day leaders in America. In Iacocca's Thoughts on Leadership[3], he states:

"It's not just elected leaders like George W. Bush and Dick Cheney either. It's many of the executives who occupy the top rungs of this country's corporate ladder. Your Kenneth Lays and Jeffrey Skillings and Dennis Kozlowskis – a few guys who took Michael Douglas' line in the movie Wall Street a little too seriously. 'Greed is good,' he said. These days, it seems more of our leaders believe that than ever before." [Chapter 12, page 137]

Sack Jack

A lot of people do not have an understanding of the corruption and erosion of values that goes on in many large companies. They lack the experience and an insider's view of the situation, and so it remains largely undetected by the general public. Let me offer you a peek.

Look how "valuable" Jack Welch was. If you read the headlines, the minute he left GE, in 2001, the whole thing went off the road into the rut. Most would believe that Jack's leadership was so great, it was his leaving that triggered GE's crash. From the outside that looks to be the case.

From what I can tell, Jack Welch was a master at "managing to his goal line," scraping off all the benefits that GE could muster for him during his tenure as CEO, and then as soon as he left, the company, sucked dry by then, began to falter.

From what I have read, what he built was a culture of threats and fear under a business model that was completely unsustainable. He propped up the company to "hold the pose" and to look successful until he left. He is touted

---

[3] http://leeiacocca.net/thoughts-on-leadership/index.html

as a leader who is a "genius," takes all his millions, and as soon as he leaves, the house of cards toppled over.

A closer look reveals less genius and more selfishness.

Jack Welch became CEO of GE in 1981 just as an 18-year bull market for big cap stocks began. During this time, GE earnings increased and beat quarterly profit projections with very striking regularity. It was discovered after the recession of the early 2000s that there was some creative accounting mischief. It turned out that GE Capital (the financial services unit of the American conglomerate General Electric) had been acting as a leveraged hedge fund, stepping in to help GE make their margins. The SEC eventually got involved and GE had to settle accounting fraud charges.

Welch's timely departure in 2001 preceded the discovery of GE's financial problems, giving the illusion that Welch was masterful at running the company, when in fact he pulled the pin on the grenade and left the building comfortably before it would go off, leaving the next guy to absorb the impact of his management "skills."

It appears, on closer examination, that his entire leadership model was based on short term gains, when in fact a CEO -- *by virtue of the job description* – is supposed to be the visionary securing long term sustainable success for their company long after they are gone. That was Jack Welch's job.

In my opinion, he was an epic failure as a leader. GE paid the price. Stockholders paid the price. The employees certainly paid the price – some with their livelihoods. Jack didn't lose a dime. When he retired from GE he took a severance payment of $417 million, the largest such payment in history at that time. Over a decade later, it looks like GE is finally starting to climb out of their financial hole.

Under most corporate values – including GE's – you can find *"We are committed to our people."* Jack Welch's "winning at all costs" management style has dominated American business conversations now for over a decade. His methods of "trusting his gut" and "blowing things up" were bad enough. He also used a threatening management style by passing judgment on "winners" and "losers" in the ranks of GE employees, instilling a culture of insecurity and fear. That's just wrong. You don't treat people like that. Only jagoffs treat people like that.

Welch's business tactics are well known, marketed and mimicked frequently by Jack wannabees. If that is the way you want to be remembered as a leader, go ahead. You will be a "winner" at leadershit.

Speaking of Jagoffs...

I was on the board of a company owned by the same firm that had purchased Chrysler before the famous bailout. The firm had recently hired Bob Nardelli, a former Home Depot CEO who also formerly worked under Jack Welch at GE, to run Chrysler. When I heard that news, I just shook my head. Not because Nardelli was a Welch follower (which he was). Not because he got passed up for leadership at GE (which he did). Not even because he didn't appear to have any automotive experience (which he didn't). Hell, the automotive guys had already proved by then that they didn't know how to get it right. Things were so bad at that point, what could hiring an outsider really hurt?

I shook my head because it was something else even worse in my opinion.

During a break at one of our board meetings, a representative from the parent company asked me, "Rande, what do you think of Nardelli being hired as CEO?"

I knew enough – not every detail, but enough. So I said, "You don't want to know what I think." I wasn't trying to be a smartass. I realized at that point that I didn't see things like everyone else who was so enthralled with Nardelli's bravado and celebrity, so I knew that my input on this topic was not going to be popular. I wanted to keep it to myself. But he kept at me.

"Yeah, I really do want to know what you think."

"No, you don't want to know."

"I want to know."

"You don't want to know."

"I do want to know."

So I said I was disappointed with their decision to hire Nardelli.

Nardelli was 58 years old when he left Home Depot. He received about $210 million in cash and stock options, including a $20 million severance payment and retirement benefits of $32 million.

That separation agreement said something like; if we terminate you – which would be because you can assume we don't like what you are doing – we will cut you a check for many millions. Nardelli received less than stellar performance ratings, and the company was not doing well, but his *bonus was not tied to performance.* So despite the company's languishing stock price, he was getting big bonuses. And he took that bonus money.

I blame the board of Home Depot for the fact that Nardelli had this humungous compensation and separation agreement payout if he left the company on bad terms. They should have been much more prudent with how they compensated him.

But I blame Nardelli, as well. He refused to tie his bonus to his performance, and then took that enormous payout on his way out, and for that reason I wouldn't have even read his resume. It wouldn't have even crossed my mind to hire him.

And the rep from the parent company said, "Well why not?"

I said, "Look, what is going on? Everybody is so overwhelmed and star struck by name recognition and celebrity. Nobody is looking at substance. What is going on here? Nardelli demonstrated in just that one act – this incredible monumentally selfish act – that he's got no honor. It is clear what motivates him."

Never mind that, as a leader, his job is to *lead people*, not negotiate an exit strategy that eliminates any incentive for him to commit to stay and work for the company. He never had his eye on the success of that company, only on his payout. Everything was put in place to incentivize him to NOT do the right thing. The numbers are one thing, but what about the people? Who knows what carnage followed Nardelli.

"From what I can see," I continued, "Nardelli screwed up at Home Depot. For whatever reason, he wasn't good enough to replace Jack Welch at GE. Why the hell did he get hired at Chrysler? Don't ask me what I think. I'm asking you, *why did you hire him?* Once everyone gets past Nardelli's name, GE and Home Depot, you're done. That seems to be all he has to offer. It seems like there is a hell of a lot more sizzle than there is steak."

The View from 10,000 feet

If you have been directly stung by this type of knockoff leadership, you may have a much better perspective of what exactly is going on behind the scenes. As someone who has held many positions and had a seat at the table with many big name leaders in countless meetings, I can tell you that things look different up close than they do from afar.

I was privy to board meetings, sat in leadership meetings, and at one time I was the only auto supplier guy on the senior advisory committee for all three of the Detroit auto companies. That was quite a ringside seat.

Unions suffer from the same leadershit system as any corporate entity. The original premise of the unions was noble and they were needed to bring about good changes in how workers are treated and how much they were paid, based on performance and value. Union leadershit – at least in the car industry in my experience while at JCI – now appears to seek pay for workers based on entitlement and leverage. What corporate and union leadershit have in common is that neither is focused on the company's sustainability.

I have been stunned by the ho-hum reaction of others to the reality of leadershit. If I were to talk about this in terms of political leadership in this country, I suspect that I would get more of a rise from folks, because the media keeps the spotlight on every move politicians make. But corporate leaders operate more in the shadows. The general public doesn't see, hear or think about them as much. Unless, like in a "Die Hard" movie, the camera happens to fall on a perp walking away from an exploding mega-disaster.

But corporate leadershit is connected to political leadershit. This is supposed to be a government of the people, by the people and for the people. It doesn't feel that way at all to many of us. We are merely a detail. Others' agendas have trumped ours. It should come as no surprise that some of those "others" are big corporations and industries that power our economy and lobby our government leaders for favors. And those corporations are run by the leadershit guys this book is about. So this matters.

Parental Pride

My son Scott worked for a mortgage lending company some years ago. He came to see me one day to tell me that he was moving back home because he was going to quit his job. I said, "What's up?" He told me, "They are coming out with a new product now called sub-prime loans, and I can make a lot of money selling these loans to people, because getting one is easy. So

I sit and talk to them about the loan, and all they see is that all of a sudden, now they can afford a home; they can have the American Dream."

Then he goes on to tell me: "I'm not supposed to, but I show them, look, here is the payment now, but in five years, the payment balloons to this. Can you afford *that*?" He said, "Dad, they don't give it one second thought. They are so locked into the American Dream of owning a home. So even though I'm going to make a lot of money doing this, I'm quitting because I'm not going to know their names; I'm not going to know who they are, but I know that some of them are going to lose their home in five years. I know. I just won't happen to know exactly which ones."

Now, of course, we know that those loans were a massive deception that caused one of the most devastating economic crises of our time, the mortgage loans and real estate bubble. I didn't know it then, but I was so proud of him for that decision even before we knew the full ramifications of those predatory loans.

An Endless Supply of Assholes

The CEO market is bad enough, but the double whammy is that it is seducing all the good people too.

In 2009, in the Financial Times, Paul Purcell, the CEO of RW Baird, a Milwaukee-based bank famously said, *"Greed will reappear. It happens every time. There will always be assholes in Wall Street because the compensation is so high."* (Weitzman, 2009)

He is so right. In the movie *Indecent Proposal,* Demi Moore plays a married woman who agrees to have sex with another man (Robert Redford) for a million dollars. Similarly, in the corporate world, there is a threshold of money that makes people surrender their morals and do unthinkable things that just one day before they would never have considered doing. That threshold for many of us is a lot less than $20 million or $10 million or even $5 million, and this is not a movie.

This type of behavior gives capitalism a bad rap. Capitalism is not bad. Capitalism is just the vehicle we use in America to carry our economy. If a drunk drives a vehicle off a cliff, why would you blame the car? We need to take a closer look at the leadershit driver of that vehicle and assess their qualifications before they get behind the wheel, and more importantly, the money that is fueling that vehicle. We should not be using rocket fuel when simple unleaded would suffice.

Buckle Up and Enjoy the Ride Straight to Hell

I was asked to consult for a company who was considering the acquisition of a once large auto parts supplier. This supplier was a spin-off of one of the Detroit three automakers, and therefore, it inherited its UAW relationship and associated wages and benefits.

In putting together a pro forma operating plan that could justify the acquisition, one key area the company needed to focus on was the "all-in" hourly worker wages and benefits that collectively totaled $65 an hour. In order to make the acquisition plan feasible, that rate would have to move to approximately $35 an hour. That is a big difference in compensation.

Among other things, that adjustment had to be discussed with the UAW. The company I was consulting for asked if I would participate in those discussions. I said that I would, but that in the interest of full disclosure, my relationship with the UAW wasn't the best. At Johnson Controls, the vast majority of our plants were non-union. The UAW called that being anti-union. I called that being pro-people and anti-losing-my-ass.

So we were in this meeting with the UAW representative, and right off the bat, I was pretty sure this guy didn't like me. We laid the cards on the table and he immediately jumped up and started yelling, "So in other words, you want me...*you want ME* to go tell my people that it's $35 and not $65? That's what you want me to tell my people? You want me to tell them that, that it's $35 not $65?"

And I said, "No, we don't want you to tell your people that it's $35 not $65. You need to tell your people that it's $35 or nothing. This is all we can offer. And by the way, those wages never should have gone past $35. This overpayment was all of us in the industry being irresponsible assholes . . . all of us and our respective predecessors who kicked the can down the line and, well, now here we are."

At the time, there was no reason on God's green earth that anybody should have to convince anybody that the work those people did was worth more than $35 an hour at that time. Everyone in the industry knew that, but everybody had an agenda. The market price for hourly wage earners went to $65, but it was way off because it was disassociated with the work that needed to be done. Instead, it was attached to UAW leadership's re-election campaigns, and the automakers management kicking the can down the line, because it was cheaper to give in than to shut down production because of a strike. So the market – which is the measure of value – got away from its intended duty and took on a life of its own, which then created a bubble that needed to be popped to resuscitate the company now on life support. It wasn't about merit anymore. It was about leverage. The automakers and the UAW both decided to forget about protecting the future viability of their workers and the industry. So guess what? Now the UAW rep has got to go tell his people its $35 or they are done.

He said, "That's one hell of a concession."

I replied, "It isn't a *concession*. It is a *correction*. And shame on all of us."

This has far-reaching consequences. Hourly workers who had purchased homes, boats, cars and built their lifestyles and a credit reach on a $65 an hour job were now going to have to alter their lives drastically and probably lose a lot of what they had built. They are now ambushed and their lives traumatized by this huge reduction in their wages. And it was never their fault. This was the fault of leadershit that cared only about hitting numbers today, without planning for tomorrow's consequences for the *people they were hired to lead.*

Human Behavior

These scenarios always end badly. Naturally, the people who cause the problem and take advantage of the situation and their position are never the ones who solve it, and worse, they don't suffer any of the consequences. As a matter of fact, many of these leaders leave a wake of tragedy for their workers and walk away millionaires. They have no shame or honor. And the people who deserve it the least – the workers – end up bearing the most pain.

You can calibrate salaries to the market, but as I have stated, human behavior is the second component – a quiet component – that plays into the equation. There will always be assholes around looking to capitalize on situations. We refer to the market, but the market is being jacked up by personal agendas and the greed of individual leaders.

Recall that one of the primary functions of a CEO is strategic planning, setting a course for the future of the company. Well, the average tenure for a CEO is three to five years, and you are asking them to make a strategic plan on a 5-year horizon. There is some obvious dysfunction built into that ask. For leaders today, establishing an actionable and measurable strategic plan for their organization under today's demanding short-term results-driven system is seen by many as essentially irrelevant. Many CEOs know this and so they simply do not bother to create long term strategic plans *even though it is part of their job description!* Many who do create a plan only do it half-assed. It may be purely conceptual, not truly actionable or measureable.

One CEO told me that his strategy was to be opportunistic. Yagottabekidden. In other words, his plan was to be there to catch whatever it is when it drops into his lap? That's your "**how?**" That is not a strategy. That's just a way of saying I'm not doing it. And did his board ever insist on a *real* strategic plan being done? Nope. If he don't wanna, he don't gotta.

In any strategic plan, there would be money and resources set aside right now to begin the build-out for long term needs, drawn off of the immediate needs of the company's *short term goals and gains,* to secure its future. The bonus structure of many CEOs is based on these same *short term gains.* When the company reaches certain numbers in a quarter or in a fiscal year, leadership receives a bonus. Is it any wonder that CEOs are not particularly interested in providing for a future they won't be around to see, that funnels away their short term bonus?

Holding Your Ground and Staying True

Why did Lance Armstrong do what he did? Why are baseball players taking steroids? What is causing them to take that risk? Because the reward is so high. If a baseball player got paid $200,000 a year (half what a US President, leader of the free world, makes) instead of $30 million, we might have something different.

While there will always be assholes out there trying to game the system, leveling the playing field a little might have a big effect on a lot of behavior.

One of the excuses you hear is that everyone is doing it, which is a giant cop out, but an accepted one. "Everyone else was cheating, lying and stealing, so I did it too." In my book, you are just joining the ranks of all the assholes. Yes, dammit, if everybody else is cheating, it *IS STILL CHEATING.* Why? Because the standard is you don't cheat.

Although it is easy to say that everyone is an asshole, there is a mindset of "If I don't do it, I'm going to fall behind." I understand this.

When I speak to business ethics classes at universities, I pose a scenario to the students. I tell them that there are three students getting straight A's consistently. Then there is one student who is working his ass off and getting a C. Now what if I tell you that the three students getting all A's are somehow getting all the answers to each test ahead of time? They are cheating and getting away with it and going to keep getting A's while the other guy is going to keep getting C's even with his best effort. So the three students are going to get all the benefits of being A students without the effort, and the C student is not receiving any of those benefits despite his better work ethic and best efforts.

One day the C student gets invited to join the group of A students who are cheating. Now he has the opportunity to get the answers to the tests ahead of time too. What would that C student choose to do? Is he going to join the A students and receive the same benefits, or is he going to continue to struggle every day for his C and never get ahead? If he decides to remain honorable and hold onto his integrity, will he ultimately lose out? How much is cheating worth to you? It's a provocative situation, but a standard ethics question. It really depends on how much you value your honor and integrity. It is the same when a similar scenario presents itself in real life.

Unfortunately, in today's leadershit system, we check the box and take the A student because results are king.

Let's Review

What are we supposed to be paying CEOs and leaders to do? We are supposed to be paying them to create business value that is credible *and* sustainable. We are supposed to be paying them for actions that meet both short term commitments and achieve long term aspirations. We are supposed to be paying them to do all of it completely, consistently and while adhering to the company's core values and meeting the highest ethical and moral standards.

It is bad enough when we pay way too much money for an authentic piece of fine jewelry. It is a whole new level of bad when you pay that same amount for a knockoff.

CHAPTER 5
GARBAGE IN, GARBAGE OUT
UNFIT LEADERS... BY DESIGN

Lemons Don't Always Make Lemonade

By 1990, Japanese carmakers commanded a 28% share of the U.S. auto market. In 1991, GM and Ford posted record losses while Japanese imports continued to capture more market share. The Japanese were competing on our soil and winning. Despite America's desire to be loyal to its natives, GM, Ford and Chrysler, there was no hiding the fact that Japanese cars were a better value. U.S. automakers became very serious about this competition, but understood little about what made the Japanese cars better.

This would have been a key time in the industry's history for U.S. automaker leaders to step up and make the transformational changes to the systems and protocols needed to deliver a competitive product. In the long run, it would have likely prevented these leaders from having to hop on their company jets and fly to Washington in 2008 to beg for bailout money. But the enormous amount of time and effort the changes would have taken certainly would have negatively impacted the short term stock price and sales.

So instead, U.S. automaker leaders took the easy route and began desperately slashing their costs.

Back in the '90s, GM, Ford and Chrysler were changing out all of their parts left and right and making constant adjustments to reduce costs, which naturally further reduced quality. During this time, I once said to a GM executive, "If a good car comes off the end of your line it's a complete coincidence. How does this chaos morph into a world class car? Do you have a station on the assembly line where someone waves a magic wand and turns all the last minute fire drills into a world class car?" I said it with enough humor so that he could brush it off. He probably shouldn't have.

From my perspective, the Detroit Three's entire developmental system then operated with the control and discipline of a band of chimpanzees lighting fireworks. Their panicked attempts to compete were not well thought out. They were buying all their parts based on price, not value, installing all the cheapest parts they could. This was their solution to competing in the industry. I don't know why they thought they were going to deliver a world class vehicle to the dealership under these conditions.

Good People, Bad Fit

I want to make sure I drive home the belief that bad leaders are not all bad people. Many of them are good, even great people trying their best. I know many leaders who are honest, upstanding citizens. At the same time, being a good person doesn't translate into being a good leader. Just as I have no business flying a 747 jet. Rest assured, I will do my very best, and it will crash and we will all die. My qualifications don't match the task at hand, but that doesn't make me a bad person or an idiot.

These good people who are not good leaders are in somewhat the same position. They are ill-equipped to achieve sustainable results the right way, but in today's system, they don't have to. They are doing the best they can in a system that doesn't offer them good choices. They are channeled into making decisions that are shortcuts, like layoffs. They are pressured into making the spreadsheet numbers their false gods, when instead they should be leading people, improving efficiency, quality, competitive differentiation, and overall performance, and letting those factors drive the numbers. Unqualified leaders are blind to this method. They do not see it. It doesn't bother them to take shortcuts because they don't know any other way to do it, and often they are not given any choice in the matter. They are immersed in a system that has made it normal, and limits their ability to do it any other way. The really bad news is that deviation from this norm of lowered expectations and standards is potentially career-ending. This I do know. I am not guessing.

Wash, Rinse, Repeat

The handoff from one CEO to the next CEO in some industries is a non-event, and the position is largely historical and for pageant purposes. These leaders are in the public eye; hired for their visual appeal and to deliver grand messages about big steps the company is taking, the vision, the innovation, the strategy….blah, blah, blah….cut the ribbon and open the champagne.

That's done. Let's do lunch.

Good dental work, PR training, a tailored wardrobe and an ever-present inflated company message are more important than traditional core competencies for this group of knock-offs. The invasion of this "Leadership Lite" reality appears to have taken root and gained critical mass. As a simple calculus of this fraudulent model, we are selecting the wrong people for the wrong purpose, and assessing their worthiness by the wrong criteria. The reality is garbage in = garbage out. As a result, the authentic leaders who could effectively run the business and deliver even better results the right way do not meet the criteria of the fraudulent model. They, ironically and tragically, are often labeled as unfit relative to the need for a shining corporate image. And that, Mr. Iacocca, is where all the leaders have gone.

"The great irony is that ego and personal ambition that often drive people to positions of power stand at odds with the humility required for great leadership. When you combine that irony with the fact that boards of directors frequently operate under the false belief that they need a larger-than-life egocentric leader to make an organization great, you can quickly see why truly great leaders rarely appear at the top of our institutions." – Jim Collins, from the book <u>Good to Great</u> (Collins, 2001)

Let's face it, if you are CEO, there is not much ladder left to climb, and the view at the top is enviable. If you are leadership lite and the company is doing well, you may think that the best strategy might be to keep doing what you are doing. Holding the pose might look like the best retention method for your position. At least until the pose gets shaky and it's time to bail. Till then, why take chances and risk a more noticeable or premature fall from grace? A conservative attitude at this height is typically agreeable to board members and shareholders if the company is doing well under current management plans. Simply keep an eye on industry indicators, and be ready to make adjustments should the need arise.

There is a dangerous inherent problem with that. Change is constant and inevitable, so any company that isn't taking measured risks to move forward is by definition falling behind. As long as the planet is spinning, there is no such thing as staying the course. An authentic leader knows that if it's broke, then fix it. If it's not broke, make it better.

So what if the company is not doing well? The approach for any leader in this position should be one of affecting change, both near-term continuous improvement and strategic transformational change. In corporate America, this is where who is in charge makes a world of difference.

Leadership is a Gift

I believe that every person is gifted with unique talents and abilities that they can contribute to humanity. Figure it out and be honest with yourself. Almost everyone can be in charge of something. But leading people, influencing behavior of others is something not everyone can do well.

I was asked whether I believe leaders are born or are made. I don't know. I don't know anything about genes, but I think that with the gift of leadership, it probably all begins early in life. I think that young children are conditioned throughout their youth. Whether by adversity or by parental role modeling, they learn to recognize and process right and wrong; what is the benefit of doing something right, and the consequences of doing something wrong, and how deeply you should commit to things that really matter.

However the gift of leadership is acquired, it includes seeing a leadership position as a privilege that must be earned.

A Steady Drip of Water Can Cut Rock

Whether they are doing well or floundering, there is an incremental loss for any large organization that does not assess their leadership properly and consistently hold them to task. This erosion can be in the way of loss of top talent, eroding morale, depletion of customers, reduced market share, unflattering reputation, or vulnerable stock price. Whatever the loss, it is too great in the highly competitive world of global economics.

I have had the opportunity to be on the inside when leaders were chosen for large corporations, board membership, university positions, and other high level posts. I can tell you that when choosing leaders today, character (i.e., principles) really isn't a necessary qualification. It isn't on the radar, either because it is assumed or just doesn't matter.

Do you know how I know this? Nobody ever asks about it. When it comes time to vet candidates, there is no mention of character. I'm not making this up. They focus in on and want to know about experience, education and credentials – which are all important factors as well, but who cares about any of that if the person is an egotistical asshole that's in it for him/herself? None of those things matter if this new hire is going to be apathetic, or undermine or even sabotage your organization's best efforts to get ahead.

Turd-Fest

There are really two points here.

The first point: Some leaders are turds, but they know how to fool us. I gave a talk a number of years ago, post-9/11, post-Enron, post-baseball steroids. There were a whole lot of turds bubbling to the top of the punch bowl at that time because the American public had taken for granted that people were who they appeared and presented themselves to be. Then we found out that they looked the part, but when you looked under the covers, there were turds. They knew how to fool us. They knew where you wouldn't look, and even if you looked there, you wouldn't know what you were looking at or what to look for. That is one way that turds bubble up.

The second point is this: Some leaders start off as good leaders and then become turds. I personally know about an individual who started off being a high quality leader. Over ten years, he slowly sold out right before my eyes. I think I know why. Power and money got traction in his life, and he hit a point where there was never enough of either of those. The business had reached the point where he simply did not have the intuition or the skill sets to take the business to the next level. He dehumanized himself, went into more of a command and control mode, and his method of motivation shifted from inspiration to intimidation. Then came the dramatic shift from managing the business to managing the results.

Some companies die a natural death in the marketplace because they lack the competitive chops to gain market share and/or effectively manage cost structure. Others have catastrophic collapse because of internal tangle and corruption. Like Enron, no company is immune to a fall from grace when leadershit players are allowed to leverage their own interests. Leadershit can be ineffective, apathetic, under-educated, corrupt, inattentive or just incapable of effectively managing success. There are many reasons a company can fail, but whatever the reason for a company's defeat, the common denominator is always the leadershit.

Let Me Hold You by the Short Hairs While I Jump Off This Cliff

What difference does it make if a company fails or succeeds? Economies are complicated networks. Our ability to survive and thrive is tied together by our ability to produce and profit as a network. No one organization stands alone. We rely on each other. It is survival or death of a *network.*

When GM closed assembly plants in Pontiac and Flint, Michigan years ago, the local restaurants, drug stores, dry cleaners and a hundred other small businesses suffered catastrophic losses and many were forced to close their doors as a result. These cities are now shells of their former vibrant selves.

One business or industry holds many others by the short hairs. Because we all ride up and down with the success and failure of our economies, and because we all invest in the products and services of many companies, and because many of us even work for them, shouldn't we all be keenly interested in the selection process of any given company's leadership that is upstream in our economic food chain? In at least an indirect way, they hold our future in their hands. Their decisions and survival impacts us all in some way.

The Devil You Know vs. the Devil You Don't

Who selects CEOs? Usually there is a board of directors who have the authority to hire and fire CEOs of large corporations. They base their decisions on various factors, and it is not the same from industry to industry or from company to company. Many board members are in positions of leadership themselves in other companies. They are sitting CEOs, COOs and CFOs, each with a large network of professional contacts. While searches are conducted and information goes out calling for qualified candidates to fill leadership positions, identifying and selecting finalist candidates usually becomes a process of finding someone who has a track record of leadership, and also is possibly known by one or more of the board members.

What is a much more interesting question is what happens next? Often when a CEO is hired – and I have no idea why – they are also made chairman of the board. So what is the process for continued accountability? How do we grade CEOs on how they measure up over the course of time? No one has ever given me a legitimate explanation why the CEO and chairman can ever be the same person . . . because there isn't one.

The best CEOs do not focus exclusively on their company's financial performances. They are hired to lead the team. Their efforts should automatically improve all aspects of the business, including the profits, service and product quality, timeliness, accuracy, customer satisfaction and loyalty. Great CEOs engage with their team, oversee the larger efforts by the company, and have an ever watchful eye on the numbers, making adjustments as they proceed.

The best CEOs educate, direct and motivate their teams and make sure to provide them with the resources necessary to meet the objectives set for them. They retain the best talent and optimize staff development. They are firm and fair and not afraid to let go of those who cannot fit into the culture or add value to their vision or the company.

Get Out Your Ruler

Today, many successful leaders are measured with a different scale. That scale is less about leading people and more about a checklist of competencies and accomplishments. The system demands immediate results. The system is looking for leaders who can deliver those results, even if it means killing bunnies.

The only way I can imagine that today's typical executive leader can successfully manage some companies in this system, operate and behave the way that they do, make some of the decisions they make, and still sleep at night, is to divest themselves of some basic virtues like empathy and integrity.

Some leaders are good people, but to really excel as a leader in this system, it sometimes helps if you are a shitty person.

There are probably phases to filling leadershit positions. Most individuals in line for these positions would start off rejecting the notion that they might need to surrender pieces of their character in order to climb the corporate ladder. Then comes reluctant adherence to lowered standards as they realize it is necessary to get along. Eventually they fully adapt and conform to the tract of the new normal – killing bunnies, abandoning the long term strategy in favor of short term gains, and planning exit packages. They are human, and as such they get comfortable with what is very wrong with corporate leadership.

Those that allow their empathy and integrity to influence their operating philosophy and decision making process may be successful leaders as well; however, in many organizations these leaders may eventually end up in conflict with the system and status quo leadershit.

In order to survive they may have to "drink the Kool-Aid." This would involve attempting to endure an environment whose leadership treats its corporate values as discretionary.

Push-Pull Short Term vs. Long Term

From 2007 to 2012, I served as Vice Chairman of the Board of Directors of a very large privately held global automotive supply company.

The entity that purchased this company had a plan to acquire it, improve its financial position and then sell it for a profit. The timeline for such a plan is typically two to three years. When you make the necessary changes to a company that generates significant improvements in the market value of the company in that short a period of time, there are only so many places where you can focus.

There was often tension between me, the new owners and the Board of Directors that was controlled by them. In almost every case, the tension was regarding my resistance to short term changes that improved short term financials, but also would set in motion longer term negative consequences.

While the company's leadership team appreciated my position on such matters, the ownership was becoming a little annoyed.

At one point, without the ownership realizing it, attrition in the Board membership left the ownership without clear control of the Board. They had lost majority control of the Board. The Board now had four members. Two were unconditionally aligned with the ownership interests, and two (including myself) were, well...not so much.

Because of the economic dynamics caused as a result of the recession, ownership was forced to hold onto this company longer than planned. Their operating model was designed for sprints – get in, make the necessary cuts, and get out. They now found themselves in a marathon. They were clearly out of their wheel house.

The ownership's investors were probably growing impatient with receiving a return on their investment, some, if not most of which went into purchasing the automotive supply company.

During one meeting, a resolution came before the Board that, in effect, would put hundreds of millions of dollars in the pocket of ownership while at the same time, put the company's financial condition and its approximately 3,000 people in far too much risk.

I was the last member to vote. My "no" vote killed the resolution. As I explained to ownership, I have absolutely no problem with you making hundreds of millions of dollars on your investment, but I absolutely have a problem with you making it like that.

Not long after, the ownership reengineered the Board both to regain majority control and in preparation for taking the company public. During that process, I received a call from the CEO. After asking me if I was sitting down, he told me that my position on the Board was changing. He said that of course ownership appreciated my experience and input. After all, I was the only member of the Board who successfully ran a global automotive supply business. However, while they wanted to retain the value of my presence on the Board, they were not at all comfortable with how I processed right from wrong, and therefore, uncomfortable with how they could count on me to vote on future resolutions.

So to have their cake and eat it too, they offered to retain me on the Board as a non-voting senior advisor.

I hung around for a while – a decision I am not proud of. Not long after, my position as a senior advisor was eliminated.

This experience was another example that convinced me that what was engineered into the leadershit system is that making money and doing it for the right reasons and the right way were mutually exclusive. And challenging that irresponsible norm just isn't at all appreciated.

One of the Very Best

Mike Fezzey, past regional President of Huntington Banks, was a good friend, a wonderful man and a truly great leader. He really understood leadership (and leadershit) and what it takes to do things the right way.

I received a call on a Saturday in March 2015, that Mike had suffered a heart attack and passed away the previous day. I was hit very hard by that sad news. We can't spare people like Mike.

Mike Fezzey was iconic. There was no decision he made, that I was aware of, that he didn't first filter through his soul. I realize it is emotional to think of business this way, but I have come to believe that it is also technically correct: Without linking your soul to leading business, you may have the position to lead, but you don't have the right stuff.

Governor Rick Snyder said, "Mike Fezzey's passing is a profound loss not just for our business community, but for our state as a whole."[4]

Mike's Paradigm Shift

Mike had shared with me that he had suffered a heart attack about seven years before this fatal one. When he and I would talk about the slippery slope of leadership, he really understood it. He admitted to me that before that first heart attack, he was on that slippery slope. He told me that he was getting full of himself and becoming that asshole. The heart attack slapped him back to reality, and he found God. He became a pretty spiritual guy, but he wasn't in your face with it. He credits the heart attack and God for correcting his course. That was good enough for me.

Mike was introduced to me through a mutual friend at an annual charity golf outing. The outing was co-sponsored by my friend's company when he was CEO, and WJR radio, when Mike Fezzey, was the President of WJR at the time. He told me, "Rande, you've gotta meet this guy. You are two peas in a pod. Your business leadership approach and values – you are like clones." I am eternally grateful to him for arranging our meeting.

We met around the time that WJR was sold to a private equity company. From my limited experience, private equity companies might have a moral compass, but it's unique to them and may only be recognizable within the borders of Manhattan.

---

[4] http://www.michigan.gov/snyder/0,4668,7-277-57577_57657-351742--,00.html

Mike was really struggling with this private equity company that had come in to operate WJR. Mike was an authentic leader who was acutely aware that one of his responsibilities was to create an environment where his people can enjoy working, and be secure and successful. He saw that that the private equity company had a different focus. Their interest was simply to make money. They were cutting benefits and salaries. I could see that Mike was pained by what was going on with WJR, the company he'd been with for over 30 years.

It seems that many private equity firms strip away everything so they can lower all the costs. They buy and flip businesses for profit and they don't care what happens to people. They really don't care. You know . . ." It's just business." Mike had to stay and watch them tear it apart. He was miserable.

Huntington Bank's headquarters is in Columbus, Ohio, but the chairman of the bank attended various events in Detroit, and he got to know Mike. Mike was connected, engaged, well-known and liked in the Detroit area. This chairman wanted to elevate Huntington in Michigan, and he saw Mike Fezzey as the guy to do that.

So Mike told me one day at one of our lunches that he got an offer to run Huntington Bank's Eastern Michigan Region. And I looked at him and I said, "What the hell do you know about running a bank? I mean seriously. No offense, Mike, but come on, really?"

And Mike said, "That's what I said to them. I don't know crap about banking."

What was so remarkable – and this guy obviously got it – was what this chairman said to Mike. "I have plenty of bankers. What I am trying to hire is a leader." He was looking for a great leader with a solid reputation who was also a quality person. The rest, he could teach him.

That is powerful. That is huge. This guy is not checking boxes, because if he was, Mike would never be considered for that position for a moment. He was choosing Mike to lead his bank because he was hiring that kind of human being. The value that Mike brought to the table was unique from what anyone else with finance and banking background would be able to offer.

"Leaders hold a position of power or authority. Those who lead inspire us to follow -- not because we have to, but because we want to...not for them, but for ourselves." - Simon Sinek

I still remember sitting there when Mike told me that and thinking wow. And the stunning part of it was that I don't think it was supposed to be extraordinary. I think that is the way it is supposed to be. It should be ordinary and routine. Huntington Bank was hiring a person, not a resume or a celebrity. Mike's profile was well articulated by Huntington's Regional and Commercial Banking Director, Jim Dunlap, who reported to PR Newswire on January 5, 2011, "Mike has a unique combination of business acumen, civic leadership and communication skills," said Dunlap."His background will enable him to lead Huntington's continued growth in the market, while working with business, civic and government leaders to play a greater role in Michigan's recovery."

Mike Fezzey left a tremendous legacy as a leader at Huntington Bank, and he left us far too soon.

Damn, I really miss him.

Alan Mulally to the Rescue

To be fair, sometimes it is a good thing to have someone come in to take the leadership reins for the auto industry that is not from the automotive industry. Alan Mulally, former CEO of Boeing Commercial Airplanes is a great example. He came in as the CEO of Ford in 2006 and set about transforming the company. I was talking to people who worked at Ford and I asked them about Mulally. When I kept hearing the word "culture" I started to get impressed.

I believe that any company's ability to generate consistent, credible and sustainable results is first and most importantly a function of the health and vitality of its culture. I once saw or heard culture defined as *"to the extent that an entity and its people live out their values."* I wish I could remember where I heard that. To hear the word used in favorable association with an auto CEO was very, very unusual, but very, very right.

Mulally's tenure at Ford was jam packed with unusual. Apparently, he was knocking down the walls that had caused each branch of Ford to operate in a vacuum. Global companies should be the same across the planet. You should be able to expect the same processes, quality, marketing, purchasing and engineering in Ford plants in Europe, as in Canada, as in the U.S., just like you can expect the same venti iced mocha latte at Starbucks to contain the same measure and mix of ingredients in Seattle as in Florida or Texas.

This is much harder for a car company. Each region of Ford – actually all the U.S. car companies – was operating as silos instead of in unison. Mulally went about standardizing Ford processes and the culture across all its regions. And with that standardization, unnecessary cost redundancies were pouring out of their profit and loss statements. Bravo.

Some of the most confounding conversations that I have had with CEOs and board members involve explaining the link between a healthy culture and extraordinary financial performance. It usually goes something like this: They listen politely and nod (as if they agree); they hope I finish my explanation sooner rather than later, then say – or don't say out loud, but think – "what the hell does a healthy culture and good morale have to do with making money? Let's do lunch." What I never heard anyone say was, "Well, you should know. JCI Automotive kicked ass while you were leading it. Come show me how to do that at my company."

The fact that Ford is still doing well speaks volumes about Mulally's years as CEO. It seems that he was another authentic leader who left a solid legacy.

"Management is empowered by titles and organization charts. Leadership is empowered by the people you are leading." - Rande Somma

Autopsy of the Box-Checking Method

There are a thousand ways that unfit leaders are brought into the fold of corporations. What motivates decisions that result in choosing unfit leaders is sometimes complicated. Sometimes it is laziness.

Most companies include diversity as one of their core values. This is a value that is turning out to be very beneficial to business, bringing in viewpoints and brain matter from all corners of the globe and every possible human angle. This is not a check-the-box thing (although you can make it that). Diversity brings deeply important issues and perspectives to light that would not otherwise be seen or heard by a more gender or ethnically homogeneous board.

I confronted the membership of a board I was on some time ago about this very issue. We had an opening for a new board member and the search committee came in and handed us the name of four or five guys. I asked were there any women candidates on the short list before you narrowed it down to these guys? The answer was no. I asked why not?

I pointed out the company's own core values and highlighted diversity for them. We were claiming that we valued and embraced diversity, yet everybody on this board stands up when they pee. We were not walking the talk. Include some qualified women in the short list for consideration, or take diversity off the company marquee. Hell, at least look like you tried.

It's simple. If diversity is a stated value of ours, shouldn't we make that an actual part of our process? This board had no diversity at all. We all know there are qualified women out there. We didn't find them because we were not looking hard enough. Actually, we were not looking at all.

One of the board members said, "So you want us to play that game where we are going to hire a woman so we can check a box."

I said, "No! What you are telling me is that if we bring a female onto the board, we would only be checking a box because you don't believe there is such a thing as a qualified woman. You are telling me that person just doesn't even exist." I said, "I'm telling you that making a legitimate attempt to find a qualified female is not even on your radar. So here is the deal, take diversity off of your list of core values because it's bullshit!"

A line _right_ out of that company's Code of Ethics for certain Senior Officers:"*The diversity of the company is a tremendous asset.*"

Just to be clear, there were really two agendas-- 1. What we are doing and 2. What we claim we are doing – and those were not the same thing.

Look, I like to get along. I am not an extremist or a zealot, but I take my responsibilities seriously, and if the job isn't being done as it should, I can be a real pain in the ass. But really, if you are going to claim one thing and do another, that's not right.

Diversity matters. It provides real value – I have seen it and it must be true for others because it is all over everyone's websites – but you can't just wave it as a banner to look good. You have to actually implement it to be true to your word and to actually benefit from it. Find a qualified woman; find a qualified African American or Hispanic, because their perspective matters. They have insight into your market that is valuable and that you need. Stop bringing people onto the board just because you feel comfortable with them because they think like you.

Bobble Headed Yes-Men

I am sure there are exceptions, but chairmen are much happier when there are board members in the room who are in harmonious agreement with their decisions. Everything runs much smoother when a CEO has board members who go along to get along because they don't know any better or don't want to know any better. That leader then has more freedom to get what they want. If the leader takes care to cover all their bases and check off all the boxes, no one is the wiser and the exterior world sees that all the boxes are checked and they don't see anything wrong.

Board members cannot provide effective oversight of a company when they really don't know what is going on and don't know the right questions to ask. Under these circumstances, they won't even know when they are being bullshitted.

Resume vs. Are You Faux Real?

I was asked to serve on a subcommittee advising a university's board of trustees as they began a search and vetting process to hire the university's next president.

The subcommittee invited input from stakeholders and professionals who could contribute to the process. They decided to get a voice from the alumni, from the staff and faculty, and several other sources. This decision to bring a diverse sampling of people and perspectives felt right.

At the initial meeting, the group was asked to go around the room and brainstorm the key criteria to use in qualifying candidates.

Someone said, "We need someone who is really good at strategic planning and implementing the plan."

Someone else said, "We need someone who is good at setting and meeting budgets."

Another recommended, "The next president needs to be good at interfacing with the various stakeholders."

They went on like this, each member volunteering their thoughts. So I am hearing all of these functional skills being thrown out as suggestions, and they were all right. We did need someone with all of those capabilities.

When it came my turn to contribute I shared, "I can only tell you what has worked for me. For me, before I even start to compare whether or not a qualified candidate has the best tangible skill sets to manage the position – what your GPA was or how many PhDs you held compared to other candidates – I need to know your character. I need to know the quality of the person and then the quality of the professional in that order." I mean after all, we are not deciding how to program a robot. We are talking about a human being.

I went on to explain, "I need to first get comfortable with the quality of the person before I fully understand the competency of the professional. If I can't get comfortable with the quality of the person, the alleged competency of the professional doesn't mean a damn thing to me."

Then somebody on the board asked, "Rande, how do you do that?"

"For me – and I would suggest for you – the most important criteria are the intangibles. Unfortunately, because there is no calculator or stop watch, they are much harder to assess," I replied. "You will hire a search firm, and the search firms that I know recognize the importance of the intangibles like character. Good recruiters are shifting their business models to put more emphasis on the assessment of these soft skill sets."

In addition to finding the candidates that fit the hard facts of the criteria laid out for positions, these firms can now offer a deeper investigative service to the organizations that hire them. This, in theory, should bring in candidates that are a better fit and more in sync with the organization's values and ethics. Acquiring a leader that is dialed into the company's mission on that level can ignite their power of purpose. These leaders naturally and meaningfully contribute, create and improve the position of the company with a solid long-term goal. To me, this kind of matchmaking really makes sense.

I have had many people working for me who had great credentials. They possessed high IQs, several degrees from prestigious universities and previously held lofty positions. That is all great, but sometimes they had a lot of knowledge that they were unable to deploy and implement in the real world because most business models are designed around collaboration and consensus. They could be the smartest person in the room, but if nobody wants to even be in the same room with them, let alone collaborate with them, what good are they?

In concluding my contribution on the advisory team for the university's quest for a new president, I added that, "We are putting all these qualifiers out there like they are all tied for first and carry the same weight. We need to put some weighting system in place when you assess your candidates."

Of course, for me it was sequential. I need to get comfortable with the quality of the person's character. It has to match up with the rest of the application. The check-box method of hiring is surely missing some potentially great leaders. I have been an applicant for many jobs, and I always hoped that the interviewer would see me for all that I am, not just the summarized bullet points on my resume.

While taking a year to select a worthy candidate for the position is not a viable option, time should not be so constrained as to unreasonably limit the ability of the nominating committee to find truly great candidates. Expand the time as much as possible to have an opportunity to explore all the options out there.

One of the board members added, "I agree with Rande. I have found that I can always teach someone to be a better engineer or better accountant or a better sales person. I don't know if I could train somebody to have the right attitude. I don't know how to do that, or even if you can."

This was an exquisite time in the history of this institution where they were going to select a new president from many qualified candidates with stellar resumes. At such a pivotal and sensitive time, it is important to find somebody who believes what you believe. What you believe is represented in your core values, your culture, and your vision for the future of your organization. The new leader should embody all of that.

CE...Oh-Oh

One day, an employee I knew who worked in the communications department of a company, Robert, said to me, "Rande, what is it with him?" referring to the CEO of his company. The company was doing poorly, and the CEO's solution: if the numbers don't work, lay off the people – kill the bunnies. What the CEO didn't realize was that meant eventually he would have to lay off more people. Whatever was wrong was likely systemic, so layoffs wouldn't solve anything. The only thing he fixed was the numbers, and only for a short time.

This was the slippery slope he was going down. And it was part of what stung him in the end. But the year before this CEO got fired, all the executives got bonuses.

Sucking + Sucking = Jackpot Bonus

Let's look at this a little closer.

I do not know the exact numbers that go along with this story, but let's say you suck, and let's say that $10 million represents sucking for this rather large company. And let's say that $50 million represents doing well.

In this given year, the CEO and leadership proclaimed they were going to make all these "improvements" to the company by killing bunnies, so they could make $15 million the next year, rather than $10 million. So they hit $15 million, maybe even $16 million, hell, maybe even $20 million – but not $50 million – and all the executives got their bonuses. One of the ways they made the additional profit that fed the bonuses was laying off around 300 people. Robert wasn't one of those people, but he was a guy without a college education who did a good job and enjoyed it. He probably planned to work for the company until he retired. He watched this process with shock, dismay and real concern for his future. They were freezing salaries and laying people off and the people making those decisions were the same people taking bonuses. Big bonuses. Super. The board is happy, Wall Street is happy. Everyone is cracking open champagne and cigars are being passed. Were there going to be consequences downstream? Nobody gave a shit.

That's done. Let's do lunch.

In the meantime, many of Robert's coworkers who were let go were left scrambling to find work so they could pay their mortgages and put food on the table for their family. Those who were not laid off were left wondering if their jobs were going to be taken from them in the future. Lack of communication, trust and job security took its toll, and distracted, worried workers were not enthusiastic or focused.

The business stopped caring about them, so they stopped caring about the business, like it works in any relationship.

That was not right. This was not success. This was not improving the business, but in a leadershit system it is quite normal. The CEO just didn't have the "stuff" to get it right, and the board didn't even know what the hell the "stuff" was. They gave him that position because he was a sitting CEO for another company. Check!

The reality is that they started off sucking at $10 million revenue for a company that should be reaching $50 million. I would never pay anyone one nickel of a bonus for $15 million, which is the equivalent of sucking less. I might pay you a bonus for when you legitimately quit sucking altogether, and get it done while observing core values (not in spite of them) – and certainly not on the backs of the livelihoods you destroyed. What kind of model is it where I am sucking less – and many heads are rolling to make me look good – so I am getting a bonus? Quit sucking! On $51 million and above, maybe leadership could consider giving them a bonus. *Maybe.*

Really, if it were up to me, I would eliminate bonuses altogether. Bonuses create behavior. Bad behavior. Bonuses have negative unintended consequences. The worst one is that executives get paid a ton of money if they hit earnings. And if you make that bonus number big enough, they are going to make sure that they hit those numbers no matter what. No bunny is safe.

Disposable Pawns

As I already discussed in Chapter 4, pay is a big part of the problem. When leadership's compensation is so huge and is tied to only one aspect of performance – near term results – it is easy to see how everything can look disposable. Seeing and treating employees as expendable becomes part of the game of getting to the bonus. When leaders keep their distance and objectify their people that way, it makes it easier to lay them off like useless pawns in order to accomplish their personal goals of promotion and the big money prize. It is justified by saying "it's just business".

Like Robert in the example above, many lower wage and skilled employees settle into their work, their job, their routine, with the intention of holding onto it for the better part of their career. They are often in it for the long run. CEOs are typically older and in the sunset of their careers. They are usually in it for three, five, maybe six years. I think we can agree that that is a completely different level of commitment.

In all honesty, the CEO performing at $15 million (still sucking level) and collecting his bonus was completely blind to this way of thinking. If I were to point all this out to that CEO, he would be horrified. He would be stunned. Laying people off is such a normal, natural and accepted way of doing business that many leaders do not even consider whether there is another way to go about being successful. It would never occur to them *that true success involves leveraging the hidden value of the very people that they see as disposable.*

"Great leaders don't do great things; great leaders get the people to do great things." - Ronald Reagan

Aligning Actions with Words

I suppose that if you have followed along this far, perhaps you agree, to some extent, that some things are screwed up in corporate leadership.

When a new leader is offered a position and a job, there is an understanding of the duties, responsibilities and criteria against which the new leader will be measured. An offer asks the new leader if they are willing to accept the job and execute those duties, and by signing they are agreeing and saying, "Yes, I am."

Our mistake is that we actually believe they were serious. We thought they meant it. Worse yet, we believed that we could hold them to it.

The website, the job description, the mission statement, the marketing brochures all report a best-in-class, world-class organization. Everything that is published reports a high standard and high quality delivery of service and/or products. The right thing is being said and published for public image. But the reality of many organizations is that marketing is disassociated with the true corporate agenda.

I know I am not the only one who believes that marketing for many companies is a ploy to fool, distract and dazzle the public and other outsiders, because corporate America has lost my trust and the trust of many others. We are suspicious of their shiny images, and with good reason.

This brings me to the word "innovation." Why do most companies have the word innovation all over their website? Probably because it is a mandatory buzzword. They don't actually have an innovation process, let alone know how to invent or implement one, because in order to have innovation, companies have to pay into it *now* to be able to receive any benefits from it three, five or ten years down the line.

True innovation is a long term investment with associated trial and error and risk, and as we've seen, Wall Street and CEOs are invested in short term wins. They are not very worried about what happens three or five years from now because remember, they will likely be on the beach with a pitcher of margaritas when any innovation they invested in is actually realized and generates a return. Their bonus and any other accolade or award is not based on innovation. They won't get credit for it, and innovation – if it is done correctly – drains the revenue from their short term success. So honest to goodness innovation is more rare than what corporate websites are claiming.

Cannibalizing innovation to shunt money to short term gains undermines an organization's ability to adapt and survive in the future paradigm of their industry. It is a short-sighted game plan, but in today's system, so what?

It should matter. True innovation is a creative process that injects powerful and eccentric ideas and concepts into an otherwise mostly rigid corporate mindset. It is the thing that gives any organization the flexibility to adapt to future changes and challenges. Throughout history, American ingenuity has always been about adaptive and cumulative innovation. Unless innovation is the core of what you do, like Apple and Microsoft, it is critical for leaders to intentionally put it on their radar and keep driving it. It should always be part of their strategic plan.

Fitting Innovation into the System

When I came to JCI in 1988, our automotive sales were $800 million, and when I left, it was approximately a $20 billion company. At some points along the way it felt like controlled chaos. We were growing so fast that we lacked the proper systems to handle all the new business, because we were too busy doing the business. We couldn't just say stop, no more orders while we put some systems in place. So we had to in essence change the fan belt on the engine while it was running.

When we put the new systems in, I asked one of our engineering leaders to oversee the process to define and implement standard operational best practices for standardized use of the systems across the board.

Innovation has its place in an organization, but it cannot be allowed to run amuck and disrupt optimized systems. We want innovation, but we want it to be smoothly integrated, to complement what is already in place. To achieve that, we need to capture and implement the best of the innovative concepts into our processes and systems, and to take advantage of them at scale. If I have 120 just-in-time assembly plants around the world, and they all operate under the same common operating systems and processes, and you come up with a better way to do something, I can take that and multiply it times 120. Now we are really leveraging innovation.

You can still be creative in large corporations, but process discipline is much more important than the process. We have to trust any new innovative process and know that it is going to benefit us before we just throw it into the mix. If you have a process in place and someone decides that they have a better idea and they are just going to go ahead and do it, they derail the opportunities for operational optimization.

Rubik's Cube

Budgets for different departments – like innovation -- have to be set. At JCI, my team and I might be at a quarterly forecast meeting, with half the year done and half a year to go, looking to see if we were still going to hit our full year numbers. There was always something going on that made that incredibly arduous. But we had vowed to do something special, and not default to the path of least resistance.

It was very complicated to navigate a new way of moving the business ahead, starting first with walling off what we would *not* do.

So we would all sit at the table together. Over on one side sat engineering, finance, and manufacturing. These guys represented the "invest-now-and-pay-back-now" departments. On the other side of the table were Human Resources – which included training and development of people, Sales, Marketing, Innovation and New Product Development. These guys all represented "invest-now-and-pay-back-later" departments, where the return on investment was longer term.

We knew what the rules were. One of those rules was that we were not allowed to rob one budget to prop up others. We were human and we were tempted . . . and it got *really* hard.

 "Hey guys, I think we are about $20 million short on the projections; maybe more." I would see one side of the table looking at the other side like a buzzard looking at a wounded rabbit.

HR had a big budget for attending to a need based on a morale survey we had conducted earlier in the year that showed there were people who didn't feel like they were being developed to be promoted in the company, so all that budget money for "invest-today-pay-back-later" needs was sitting there like a big piece of juicy meat, with manufacturing and engineering eyeballing HR like a bunch of hungry jungle animals.

But we had walled off the option of robbing one to cover the ass of another, so I remind them, "Hey, remember that the budget for Innovation and that budget for HR and Sales and Marketing? Those are all *my* budgets. They don't belong to anyone else at this table. They are my budgets and you can't have any. So now what?"

It was always entertaining for me – actually for all of us – but not taking the path of least resistance was never easy. We could have had that meeting done in ten minutes, and I bet it took us a week to figure out the right answer. Our calculations went from a tic-tac-toe board to a Rubik's cube. More hours; more brainstorming, but we always – I mean *always* – found the right answer.

By the way, if we had just done the tic-tac-toe method, we would have blended right in. Everybody would expect us to do it that way. Nobody was paying us a bonus to do the Rubik's cube. Nobody was incentivizing us or even caring if we did it one way or the other. Those who do not take the time and effort to do it the Rubik's cube way, they are getting paid *way* too much money to play tic-tac-toe.

Pulling the Pin on the Grenade

I used innovation as an example of how leaders can rob Peter to pay Paul (or pay themselves), but there are many other ways that this is accomplished in the corporate setting. Nothing is safe when leaders decide that the pot of gold is more important than the company, the people they are leading, or the quality of their product.

There are no immediate consequences for deciding to satisfy the short term goals that at the same time put the future of the company at risk. Those consequences are typically years away. We have allowed leaders to leverage all the long term resources for innovative strategic plans for the future of the company, in order for them to accomplish short term goals which elevate their bonus and/or celebrity.

If you had a grenade and pulling the pin on the grenade was the answer to your short term problems, why would you even hesitate to do that if you knew you were not going to be in the vicinity when the grenade actually detonated? The consequences are so far removed from that irresponsible decision that it seems a very viable option for leaders with little character and a retirement plan to go ahead and sell out the company's future for their short term gain.

Corporate Infidelity

I believe that people are generally starting to notice the dip in standards. There is a growing murmur of discontent in this country. I believe we are starting to watch and pay more attention to the quality and character of leadership on every level.

With that in mind, let's talk about how the system in corporate America grades its leaders. Performance reviews given by boards of directors are designed to grade CEOs on their performance. The performance of any good CEO is partly about near term performance, but it is far more about assuring a better future. But that future rarely ever has the same CEO at the helm.

Many CEOs in public companies are in the twilight years of their career, so for some, this job may be their last four or five years in the workforce. More importantly, because the compensation packages have continued to inflate beyond reason, after just a few years at one company, CEOs are frequently already shopping for their next CEO position or being wooed away by another company that is trying to fill their leadership ranks with a sitting CEO. The result of both of these scenarios is that the market for corporate leaders actually works against the future-focused job description for those same leaders. Hello. Does anyone else get that?

If someone has proven that they are not going to be loyal to one company, why in the world would you think they would be loyal to you and your company? If they left a company to come to work for you for more money, they would likely do it again. That sitting CEO was not future-focused when you met them. He/she was "me-focused."

Corporate infidelity has massive upside incentives for leaders to dump their corporate bride and go be with a new, hotter, sexier company seducing them with a lot of money . . . and yet, unlike romantic infidelity, there is nobody saying it is wrong or immoral or shameful. In fact, everyone (which is corporate America, the media and the market) is saying, "Awesome! Go for it! Do it as often as you can to get all the booty!"

If a leader can always get more money – a LOT more money – with a new company, and the system is encouraging them to bail time and time and time again on their long term obligations with the "old" job, why would they ever make a long term plan to stay? Why would they ever develop a plan for your company that protects its long term future, knowing they will not be around for it? The system is rewarding leaders for becoming "players."

Retention bonus you say? That is just a big price a hiring company is willing to pay to keep you whole. It should be called the "buyout price," one of the many seducements.

A good board and a good CEO will look at the center of gravity for any person being considered as a candidate for CEO. They examine where the CEO focuses their time and energy. The majority of that is supposed to be focused *on the future*, with a little bit left over to make sure that everyone is doing their "today" job, and all along everyone should be trusting each other because that is the culture that an authentic leader installs. That is what they should be looking for; not a serial CEO who is easily lured away as soon as a better offer shows up.

Be a Winner Once, Receive Trophies for Life

Boards frequently restrict their CEO searches to sitting CEOs, as I described earlier. The theoretical reason behind this is that a company then doesn't have to suffer through the learning curve of someone untested in that role. Of course, if the former CEO had done their job creating a succession plan, the company wouldn't have to suffer through the learning curve of any new outsider CEO, sitting or otherwise, but that's another story. When a new CEO must be found, one who is already a sitting CEO somewhere else supposedly comes preloaded with the skills and the experience that makes them a wiser and more effective leader.

This is another manifestation of the path of least resistance for so many processes in business today. Easy is right; easy is right; easy is right. The "easy is right" standards are lower than "right is right." Now, all of a sudden, you are getting people in leadership positions that you wouldn't want running your lemonade stand, and they are getting paid $10s if not $100s of millions.

Board members, who are responsible for oversight of the business and hiring of CEOs to run it, sometimes get money and stock as well as a title. The idea is that the stock will incentivize them to do a good job so that the company will do well, and as a stockholder they will benefit by keeping the company on track. But the salaries and other immediate compensation are so high for these leaders that the stock just does not hold that much value. They are current or former executives who have made a lot of money already, and who are individually well vested in the stock market, so the incentive to work hard is really non-existent for many of them. They have their growing IRAs and their millions that they contracted in their hiring negotiations.

Many of these board members have held CEO jobs or other big positions, but how many of them were on the leadership team of a company that went Chapter 11? Shouldn't we wonder about that history? They may not have done a great job as a leader, but they have CEO, COO and CFO all over their resumes, so they are considered good candidates for board positions.

Additionally, and similar to the "sitting CEO" phenomenon, if you are on the board of one company, that usually weighs in very positively for putting you on the board for another. There is little investigation into the details of how good of an executive you were or how good of a board member you are. You are allowed into the club because you have the credentials. Nobody much cares about your record. You have a great bio, so you look attractive. You're hired. Let's do lunch.

It is not unusual for a CEO to also serve on one or more boards. I am not sure how in the hell they find the time to devote to those obligations unless their standards of performance are so low that the amount of effort required is minimal. They might just show up at a board meeting, pretend like they actually give a shit, don't make any waves and don't piss off the chairman. Can a corn!

In order to be a truly great leader you need both character and competence. But it seems like lately you don't really need the character part to be awarded a leadership position. In fact, it may be more of an inhibitor in the process than anything. Leaders with integrity are not willing to go the path of least resistance, but the system is somewhat geared for leaders who can quickly make numbers work and deliver results. The system demands big results, and more importantly, it demands them *now.*

When it comes to some leaders I know, I wouldn't let them run my kid's lemonade stand. They might be great people with great talent, but leadership of a business is not everyone's bag. Some of these leaders kept landing those leadership positions because they already had them. Why did they get the second one? Because they had the first one. Why did they get the third one? Because they had the first two.

At some point your resume alone carries you. It's box-checking. I personally know of a few CEOs who ran businesses that under-performed terribly. Some filed for Chapter 11 either during or soon after their tenure. It was the same thing; all were sitting on at least one corporate board. Why? Because there are no boxes to be checked for quality of prior performance, the legitimacy of the prior performance, or how the performance was generated. This lack of insight into past performance of leaders lowers the bar and perpetuates the current broken system.

Crickets

When I was on the board of directors of a large publicly traded company, their CEO refused to generate any succession plan or strategic plan – two things he was required to do, as you will recall from my prior discussion. For years he stonewalled the board showing up at board meetings without even a valid explanation for why he hadn't done either of these things.

I kindly confronted the CEO frequently, and asked him where his plans were. I needed to see them because I would have to fill out his performance reviews – one of the duties I had agreed to as a board member. I asked him this same question at almost every meeting.

One time he got angry and raised his voice at me. I stopped him and said, "Hold on. Take a deep breath. With all due respect, I don't report to you. I am responsible to shareholders. They have put their trust in me that in some way I am going to be a good steward of their investment by overseeing the operations of this business and that it is being run correctly, and thereby giving them some comfort that their investment is in good hands. I work for them. This is my job and I intend to do it. Actually, I do care whether we get along. I really do. But when push comes to shove, if you are asking me to ignore my obligations in the interest of getting along with you, that's not going to happen."

Now, I didn't decide the rules. I am just following the job description for being a board member. The succession plan and strategic plan are pretty common assessment indicators for a CEO's performance. They are on this guy's performance review. They were on there before I ever arrived on the board and they will be there when I leave. There they are. Right there in black and white on the form with little boxes for me to check off. And I am being asked to check off the appropriate box to evaluate the CEO's performance. That is my job.

As crazy a moment as it was virtually standing toe-to-toe with this CEO arguing with him to do his damn job, it paled in comparison to the stunning peripheral drama taking place around us. There was not one person in the room who backed me up with even so much as a nod of the head. Everyone is looking at their watch, looking at their shoes. Crickets.

Who's Zooming Who?

Then in a moment of clarity while the crickets played, it occurred to me that these guys on the board with me all think they work *for him*. And he thinks that I work for him, too. They are all here because they are *not* going to say anything that engages this CEO in conflict. That's how they got the job and that is why they are not aligned with me. They are going to go along to get along and this CEO will do as he pleases.

Hell, I am the first one to admit that I am not always right. And I don't even know when I am right sometimes, but I knew that I was so absolutely right this time because I was just repeating what was on my job description – the damn piece of paper in front of me that *they gave me.*

I went into the restroom later during that meeting. The CFO of the company came in and stood at the urinal next to me. He looked under the doors to the stalls to see if he anyone was in there with us. Then he quietly said to me, "Rande, you are 100% right, but you know how he is."

I guess he had to be careful who heard that.

The Envelope, Please......

After that came the CEO's performance review. The process was this: each board member receives a form in the mail that has eight categories to evaluate the CEO of this publicly traded company. Scoring is from one to five. Each board member completes the form and returns it to the compensation committee chairperson who consolidates the scores for each category.

Once the forms are all completed and handed in, the board convenes for the meeting. Without the CEO in the room, the compensation committee chairperson reviews the scores with the board. After discussion of the performance review scores, the chairman/CEO is brought into the room to receive his review by category.

So I receive my review form via mail and I fill it out. In terms of scoring, this is how it basically works: one = "you suck" and five = "you're awesome." So there are some fours and fives, you know, the company has enjoyed some significant success to this point. The CEO had done some very good things.

Then I come to "Succession Plan".

You probably know me well enough by now to know that we are now officially headed down the crapper.

The performance review – the form that they gave me – describes what criteria to apply. I do not get to make up my own criteria. According to their criteria, I was obligated to give the CEO a score of one = "you suck" for Succession Planning only because they didn't offer me the option of zero = "I'm throwing up a little in my mouth."

I go down the list some more. There are some more threes, fours and fives. Then I come to "Strategic Plan." Again, I do not get to make up the criteria for this category. I give him another score of one = "you suck" only because, again, zero doesn't exist.

The head of the compensation committee collects the completed forms from the nine board members through the mail. He consolidates the scores. The board meets.

Before the CEO is invited into the room, the consolidated scores are then read off so the board can have a free and open discussion about the scores without the presence of the CEO.

I honestly don't remember the exact score. I am going to just give the score that gives you the essence of what it represents.

Succession Plan: he receives an overall three (which is satisfactory.) That's with my score of one. If you removed my score of one, his score would jump to at least a four. That is a four out of five.

Strategic Plan: He receives a three again.

I stop the meeting because I am an idiot. "Wait. Stop. What did we just do?"

"These are two areas of the performance review that are critical to oversight and assessment of what this CEO should be focusing on and doing well" – which is the reason they exist on this form (*that you gave me!*).

I continued to give myself enough rope for the hanging, "These are two plans regarding the company's future, and by any definition simply do not even exist. There is no succession plan or strategic plan in a form that we can provide oversight" *(which is our job!)* "We just said that we are good with that; we are satisfied that it doesn't exist."

Then came a little muttering and then the damn crickets again.

So I went on, "What I believe is true is that over time and totally unintentionally, we (the board) have morphed to a place where we are not holding this CEO accountable for what he is _obligated_ to do; instead, he has conditioned us to hold him accountable for what he is _willing_ to do." (Boom. The sound of standards dropping.)

For whatever reason, he is unwilling to provide the board with a strategic plan or a succession plan. He doesn't want to. This board said ok. They have said they are ok with it because their expectations have been lowered to a point where you already assume those plans are not going to be there. So it fits. We assume it's not going to be there. It's not there. We're satisfied. You know how he can be.

Good. Done. Let's do lunch.

In an ideal situation, what the CEO wants to do is irrelevant. That is not the deal. He does not get to alter the standards and lower expectations. His persistence over several years of disregarding critical aspects of his job is really a dismissible offense. The best leaders do what they are obligated to do. They just do their job, without looking for the wiggle room of getting out of doing their job, and the board is there to ensure it. Or in this case, I guess not.

Just Do Your Job

When I was up for my third term on this board I decided not to return. I expect I was going to get nominated and the CEO would not have stopped it. He probably would have hated to have me return, but what was he going to say? I don't want Rande on my board because he keeps trying to make me do my job? I went to see him because I wanted a respectful departure. I gave him the news and tried to explain to him why I wasn't going to return without being too judgmental or critical. I told him I don't think I can provide a lot more value here the way things operate. I didn't feel the need to create a controversy . . . which eventually then went on to happen. Go figure.

He said something to the effect, you did a good job, Rande, but in the end, you really didn't fit.

Wait. What?

And I just had to know, "What do you mean?"

He went on to explain that, 'Well, you came from two Fortune 500 companies and we are a big, but a much smaller company than what you are used to, and we just don't have all those bureaucratic policies, and this stuff and that stuff, and so we are more nimble, more elastic. We are more this and that. So your standards are used to a bureaucracy of the Fortune 500 companies, so it was a mismatch."

Hmmmm. Nope.

"I respectfully disagree," I said. Here we go.

"First of all, I understand that you associate very large corporations with wasteful bureaucracy. While I've had a lot of exposure to that crap, it is not something that I naturally do. I can recalibrate and shift to the context of this company and how it operates. But I do agree with you. I don't fit, but that's not the reason I don't fit."

I was just trying to make sure he understood.

"I don't fit because I am not going to accept you not doing your job. Board members that fit are willing to do that."

This is why I am all for term limits for members of the board of directors. When you walk into a room that is freshly painted, it stinks. After being in that room for a while, though, you don't notice it. You don't smell a thing. As a human, if you are in a situation long enough, you will conform to the circumstances in which you are immersed. Humans do that. They adapt. They become crickets.

I was one of three board members up for re-election that term. I found out at the last shareholders' meeting that one of the other two board members up for re-election had pulled his name from nomination. He was leaving the board. That was stunning, because he had been on the board for years and was a friend of the CEO. I really liked and respected this fellow. I pulled him aside and asked him, "This is none of my business, but why are you leaving?"

He said, "I kept reflecting on what you said in that meeting, Rande, about how we are not doing our job. We have shifted to a place that just allows whatever the CEO wants. That is not our job. And I got to a point where I either had to be a good board member, or I was going to preserve my friendship with the CEO. If I was going to be a good board member, he was going to resent me like he resents you (I knew that, but ouch). So I decided I'm going to stay friends with him, and withdrew my nomination for re-election."

So I was left wrestling with whether any of that was a good thing or not. It was kind of validating because it told me that I am not so screwed up, and I was not entirely alone fighting against a normal that had set in so deep that most people did not realize it was bad.

This was my last meeting and I was saying good bye to everyone. A newer board member came up and asked, "Rande, do you have any advice as you are leaving?"

I turned to him and said, "Yes. Just do your job."

CHAPTER 6
ALL HAIL SHORT TERM RESULTS
LIGHTING THE FUSE ON INEVITABLE CONSEQUENCES

There was a point in time in recent history when the drifts toward allowing lower quality, lower standards and unqualified leaders began to leak into our leadership system. It seems that the system began to fluidly allow greed and shortcuts to success that undermined long term viability of corporations.

I believe this resetting of standards has introduced a greater need for character vetting of leaders, but to date, it doesn't substantially exist, as far as I can tell. So for now, the "me" and "now" way of thinking may have taken root in our leadershit system.

Maybe part of the problem is that we are so overwhelmed by the flood of leadershit that we feel paralyzed and powerless to do anything about it. We seem to be in the midst of a time in our history that I call the "generation of surrender."

There are people who see leadershit and want to do the right thing, but they don't know what to do. Not exactly apathy, but more a sense that they are just caught, because they don't see that there is anything they can do about big problems like leadershit. So they just let it go. They don't want to be me – frustrated and almost frantic for an answer to fix things. They just see it as something they can't control or do anything about, so they turn and walk away.

Maybe we can come up with some ways to change this sense of powerlessness....

We Can't Be Great if We Can't First Be Good

There are few impactful consequences for irresponsible, unethical and immoral leadership. Few offenses rise to the level of breaking the law. Even the ones that do cannot always be effectively brought to justice or even be made public.

I was part of a team from JCI that negotiated a deal with a team from one of the Detroit Three. We paid approximately $25 to $30 million dollars for one of their plants that made seats. I dealt with their team leader through this transaction.

Part of the agreement said that they would not market test the seats for two or three years after we bought their facility; in essence, committing their business to that facility for that period of time. Market testing in this case would be the act of soliciting competitive proposals for the purposes of shopping the sourcing of the supply of the product. The purpose of this market testing restriction was to give JCI time to get oriented, integrated, organized and optimized in the new facility without losing the seller's business. It was a negotiated term that added to our purchase price for the facility. We paid them for that loyalty, for that component of the deal.

Virtually within days of signing that agreement with us, that automaker intentionally broke that contract with JCI and started market testing.

This meant that I needed to approach and talk with their leader about this intentional breach of contract, but think about that. What do I say? "Hey, you are violating the agreement we just made." He knows that. Hell, he planned to do it before the ink was dry! What do I say? "Don't do that anymore?" "Please stop that?" I did not know how to have this conversation with this jagoff.

Because although we paid $25 to $30 million for the plant, they were a $2.5 billion, approximately, global customer of ours.

So we get into this discussion, and after some small talk, he simply says to me, "Rande, what are you going to do -- sue us?"

Boom. Conversation over.

We had an entire team of attorneys who put together this pretty complicated contract that delineated what we committed to do and what they committed to do. A lot of time and money was spent constructing this thing.

And right there I got it. Forget the lawyers. Forget the contract. That document clearly stated that this automaker had to hold off market testing for a couple of years. They know that, but there were no consequences for them if they didn't. So they didn't.

I couldn't sue them. I couldn't do anything to them because it would end up a net-net loss for my company. I might win the battle, but I would surely lose the war.

And here is the point:

All I ever really had this whole time was this leader's word that he would honor the contract that he signed. All I ever had was his integrity and that he would be ashamed of himself if he violated his word. That is the _only_ thing I really ever had. And in the end, clearly I didn't even have that.

As a practical matter, in the end, all we ever really have with any agreement is whether we can trust that someone we are doing business with will honor their commitment.

With this event, I knew then that the old handshake honor system was surely dead. Somehow we have shifted to this place where "it's just business" has trumped morals and values and honor.

To trash common decency and courtesy and eliminate decorum has become so onerous in this country that Americans cannot afford to do business here anymore.

Now we have attorneys and subpoenas and documents and contracts piled high on everyone's desk and in courts across this country, increasing the cost of regulating people when they choose to violate their own word.

The almost predictable and routine unethical professional behavior of our leaders is driving up the already oppressive cost of doing business in this country, plain and simple. We have disintegrated to a society where now nobody deserves to be trusted, and it has added billions to the cost of doing business in America. So we cut costs and move operations to other countries to compensate for our leadershit decisions. We are literally paying for our lack of basic integrity and honor. And that is a real overhead cost that adds absolutely no value.

Should we just add more and more lawyers to concoct more and more clauses in more and more contracts in a futile attempt to head off more and more deviations from ethical behavior? Should we take more fights to the courts, so we can end up on more and more court dockets, and we pass more and more expensive legislation to try to control it all, forcing businesses to pay the high price of this legal load? And it is all really just putting lipstick on a pig.

And we are the pig.

In the end, the business reality is that the only real consequences for unethical or irresponsible leadershit behavior might be the self-inflicted hit that one would take to his or her sense of honor and integrity – the very virtues that obviously don't mean a rat's ass to many of those we select and accept as our leaders.

Somehow, when standards and expectations are lowered, a leader's sense of pride and fulfillment for doing great things the right way – which is a prime motivator for authentic leaders – vanishes. At the same time, the power of guilt and shame that any leader might feel as a deterrent to taking illegitimate shortcuts evaporates from the equation. Obligation, duty, pride, guilt and shame are all internalized traits that motivate us and keep everything on track for many of us in this country. In corporate America it seems that these internal traits are lacking and the things that motivate leaders are largely external.

I don't often see leaders being ashamed anymore. I see excuses.

Legacy for leaders really should include pride of accomplishment in what that leader did for the company, its people, the stakeholders and the future of all the communities connected to his/her decisions. You just have to read the headlines today to understand that legacy now mostly has to do with celebrity, power, and the size of compensation packages for leaders. And let's face it, when you measure leadershit this way, size matters.

"An organization whose morale is not high and whose leadership is not trusted can only establish mediocrity as its highest legitimate aspiration." – Rande Somma

I sit in conference rooms and listen to qualifications being checked off for a new leader. I think about how many people looked exactly right. They went to the right school. They had all the correct qualifications. They said exactly the right script. They rehearsed answers to big interview questions, and they landed the job. And that was their touchdown. Many people devote more energy and time to studying how to land a leadership position than how to be an authentic leader. The threshold is low enough to allow this to happen. This can be so destructive if that leader turns out to just be a very good salesperson, and companies and employees pay the price sooner or later when the wrong leader is chosen.

Just like politicians who say all the right things before they are elected. This is what we all recognize as their "promise" to us as to what they will do. After they get elected, the promises frequently get substituted with excuses and a new agenda.

When the discussion around criteria of who should lead an organization is done, the discussion about character is not skimmed or even glossed over. It is skipped entirely. They might choose the equivalent of Charles Manson as long as he has the right stuff on his resume and demonstrates that he gets results.

There will be an end to this ignoring of character and acceptance of bad behavior. This is not sustainable. This is hurting too many people, companies, communities and ripping the very fabric of capitalism.

Terrorists are trying to kill us and blow us up, but there are also people in leadership positions in this country who by their behavior are slowly, quietly and systematically destroying American livelihoods, families and lives. Until you wake up one day and realize that you are one of those people, one of those families, you may never appreciate the tragedy and depth of destruction that occurs when leaders focus on self-interests versus obligations.

It's Just Business My Ass

Leaders can show a blatant disregard for the consequences that others must suffer as a result of leadershit decisions. Often, the only defense for their ineptitude or failure –quietly accepted by the business community as an inevitable part of the capitalistic system – is that "it's just business." We have all heard that phrase. Somewhere along the line Americans started to believe that they must accept "it's just business" as a God-given right of big business to diminish anything that has tragic fallout, results from poor leadershit, and/or is ethically questionable.

In my view, when leaders bring out the "its only business" comment, they are really asking to be let off the hook. It is never *just* business. If you are supposed to be leading a large organization, somewhere along the line, you are either positively or negatively impacting human beings, society and our culture.

It has likely happened many times where a leader has to stand up and say, during the announcement of layoffs, "Don't take it personally. It was a business decision. It's just business." What they are really saying is that although you have been working hard and doing the right things, I seem to have run this organization off the road into the rut because I didn't foresee something, didn't prepare properly, or didn't pay attention to the trajectory of our industry, or just didn't give a shit about any of that . . . and now you will pay the price for my shortfall. I'm gonna collect my bonus and go to the beach."

If I were an employee listening to the "it's just business" line, I would have some thoughts and questions. If it is "just business," then I'm really working for the wrong person. If all this means to you is a business decision and I just got caught up in it, I have to question your leadership ability as well as your sense of decency. Where is the explanation of your part in this? Why did you let us get into this situation? Why didn't you lead us better and what price are you paying for your failure? And where was the board of directors while you were running this business into the ground and ruining my life? Any leader that does not comprehend his or her weighty responsibility to the rest of us should not be a leader.

And yet, we have grown to routinely accept the "just business" explanation, letting our modern leaders slide through the cracks without explaining the part of that "just business" that was their responsibility. What about an explanation of how they are going to make changes to make it right? How are they going to make it up to the company? To the employees? To stockholders? How will they suffer when the rest of us lose our shirts, our security and our jobs? Or will they suffer at all?

We need to snap out of our apathetic acceptance of leadershit. We need to get back to valuing, and demanding, results built on long-term vision and strategy. With a steady gaze set on the long term, and an *acceptance and expectation of short-term setbacks as part of the process for long-term success*, with the right team and culture working towards all that, authentic CEOs can navigate their organizations through many economic storms.

At the end of the day, any leader who is continually boasting about stomping out brushfires at work; "I stomped out this one, and this one, and this one," is probably not doing a good job. One day someone needs to ask, "Why are you always stomping out brushfires? If you had established a long-term vision for success, you wouldn't have to stomp out brushfires every day." The downside to thinking short-term is that you are always using your time and resources, jumping to take care of things in a reactionary way. Short term responses dramatically limit your options, and those options are pretty much all bad.

"What you accomplish is of importance, but far less important than how it was done." – Rande Somma

CENTER OF GRAVITY

Manage the Business *(Authentic Leaders)*		OR	Manage the Results *(Leadershit)*
• Culture/People • Competitive Differentiation • Short and Long-Term Focus • Morale • Functional Expertise • Balance Centralized & Decentralized • Create Scale • Optimize Utilization • Process-Centric • Process Discipline • In-Cycle Metrics • People Selection & Development • Communications	• Apply Methods • Leverage Technology • Optimize Efficiency, Productivity & First Time Capability • Assure Consistent Stream of Creativity & Innovation • "Why" & "What If" Focus • Quality Systems & Improvement • Product Portfolio • Program & Customer Management • Diversity & Inclusion • Customer Satisfaction		✓ Financial Statements ✓ Shareholder Value ✓ Market Valuation ✓ Executive Compensation

CHAPTER 7
WHEN IT BECAME ABOUT THEM
LEADERSHIP CULTURE WHERE SELF-INTEREST OVERRIDES DUTY

"A leader's interest is finding the best way...not having his own." - Wilfred A. Peterson

Bless Us All

My wife and I have been members of our church for over 30 years. It was built in the mid-60s, and my wife, a native of the Detroit area, attended it as a young girl.

In 2009, the senior of its two priests approached me to ask if I would run for president of our church's Executive Board. He explained that he felt that the church was in financial trouble and that it might be time for someone to get involved who could bring significant business experience to the table.

I have helped the church in the past, leading some major fund raising events, and I was one of the leaders of the youth basketball program. However, I had never served on its executive board.

The priest didn't know exactly what was wrong and how bad the financial situation was, but his alarm was going off in his gut and it's a good thing that it did.

This was during the 2008/2009 national recession, and the church – as well as almost every other entity in Detroit – was faltering and on the brink of collapse. They were caught in the fallout of Detroit's economic disaster resulting from years of corruption coupled with the collapse of the auto industry, both of which were a result of leadershit.

The members of the church's executive board were good people who were willing to donate time and energy to serve their church. However, none of them had significant experience in business management.

I agreed to take on a volunteer role, leading members of our parish through a root cause analysis of the financials. From that analysis they could build a recovery plan. I was teamed with the church's president to implement the recovery plan as well through operational committees we put together.

I had a suspicion that our liquidity situation was worse than we had thought. I asked one of the parishioners with extensive financial expertise if he would work with the church treasurer to translate our bookkeeping system into accounting statements. I had a particular interest in a cash flow statement based on an ordinary operating run rate, which is an extrapolation of known recurring income and expenses.

The diagnosis was not good. If they kept bringing in money in the following months at the rate that they had been, and if they kept spending money the way that they had been, it was clear that, unless we took immediate drastic action to slow down the cash burn, the church could be insolvent within a year, and certainly before we were able to realize the benefits of our recovery plan. I conveyed the gravity of the situation to the president and estimated that, given their financial profile, they had about eight more months before they would be insolvent.

Soon after, I presented the findings at a full board meeting, and told them they needed to make dramatic changes. That was the first time that they fully grasped how bad the situation really was. They had no idea that they were that close to insolvency. They pressed me for my opinion about what to do.

I said, "Look, you have a few options, and they are all ugly." One of the priests wanted to know what I meant by that.

I told them the true story about the young hiker who went hiking in the mountains alone, fell into a ravine and got his arm stuck under a rock. Nobody knew where he was, and after a few days of not being able to free himself, it became clear what he had to do to survive . . . he had to amputate his own arm.

"That's where you are," I told them. "If closing the church is not an option, you will be forced to make some very difficult decisions."

The church had waited too long to start bailing the water out of the sinking boat. The board now had to take immediate action to slow the cash burn to buy time. A large portion of the "bleed" in terms of costs was the support of the clergy. As a result, they realized that one of the two priests had to be reassigned to another nearby parish. The junior priest had been with our parish for a long time, so it was not lost on anyone that this, while necessary, would at the very least be disruptive for this man and his family.

Financial forecasting is something leaders want to stay out ahead of in order to prepare for difficult times. When those difficult times take an organization by surprise, you are left with few choices to stave off insolvency. One of the worst options is to cut the payroll and layoffs.

This was the beginning of a long and very bad time for the church . . . and for me and my family.

The one priest who was to stay was concerned. He said, "Rande, we are a cathedral with several hundred families. We stretch from Chesterfield to Ann Arbor...we need two priests."

I explained, "That's true, Father, but right now it doesn't matter if you need 20 priests. You can't even afford one priest, but you aren't a church without one."

The new plan included a number of significant changes that were expected to bring the typical resistance. But since closing the church was not an option, neither was kicking the can.

And then there was one means of resistance that I had no experience handling, and never saw coming.

Holy Hell

Not long after we kicked off the recovery plan for the church in the spring of 2011, I received a call from our church president.

"I got an anonymous letter bad-mouthing me," he said. I told him that it sort of means that we are being effective, because change is difficult for any organization, so of course there will be those who are unwilling to change, even though not changing means extinction. Push back is expected. It is part of the process.

Then another disparaging anonymous letter came to the church. Then another.

In January 2012, I opened the mail at our home and read an anonymous letter claiming that the changes being made under our new operating plan for the church are meant to destroy the parish, and that I was the primary person responsible. The letter went on at length, specifically threatening my life, my wife's life, and the lives of the three daughters of the church's president – all of which were under the age of 10. The letter revealed details of violent and malicious things that would be done to my wife and the little girls.

I made a police report the same day, and a detective was assigned to the case. He said there was a time in the past when it would be a safe bet to believe this was only a scare tactic, but not in this day and age. Treating this like it was a scare tactic today would be reckless. And so we didn't.

I was extremely concerned, first and foremost for those little girls and for my wife. To add more resources to the effort to find who was responsible, I also hired a private investigator. I just took the position that more was better.

We reached a point in the investigation where it became necessary for the Bishop, who was the leader of all the parishes in the Midwest region, to engage in the process. We had hit a road block that only he could clear. Under the circumstances, we expected that he certainly would address the situation. But then he didn't.

While talking to the Bishop's assistant to express my frustrations with his astonishing inaction, the assistant told me, "Rande, you have to understand that His Grace is not very comfortable with contentious situations."

He is not comfortable? Now I am pissed.

I responded that first of all, a death threat aimed at women and children is something far more extreme than a "contentious situation." Second, the fact that the Bishop was not comfortable giving us help that only he could provide – especially where lives may be at stake – maybe doesn't mean that he is a bad person, but it absolutely means that he is completely unqualified to be a leader. This was not about him or his comfort level with the situation. Real leaders never even consider choosing their own comfort and their self-interests over their duties and obligations. Never.

I regarded his refusal to step up and get to the bottom of the issue as a blatant lack of responsibility to his duty as the leader of the church. If he wouldn't tackle this problem, who would? Nobody. It was despicable.

If there was ever a good reason for me to kick the can and pull out of any further involvement with this recovery project with the church, this might be that reason. But after talking with our wives and our priest and with a lot of faith, we carried on.

We finished the recovery plan, the church avoided insolvency, and their debt was paid off. In general, there was a bit of revitalization that gave the parish real hope for the future.

Today, the church's financial situation is fairly good. In October 2015, the church celebrated its 100th anniversary, an anniversary that was in real jeopardy of never happening just three years earlier.

To make a long story short, the persons of interest refused to speak to the investigator, so the case was never solved, thanks to Holy Leadershit. More importantly, the threats made in the letter were never carried out...Thank God.

Ivory Towers and the Wiz

Some businesses occasionally or routinely ask their employees to fill out what are called engagement surveys. They are also referred to as employee satisfaction surveys or morale surveys. These surveys measure employee sentiment on such things as passion and pride in their work. The surveys ask questions of employees like, do you feel like your talents are being well utilized and developed, and do you believe in the organization's mission. This helps the employer locate gaps between leadership and the people under them, as well as get an understanding of how to improve employee engagement.

While speaking about engagement surveys to Business Schools' MBA classes, I remember two remarks that I hope are not examples of how these surveys are typically treated.

The first one was from an individual who said he participated in a survey conducted by the company where he worked. I asked him, how long ago did they collect the surveys? He said about six months. I asked, what was leadership's response to those surveys? He said, so far, they've heard nothing . . . and don't expect to.

The second remark was from an individual who said his company had done some surveys in the past. Then, after some time passed, they sent out a new one. He said the question on the new survey that got, by far, the most negative response was "do you expect anything to be done in response to the messages that leadership gets from this survey?"

Without question, the number one thing that any leader needs to develop as a foundation is trust. Without trust, performance suffers. In order to develop a deep sense of trust, it is up to leaders to humanize themselves. People don't trust titles. They trust people, so being human in their eyes is critical, as well it should be.

The _second worst_ thing that a leader can do is not get honest, candid and constructive input from the work force. The _worst_ thing they can do is get that input, check a box and file it without making any effort to respond to it.

Leaders who pass out surveys from their ivory towers and never provide the courtesy of a response, or never implement change that would reflect that they cared about their employees' input – or that they even read their survey responses – are inviting trouble. It is a sure way to confirm employee suspicions that leadership doesn't care about them. And if they know leaders don't care, they don't trust them. Now they don't even like them.

Trust can be created through several different methods, but leaders certainly cannot generate trust if they don't have self-confidence. Leaders who lack self-confidence have what I call the Wizard of Oz Syndrome. That little gray-haired guy behind the curtain didn't have the self-confidence to lead, so he dehumanized himself and relied on intimidation, creating a whole new huge terrifying persona to get the results that he wanted, and that he thought he couldn't get by being himself.

Rock and a Hard Place

When I was running sales at JCI, I hired a fellow – we'll call him Joe – who I got to know pretty well over the years. I knew his wife and family and we became friends. Fast-forward to several years later. I am the president of North American Operations at JCI, and the VP of Human Resources walks into my office. He said, "We have a problem with Joe."

I asked, "What's that?"

He continued, "We have a paper trail that shows that he is falsifying his expense reports and he is taking large amounts of money."

He sat down and he walked me through the numbers. He wasn't kidding. It wasn't a few bucks here and there. It was a significant amount of money.

Then he looked at me and asked, "So what do you want to do?"

It was one of those "ah-ha" moments, and I hope that God made me remember these for a reason.

What do I want to do? What do I, Rande, want to do about this? I like Joe. I know his wife and family. I knew the impact termination was going to have on him. I know the difficulty he will have finding the next job, under the circumstances. What Rande *wants* to do is ignore it and make it go away. But what Rande wants to do isn't relevant at all. What is relevant is what the President of the North American Operations is obligated to do.

We tell people, here are the rules. Here are the boundaries, and if you go outside of these, there will be consequences. If Rande does what Rande wants to do here in this situation, where someone he knows and likes is caught outside the boundaries breaking the rules, and gives him a pass, why would anyone in this organization ever again believe or trust Rande?

I don't know how many nights I laid awake in bed. One choice served my self-interest, and one choice served my obligations to the company. I knew what I had to do. I called his supervisor in the morning.

Soon after his supervisor terminated him, Joe asked for a meeting with me. I was sure he was going to beg me for his job. He looked at me and he was emotional, and so was I. He said, "I just wanted time with you to tell you that I am sorry for letting you down."

Damn. Leadership is hard.

Inserting Actual Humans and Humility into Humanity

What do I think is one of the most important, if not *the* most important, trait of a leader? Humility.

People with humility never fall in love with themselves. Leaders with humility are sometimes misunderstood. Because they do not pretend to know the answer to everything, what is sometimes perceived as weakness is really strength. Humility breeds pragmatism and other great leadership qualities: delegating and empowerment.

Authentic leaders don't have an overriding need to always be right, to bask in the spotlight, or take the credit for everything that goes right. They also don't blame others when things go wrong.

There are many leaders who sit in a room and feel like they have to be the smartest one in the room. This is what I call the command and control person. They fail to realize that the goal is not to be smart. The true goal is collaboration and consensus. That is why I love diversity. Everybody is looking at the same problems through a different prism. We are looking at all the angles and we are minimizing the blind spots in the process of crafting our solutions.

As I have told members of my team, not only are dissenting opinions welcome, they are expected. And then you back it up.

"Humility is not thinking less of yourself, it's thinking of yourself less." – Rick Warren

Humility is a great humanizer. It is a great and natural fit for authentic leaders. If you remember the leadership scale designed by Jim Collins and his research team, in his book *Good to Great*, the one that scores leaders from one to five, humility is the distinguishing feature between what he calls level four leaders and those at the top of his leadership scale: level five leaders.

Morale

In about 1999, I read our mission statement at JCI and it said something like "World Class Global Leader in Automotive Interiors." We spent quite a bit of time and money measuring quality, cost, on-time delivery and all these tangible things.

At the time, I was really focused on our culture and the people at JCI. Our corporate values included something about "People are our Number One Asset," and yet we weren't measuring morale at that point in the late 1990s. Morale was a big question mark. What if we had a lot of employees who were not very motivated and had low morale? How would we know? Would it make a difference in our outcomes? We didn't know anything about our people and hadn't done any investigation or support of that core value, but we sure knew our way around an income statement.

We decided to find out what the morale was to make sure that what we were proclaiming in our corporate values matched the reality of our employees' attitudes, because if it didn't match the proclaimed values, we would have to change that. Or change our core value statement to *"People are our Number One Asset Most of the Time, But Not Always."*

We did a morale survey through an independent third party organization for three years in a row at JCI. We did it for three years because we wanted to act on the first year's results and then see if there was any improvement in survey results the following years. The idea was to make sure that what we were doing was actually working. A number of questions were asked. One of them was "Do you trust leadership?" 62% said yes. That meant 38% either didn't know or didn't trust leadership. That was just not good enough.

So we set about finding out why 38% don't trust the leadership. The third party who administered the survey went back, and through their process they reported that the reason was that, they "don't know you." They didn't know me, their leader. Now, I had been there for a number of years by the time I was President of North America. Members of my staff weren't new either. I told the survey team, "I have been here a long time. They know me." And they said, "No, they don't know *you*. They don't know Rande."

Go Steelers

To address this issue, we decided to set up an internal website and post a profile of each leader, with a heavy personal emphasis. One of the things that my friends all know about me is that I am a huge Pittsburgh Steelers ("Stillers") fan.

At the office, our executives often ate at their desks. To help us connect with our entire working team, we broke out of our executive cocoon and spent our lunch time in the cafeteria. You wouldn't believe the looks and the response we got when we started showing up for lunch there every day. Mingling with the entire workforce seemed energizing for everyone.

Weeks later, as I was leaving the cafeteria with a member of my staff after lunch, a guy tapped me on the shoulder and said, "Hey Rande, I have a cousin from Pennsylvania. The guy is nuts about the Steelers. He has black and gold all over his house!" We had a very nice quick exchange talking about the Steelers and his cousin.

My staff member said, "Well, ever since that website went up, we sure have a lot of Steelers fans around here!"

I got his point, or his dig, but I thought for a minute and said, "Do you think that fellow would have been able to approach me and talk to me without giving him the opportunity to know me as a person?"

We connected as humans. It was simple but magical. And I told my staff member, "You don't think he isn't going to go back and work a little harder this afternoon?" It is fulfilling and feels more human when you are doing things for each other, for people, not just for paychecks or promotions. I know that I went back and worked a little harder that day. You could sense that things were starting to click between upper management leadership and the workers.

I saw and felt the value in humanizing myself as a leader. I know that many leaders are afraid of doing that because they fear over-familiarity with the workers will lead to less respect from them, leaving them vulnerable and undermining their ability to lead.

I believe they really have that upside down.

Social Capital

I didn't invent this way of thinking. I had to learn it too. The value of people coming together creates social capital and has been recognized in many industries for a while. It's what every civic organization seeks to create. Social capital has value in fellowship and shared information and common goals. Social capital thrives in communities that provide platforms and places for people to come together to share their knowledge and information, to collaborate and communicate. This raises the value you get out of your network and relationships. This is why cities place so much emphasis and value on green space, benches, parks, bike trails, playgrounds and porches. Bringing people together has long been known to produce value in a society.

Social capital is built from human capital, which is the individual value that each person brings to the table. If you insert this concept of social capital within a corporation, you break down the walls of rank and pay scale for the greater good. When everyone is treated well and given access to leadership and allowed to share their ideas openly and without fear, they become familiar, they become trusting, they become invested in the outcome. This is the birth of a culture.

Reciprocal Dynamics

Throughout my career, I have worked alongside people who do things that I don't know how to do. As their leader, I would admit to them that I don't have much training or experience with their expertise and ask them to teach me so I can have a functional working relationship with them. It was my job to understand enough in order to support their efforts and help them get where they are expected to go. Everyone had a value, and it needed to be fostered. We mutually helped each other.

This is reciprocal dynamics, and it is a powerful tool for business. With reciprocal dynamics, leaders are personally plugged into the processes that their management and employees are using, so there is no disconnect between expectations and performance. There is mutual respect and recognition at all levels through familiarity and working together. That respect is earned.

One of the biggest and most common mistakes a leader can make – and I have done this myself – is to set expectations for employees and then fail to provide them with the necessary resources that enable them to reach those expectations. I learned what I was doing wrong through engagement and morale surveys at JCI. I discovered that while I was asking engineers to perform at a certain level, I had been giving them inadequate resources to achieve those goals.

Reciprocal dynamics produces good will, fellowship and familiarity. In turn, these breed trust and loyalty, leading to collective value and economic benefit. It all starts with a leader who is willing to professionally engage on an honest level with those under him or her and learn from them. The return on this investment can be profound.

Closing the gap between expectations and performance by understanding where leadership is falling short through reciprocal dynamics is a big deal. I am not sure how many people have been fired because they did not meet leadership's expectations, when in fact it was leadership who had little or no understanding of the level of resources needed in order for that employee to perform at the expected level. Sadly, I am sure it is some astounding number.

Additionally, as leadership continues down a blind path of never finding the "right" people to meet their unrealistic expectations, you see this revolving door of employees who serially "fail to perform." Hiring, training, on-boarding new employees and firing them gets very expensive for any company, and the lack of continuity becomes disruptive to its business. It is a destructive way to do (or not do) business and it is the fault of a poor leader. The more a leader continues to respond to his failed employee situation with the same reaction, the worse it becomes. The remedy gets less and less legitimate because the climb from where you were 3 or 4 or 8 employees ago has become steeper.

Reciprocal dynamics, social capital, and culture were the foundational concepts that the JCI Automotive business was perched upon in my final years there. It had never been done before and the financial numbers skyrocketed as morale and familiarity with leadership grew. It was remarkable.

Leadership is not about the person in charge. It is about people. It is about everyone, from the highest paid CEO to the minimum wage earner in the company. It is about customers, vendors, suppliers, shareholders. It is all of us, and that concept has largely been lost by too many leaders who think it is all about them.

"Humanization of leadership breeds a culture of people committed to and supporting each other. The power of these reciprocal dynamics establishes a higher capacity for excellence than when people are working for a title and a company." - Rande Somma

Turns Out Being Human is Profitable

At JCI, we also started to have a 'President's Breakfast' every month, where I could sit down with selected rotating groups of employees and talk with them about their views of the company. We held other meetings designed for our people to talk to leadership, not for us talk to them. The cumulative effect was that I learned so much from these forums about the company that I didn't know, and I learned a lot about the fantastic people who kept its wheels turning every day.

We gave morale or engagement surveys to our employees for three consecutive years. What I was most proud of with the surveys was the demonstrated improvement in responses over those years, and the correlation with the financial performance results for those same time frames, as demonstrated in the following charts. The overlay is stunning. All of our business performance numbers followed the improvement of the employment morale survey. All of them.

DO YOU (EMPLOYEES) BELIEVE WE ARE LIVING OUR VALUES? (PERCENTAGE OF EMPLOYEES ANSWERING YES)

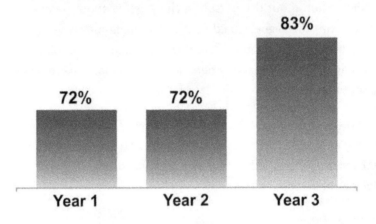

Independent Third Party Survey of Automotive Group, North America Employees During Rande's Tenure
2000-2003 Economic and Automotive Industry Recession

DO YOU BELIEVE IN AND TRUST THE LEADERSHIP TEAM? (PERCENTAGE OF EMPLOYEES ANSWERING YES)

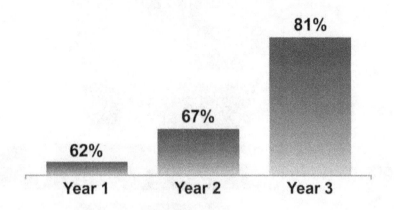

Independent Third Party Survey of Automotive Group, North America Employees During Rande's Tenure
2000-2003 Economic and Automotive Industry Recession

PROFITABLY GREW SALES DURING ECONOMIC & AUTOMOTIVE INDUSTRY RECESSION 2002 AND 2003

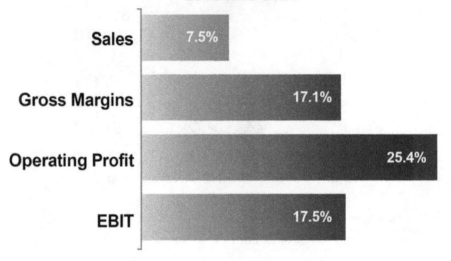

Automotive Group, North America During Rande's Tenure

RECEIVED 42 AWARDS WON OVER THREE YEARS

Customer

- Ford World Excellence Award
- GM Supplier of the Year
- Nissan Quality Master Award
- Toyota Excellence Award
- Honda Quality Performance Award
- Toyota Certificate of Achievement Awards for 15 Plants

Industry

- Fortune Magazine's Most Admired Companies
- J.D. Powers Highest Quality Seat Supplier
- Sales & Marketing Magazine Top 25 Sales Organizations
- Automotive Interiors Magazine's Industrial Design Excellence Award
- Shingo Prize for Excellence in Manufacturing
- Design Society of America's Design & Technology Award

Community

- Michigan Minority Business Development Association Corporation of the Year

---

Awards Presented to Automotive Group, North America During Rande's Tenure 2000-2003 Economic and Automotive Industry Recession

SHAREHOLDER RETURN

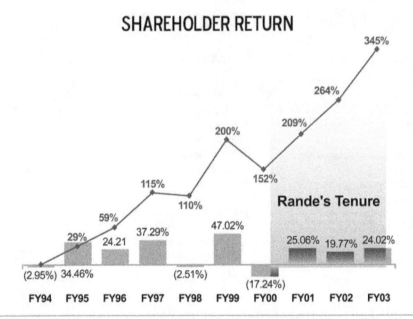

* Rande's Tenure as North America and Worldwide Automotive Group Leader. During the 2000 through 2003 Automotive Industry and Economic Downturn, the Automotive Group Represented Approximately 75% of the Corporation's Overall Sales and Earnings.

STOCK PERFORMANCE

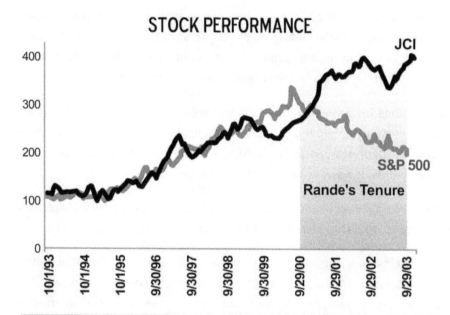

* Rande's Tenure as North America and Worldwide Automotive Group Leader. During the 2000 through 2003 Automotive Industry and Economic Downturn, the Automotive Group Represented Approximately 75% of the Corporation's Overall Sales and Earnings.

When you really have the opportunity to get to know people, it dissolves any objectification that was in place before that made it easier to pass judgment on them or to dismiss their value. We developed friendships, tolerance, understanding, empathy and patience. These are the valuable intangibles that rocketed JCI to the top of the charts on Wall Street when the rest of the planet was struggling with difficult economic times. We became a community with a common goal. This is how mutual respect is earned and a culture of inclusion is constructed. It was powerful and successful.

Corporate Moses and the Script

By 2003, morale was high at JCI. Our people trusted their leadership and it directly translated into outstanding financial performance. In every measure of business performance, our numbers were aligned and on the upswing. We were consistently hitting big numbers each quarter while most competitors and other corporate entities inside and outside our industry were falling off in the economic downturn of 2000 to 2003.

Our methods for achieving great success were very unconventional at the time. Elevating employee morale and engagement were viewed as intangible, theoretical paths to success. And they required time and effort. In other words, it wasn't easy or instantly measurable.

"Getting it right takes time. Right has no short cuts, yet today's leaders are measured using a stop watch, not a calendar." – Rande Somma

But in reality, our methods were no more or less than the script most businesses claim to follow. It is the script on the company website; the script in the employee manuals and in all the collateral marketing publications. That script contains the words we are supposed to be following. That is what we are promising to the stakeholders and the public. Corporate America's Moses came down from the mountain with that script. The only problem is that leaders talk about it, but have not followed it, and based on today's standards, they are not expected to. When did lip service become good enough for us?

The Newbie

I was working as the Purchasing Manager at an axle plant in Ohio back in the '70s, when I had my first career change opportunity. I became the production control manager, at the age of 27 or 28. I also became the boss of three guys who had been with the company longer than I had been alive. Scary.

My office was in the plant, and I will never forget walking into that office my first day and seeing this written on the chalkboard:

"I must hurry to catch up with the others for I am their leader."

So I got together with these old coots and I asked them what they meant by that. They told me, "Look, the biggest mistake you can make right now is to come in here and act like you know what you are doing. We know you don't know what you are doing. We will help you get there. The only way you can screw this up is if you act like you think you already know everything."

These men who reported to me taught me the value of humility. Don't try too hard. Don't come in here and act like you have to show everyone that you know what you are doing. They were offering to take me under their wing and help me learn. They told me that they would get me there, and bless their hearts, they did. They got me there.

The plant manager at the time, the boss to who we all reported, was an intense guy who expected to receive and deliver high quality products and achievement from the plant every single day. Like my father, he never felt it necessary to separate himself from everyone else or to remind everyone he was everyone's superior. He never acted that way. He never needed to pull rank on anyone. He led by example, working hard and elevating expectations for himself as well as for everyone in his charge. He was greatly admired and respected by all for his devotion and ethics. We worked hard for him because we wanted to.

Then they made me the Plant Manufacturing Manager, overseeing almost 1,000 people in the plant. That was my first opportunity at managing the manufacturing operation.

The Great Good...Even When it is Bad

Not long after my promotion, the plant closed even though it was doing very well. The closure wasn't a result of the plant's production or performance. The company's leadership decided it just wasn't economically feasible to continue having certain plants making components, and other plants assembling them. So they were going to vertically integrate component manufacturing and assembly under the same roof. That shook things up.

A large meeting was organized in the cafeteria to convey this terrible news. All managers, including me, were to attend. I had to be in the room when those 1,000 people were going to be told that they no longer had a job. Some of my best lessons are the ones that make me sick. This was one of those lessons.

I remember sitting at the table looking out at the audience contemplating what was about to happen and thinking about the impact on them and their lives and families when they lost their jobs. I had a view down the hallway to the plant manager's office. I saw him – this big tough guy who demanded so much of his staff – walking toward the cafeteria with some papers to make the announcement. He stopped a couple of times on that long walk. He was clearly trying to gather himself to do what he needed to do the best way he could. He was sensitive to what was about to happen to these people who spent so much time with him, many of whom he got to know very well out on the shop floor. It was never just about him. It was about everyone pulling together and doing good work.

The struggle he experienced before delivering the bad news was testament to who this great gentleman was; someone who felt so deeply committed and frankly, hardwired to care about the plant and all of us so much. It was from him that I learned that leaders who treat people well and genuinely connect with them, create an atmosphere of mutual respect and trust that does not diminish their stature or status as a leader. In fact, that stature gets better. Still today, I do my best to stay in touch with Gerry Nadig, that plant manager.

The Big Three: Larry, Curly and Mo

During my tenure at JCI, I was the only supplier executive that was a member of the supplier advisory councils of GM, Ford and Chrysler concurrently. These advisory councils were formed so suppliers could meet with the car companies and tell them, "Here is what you could do differently where you would win and we would win." Theoretically, these meetings were supposed to improve circumstances for everyone in the process. JCI and all the suppliers brought a lot to share and contributed many ideas.

I sat in on all of the meetings with each of the three automakers. These were three completely different companies, in three different cities, different board rooms and with different participants, but boy, did they have a lot in common. In every meeting, suggestions were made on how to improve processes and relationships with suppliers. None of them were implemented. Not one. Win-win was not of interest to these automakers. It was "we-win-and-gotta-go." They didn't have to be concerned with the suppliers' circumstances. The minute automakers had to put skin in the game, it was time to go. They already got their annual price reduction. That was the only win they were interested in. So why all these meetings? To check a box.

Post- Stallkamp Chrysler

In late 2002, I was President of the Automotive Systems Group Operations-Worldwide for JCI and scrambling to figure out how to replicate and export North America's successful operational business model to Europe, South America and other global JCI centers. And there was a lot going on in America at the same time.

Tom Stallkamp had been gone from Chrysler for a couple of years by this time, and everything that Tom was about left with him. The new VP of Purchasing at Chrysler was not like Tom, and Chrysler quickly reverted back to taking their 5 percent price reduction up front like Ford and GM without investing in the innovation that was going to help suppliers offset that reduction.

Despite this, JCI turned in remarkable earnings reports during this time while many other U.S. companies were feeling the sting of the economic downturn.

I was busy trying to negotiate a $224 million price reduction that Chrysler demanded over three years – which was a hard discussion to have with their new VP of Purchasing, because it was simply a stunning and brazen grab for money. Our relationship with the U.S. automakers was always, always, always all about leverage. There were constant ridiculous requests from GM, Ford and Chrysler that we had to navigate, but antics of this magnitude had never before been attempted.

As I am having this conversation with the new VP of Purchasing, I noticed on his desk, on top of the pile of papers next to him, a piece of paper with a bunch of yellow highlights. It was JCI's recent press release and it was next to our quarterly earnings release. And our numbers were awesome. And he knew, as did everyone, that JCI Automotive North America was far and away responsible for the company's overall outstanding earnings report.

In reference to the $224 million price cut they were demanding from JCI up front (which is, effectively, the same thing as asking JCI to just pay them that amount), the Chrysler VP said, "You guys are making money, so you can afford this." It was a general statement, but it reflected the adversarial culture between American automakers and suppliers at the time. If suppliers made money, automakers immediately came after you claiming that it was evidence you were charging them too much for parts. It was outrageous.

And here is the contrast.

After conveying to my chairman at JCI the conversation with Chrysler's VP of Purchasing, my chairman told me that at almost the very same time that I was negotiating the $224 million with Chrysler, the CEO of Toyota, also a JCI customer, had stopped him at a speaking event they were both attending to congratulate him on the press release and the earnings report.

So we were criticized and hounded for money by Chrysler for having a great earnings report, while Toyota congratulated us for the very same thing. This was an iconic representation of the exact opposite approaches to the business that made one automaker a failure and one a success.

In order to justify this ridiculous claim that we have to pay them more money, Chrysler brought in a consulting company. Chrysler needed to figure out ways to get more money. They came up with this abstract wild-ass cockamamie reasoning for a 20 percent price reduction from suppliers. We could barely make a nickel with them because they were so screwed up. It was absurd. This 20 percent was on top of the 5 percent a year, and the extra 5 percent they took a few years before when we had that nice dinner with Dieter. Now they wanted 20 percent *more*. And their rationale was that they thought that JCI was overcharging them. So in essence, they wanted their money back, and they thought that added up to $224 million from JCI.

We were selling seats to Toyota as well as to Chrysler. It was apples and oranges. It was different seats, different fabrics, different mechanics, different everything. The only thing that Toyota had in common with Chrysler was that they built cars. And Chrysler wasn't even building good cars, so they didn't even have that in common at the time.

Chrysler somehow tried to connect those dots and the VP of Purchasing told me, "Yeah, but you charge Toyota less than you charge me."

My response was, "Yes, I do because they don't have the shit in their system that costs money to clean up while we are delivering the product." The total monstrous non-value-added cost that our relationship with Chrysler generated didn't exist with Toyota, and despite the fact that JCI charged Chrysler more than Toyota for seat systems; we still made way more money with Toyota. *Way* more. What JCI made off of Toyota was legitimate profit because that system and that relationship were healthy. At the time, we actually were using some of that Toyota profit to underwrite our relationship with Chrysler. So what this guy was actually asking me to do was to make JCI a pass-through conduit for Toyota's success in the market. He wanted Toyota to underwrite Chrysler even more.

Because Chrysler didn't look for or deal with the root cause of their troubles, the symptoms worsened and they had to keep coming up with more and more creative ways to rationally explain why they kept falling short. And they crossed over the line and kept scraping at the suppliers. Why? Because they could. First the 5 percent, then an additional 5 percent, and then this truly insane 20 percent. Really, it became embarrassing to have these conversations with them because it was so obvious that they were desperate *and* they had no plan to save themselves.

During this time of intense negotiations with Chrysler, an entirely separate set of circumstances were unfolding internally at JCI that would eventually lead to my being fired. As a result of those events and the personal impact they have had on me, I cannot recall exactly how we ultimately navigated this particular conundrum with Chrysler.

It wasn't long after these events with Chrysler that I was let go from Johnson Controls. Some have speculated that I was let go because I pissed off Chrysler.

Let me assure you, that was not the reason.

Steve, the Marketing Bunny

Steve was a guy at Chrysler in charge of warranties and the rating of their cars in the market. He was a technical marketing guy, but his main job was to get Chrysler cars to achieve high scores in Consumer's Report, JD Powers, etc. His bonus was based on those scores. But he had no power to influence the quality of the building of the car. He only managed the brand.

Some of you can probably already smell where this is going.

As Chrysler was heading down that slippery slope and losing market share, the next set of bunnies that they aimed to kill was us, the suppliers. At one point JCI was doing about $2 billion a year with Chrysler. So they pretty much had us by the short hairs. They had all their suppliers by the short hairs.

I ran into Steve when I was in and out of those meetings at Chrysler with their VP of purchasing because of that hocus-pocus jumbo baloney that supposedly justified why I had to give them $224 million price decrease over three years. The purchasing department is only getting measured on how cheap they can buy the parts needed to put their cars together, so it was a full-on bunny hunt.

I'm trying to figure out a way to stay in business so we can meet Chrysler's crazy demands. Something's gotta give. If you're going to take $224 million from me, I've gotta take $224 million out of my cost structure. I can't eat it. I've got shareholders. So what am I going to do? They must realize that if they want to pay so much less for a part, the part won't be the same quality.

When I saw Steve, Chrysler's marketing guy that day I told him, "Steve, you're in big trouble, man. You've got about three years to get the hell out of here."

He asked me, "Why?"

I said, "There's a blue light special going on down in your purchasing department. Your VP of purchasing is ripping and tearing at prices, and he is going to make a bunch of headway to get costs down. That guy is going to receive a banquet, a parade and a big bonus for achieving those goals . . . and for those very same reasons, three years from now, you're going to lose your job because all that money he is stripping out of the price of parts is coming out of the quality of the product. So when you get your JD Power scores, they are going to suck. Hell, you might even have to spend ten times what he is saving in parts today to pay for recalls in a few years."

He looked at me and he understood *exactly* what I was telling him.

It takes about three years to get a car from concept to the dealership, so the poor quality that was being agreed on then was going to show up in the car scores three years from then, and although Steve had nothing to do with the decisions that lowered the quality of products being put in those cars, he was going to be the bunny to die because of them. JD Powers would crucify the crappy quality coming down the line (and of course there were lists of recalls) and there was not a damn thing any marketing person could say or do to rectify that. There was no way Steve was going to make chicken salad out of that chicken shit.

These two guys worked for the *same company.* They were supposed to be on the *same team.* Purchasing pulled the pin on that grenade. The purchasing guy will receive a big bonus, and the sales and marketing guy will suffer the impact about three years down the line and probably pay for it with his job.

I don't know what became of Steve since my departure from JCI, but not long after, Chrysler went to Washington asking for bailout money. JD Power scores and the quality of their product wasn't their biggest problem.

The fat lady wasn't singing yet, but she was sure warming up.

How the Mighty Do Fall

It is far, far more difficult to manage success than to manage adversity. Adversity is easy to manage. With adversity, you have to fix stuff or you die; you are pressed into action and what needs to be done is crystal clear. Your tasks are clearly laid out before you and you execute them with laser focus. Attention to detail isn't a good idea, it's mandatory.

But success can lull a leader into complacency, so they become sloppy and forget that there is a tradeoff. Success involves less pressure, demands less clarity. It leaves you alone with your triumphs and you begin to feel invincible. Your sense of humility becomes vulnerable and the process of getting full of yourself is primed to be set in motion, and what it takes to overcome adversity fades from the memory, to be replaced by what it takes to keep and get more power and money.

Remember when the three auto executives from GM, Chrysler and Ford flew to Washington in luxury jets with a tin cup to ask for a handout to save their companies? The optics of that never occurred to them, let alone how much money they burned traveling that way rather than hold themselves to the *obligation* to seek out more economical transportation and travel *like the rest of Americans.* It never occurred to them to curb their excesses to help cut costs. That was leadershit entitlement on display for the world to see.

North American Operations and the Path of Least Resistance

I was sharing responsibilities for North American Operations of JCI Automotive with another executive in late 1990s before the position was given to me exclusively. It was an $8 billion business at that time, and we had just come off of a very good year at JCI – 1998.

1999 turned out to be a little peek at the very beginning of the national recession that we didn't yet know was coming. We were doing well up until the sixth month, but as we looked ahead, external conditions were changing that were really putting our forecast in jeopardy.

We were looking at the risks and opportunities we had used to establish our projected numbers for the year, and now questioning them. What was our production build really going to be? Can we collect this money? Can we win this negotiation? Can we hold our margins with this proposal? The forecast said one thing, but we had to maximize the opportunities that were not in the forecast. In other words, and for example, the full opportunity on a particular negotiation might be $10 million, but we might conservatively only put $5 million of it in our forecast and list the other $5 million as an opportunity.

Conversely, if you decide to put all $10 million of that in the forecast, then you would list some of that in the risk category. The first thing corporations try to do is remain conservative; minimize the opportunities and optimize how much of the risk is going to happen. That is the basic dynamic of the balancing act with trying to give forecasts to Wall Street.

At this mid-year point in 1999 we began to get concerned about the numbers themselves, and also the likelihood of certain claimed opportunities happening in light of the changing economic environment. There were opportunities that could get us to our projected numbers that we had already given to Wall Street, but we didn't know if we still wanted to bet on those.

Companies don't ever want to go back to Wall Street and restate projections because it means that the next time they state projections, Wall Street may not believe what they are told. Should they believe your projections? Their reputations are on the line too because they turn around and go to their clients and say 'buy that stock' based on projections. You want them to keep saying that about your stock! If they can't trust the forecast, they won't recommend the stock to investors. Restating projections can fracture that trust with Wall Street, and trust is everything with those people – and well it should be. They have to run with the numbers that they are told.

So whether we decided to restate our projections, or to simply make sure we hit those original numbers, was a big deal.

In that mid-year meeting, it came down to my associate who shared North American Operations with me. He was questioning why we should take any of those risks. He said, "If we say yes to making these opportunities happen, and yes to minimizing the impact of these risks in our projections, we are just signing up for a whole lot of work and a whole lot of risk. Why don't we just lay off 10% of the workforce? It is easier and it will keep us safe. We will make our numbers." He was correct. With his strategy, if we lay off 10% of our people, anything we landed in terms of opportunity would be gravy, and anything negative we get from risk, we have already accounted for in the layoffs.

It was the safe and easy answer.

I understand. If I take my calculator and crunch those numbers, yeah, you get 10% and yeah, that's X amount of costs, and if you adjust that, then profit will match the original projections that we told Wall Street we would get. Problem solved.

And I said, "I'm not doing that."

Some of it has to do with knowing that letting people go keeps me awake at night – but on top of that, it just didn't make good business sense to me. He got frustrated because I wouldn't agree to do it his way. He was a good guy, but he was trained and tuned to run the path of least resistance. Lay off 10% of the people. Done. Let's do lunch.

I refused. "Look, here's our mission statement. I'm not trying to be an ass. I'm not making it up. It's just right there in black and white. We want to be world class in automotive interiors and care about people. Let's make an attempt to be that."

I explained to him that it wasn't impossible to end up in a position where we would have to lay off some people. I can't say that I will never do that. But I didn't want layoffs to be the first on the list. Let's try some other strategies first. There were a bunch of other things that we could try to deal with this predicament, but it had become normal for leaders to look to layoffs as the quickest, easiest and safest way to hedge a bet against any looming risk. It works and nobody blinks an eye. The system waves that decision through every time with no questions or consequences.

Now he's pissed because we can't go to lunch because the problem is not solved. Plus he probably had low blood sugar. He was cranky.

Here is how that breaks down and why it mattered – at least to me: We had 3,600 people on two campuses combined. My colleague wanted to take 360 of those people out of the rotation on the floor. Our operations are designed and finely tuned around an operating model that requires 3,600 people to run it. If we take 360 people out of that equation, we can get the numbers to work short term, but we will be running on a sub-optimized operation model that will begin to erode our performance and then our customer satisfaction. Then we will be talking again three months from now, and we might need to lay off another 10% to make the numbers work again. Obviously, at some point this strategy hits the wall. You can't just keep laying people off to reach numbers. You are not getting to the root of the issue. You are playing whack-a-mole®.

I told him that we have to re-engineer our operations so we can hit our numbers and at the same time stay true to our values and mission statement. We have a commitment to our customers and to our employees to try our best for them. This wasn't anybody's fault. JCI Automotive operations were designed to be inefficient. Our workforce grew in direct proportion with the increased volumes. So we had to reconfigure our systems and engineer out the inefficiencies.

The main point in this story is that certain things need to happen in business in order to be successful. But this is about a mindset. It comes down to doing it one way, or doing it another way. Both of them can get an organization to the same place. One is easier than the other, but leaders have a choice.

We didn't lay off anyone that year. Because we blocked that path of least resistance, we put an all-out effort on optimizing all of the legitimate opportunities that we had in front of us. With that "have-to" factor motivating us, we were able to meet our full year financial commitments.

My colleague went on to run another company in 2000, and I started running JCI North American on my own.

As we went forward to 2001 and 2002, I saw real evidence of a downturn, later to be the full blown recession. Up until this point, we had depended quite a bit on production volumes to drive our earnings, and those were subject to external circumstances that were mostly out of our control. If we were to become less dependent on volumes, we had to look internally for a transformational change in how we ran our business. Rather than just slashing our workforce every time we needed to make the numbers work, we tried harder to insulate ourselves from layoffs always being the solution to profitability.

In the end, we did become more efficient, and that efficiency meant that we needed fewer people to accomplish our work. Depending on how bad things get, nobody can offset everything when the going gets tough. We did have to eventually let some people go. The layoffs were not about using employees as place markers on a spreadsheet. They did not happen just to make our numbers work. They were let go because we optimized logistics and systems to run leaner with fewer workers. That was so hard. We tried to do as much as we could to retrain them and move them into different operations, but not everyone could stay.

The good part of that story is that it took almost two years more before we had to do any layoffs, and the number we let go was under 100. Much better than 360. Many of those people also got an opportunity to return because, as a result of operating leaner, we got more business and grew more, so we once again needed more people.

When I look back on that time, I know that my colleague and I could have lain off more people, done it faster, hit our projections and nobody would have been the wiser . . . or cared how we did it. The board doesn't know what we are doing in day-to-day operations – nor do they care. Wall Street doesn't know because they are a bunch of good folks who never ran a business, but who are really good with algorithms. So as long as the results are what everybody wants, nobody can attack your methods.

Hindsight is 20/20. In 1999, the number of employees that we carried was directly proportionate to the high volume of business we had been enjoying up until that time. Had we simply laid off 10% of our workforce in mid-1999, we would have been crushed in 2000 when the full blown recession hit. Without making the necessary adjustments to the business model to make it more efficient, JCI would not have weathered the recession as well as we did.

When It Became About You (Path of Least Resistance)

I am a simple guy. I need things to be obvious. I always knew what to do because I just looked at my job description, and I'm quite sure it never said that I could blow something off if it gets too hard. It never said that.

The nuances of quiet personal agendas always tripped me up. I came to find out that those in the know would be alarmed if the job description didn't say what it was supposed to, but often they didn't necessarily expect you to do what it says. You know what happens when you dummy-down leadership expectations? You get dummies.

The one thing that motivated me all the time was that I was a weak person when it came to layoffs. I didn't have the stomach for it. I had been there, seen it and hated how it made me feel. I also know what it feels like to be suddenly out of work. I have sensitivity to what kind of tailspin that puts a person and a family into. The people laid off aren't the cause of whatever problem necessitates the layoff, so there is a certain injustice to it that I find very difficult to tolerate. At all costs, I felt the need to avoid layoffs as an option for fixing what was wrong with business. It was this disposition that really motivated me to be proactive and look ahead for solutions that wouldn't cost people their livelihoods.

Too often I would hear all those infuriating phrases that got invented to relieve leaders of the burden of responsibility of letting people go. You know them too: *"It's only business"* and *"You've gotta do what you've gotta do."* Ok, that's done. Let's do lunch.

What a bunch of junk!

When I hear that, I hear somebody distancing themselves from the pain of a bad decision they made so they can sleep at night because they picked the most toxic and sometimes selfish ways of getting from A to Z.

The fundamental reason why I am angry about leadershit – and why you might be angry too – is that it feels like betrayal. Candidates are interviewed and their credentials and experiences are assessed. Board members who are hiring CEOs and other leaders listen to candidates' philosophies to get an understanding of who they are and how they might fit the position. Due diligence is done and leaders who seem qualified are selected for the job. The job, tasks and corporate goals are agreed to be executed under the contractual obligations set forth in the job description. This is the agenda that is agreed to. Leaders are hired to serve *people.* They are hired to improve circumstances for everyone.

But there sometimes seems to be another agenda that is inserted – a quiet and frequently personal agenda – that was not shared with us prior to signing their contract. And this agenda trumps the agreed-upon one.

 When knockoff leaders turn to the easiest route; go off script and default to another agenda, the sting of betrayal affects all Americans – all of us.

Smoke and Mirrors

Paths of least resistance were always options, but they used to be unacceptable options at the bottom of the list of other options. Under today's broken leadership model they are solutions that have shifted from unacceptable to acceptable to typical, and possibly even preferred in some instances. Easy routes are almost always now accepted as the usual course of business, standard operating procedure. People are objectified as disposable line items, so layoffs work because the "math" works and because the collateral damage simply falls into the column on a spreadsheet making it palatable. The real things that are happening to real people are not considered...or felt...by those slashing the ranks.

This goes deeper into the operational course of business. Investments that have been allocated for building the "future" are hijacked and redirected to underwrite and optimize the anemic "present" to show short term gains and guarantee bonuses and compensation bumps for current leadership.

Shoring up the financial façade of the company increasingly depends on skill sets required for financial and accounting creativity. The cost efficiency model (do more with less) erodes to a cost reduction model (do less with less). Relationships with partners and suppliers are abused in this environment, and any honor of the core values only happens now if it is convenient.

This is when the "talk" is still the "talk", but the "walk" is anything but what is portrayed publicly. The motivation center of gravity shifts dramatically under this leadershit model to intimidation and threats. The belief that the "ends justifies the means" is fully installed as the business model.

What is really incredible is that the businesses running like this become fantastically proficient at projecting the appearance that their results are a function of a well-run business. It appears that the vitality of the enterprise is robust. They report grand decision-making events, "solid" short term gains, and a good investment strategy. They may claim that selling off components/sectors of the business is part of their transformational change consistent with implementing the strategic plan, but many times they simply need money to buy time. However, when it is announced it all sounds very strategic.

Big Three-Alarm Fire

I don't' know Mary Barra, CEO of General Motors Corporation, but I am going to assume that she means well and she is going to try to do the right thing where GM is concerned. She was elected to CEO position on January 15, 2014, and less than three weeks later received news that GM would need to issue a massive recall of a failing ignition switch that was leading to driver injuries and deaths.

By the end of March, she found herself in Washington, D.C. sitting in front of a Congressional investigation committee attempting to answer harsh questions regarding the faulty switch and how much the GM leadership or anyone in the organization knew about it. Some might say when she took the reins at GM she was handed a hot potato. I would say she was handed a live grenade.

Barra is dealing now with the consequences of business decisions made eight or more years back by her leadershit predecessors. They knew things could get bad and they let those problems grow rather than make the effort to deal with them. I just wonder if she has identified, has the capacity and resources, and is taking action against other growing problems that began two, three, four, five and six years back, if there are any.

To really correct the course of GM, there will need to be some enormous changes made in the GM culture. It will be like trying to steer a freighter with an outboard motor. An entity of that size is not going to be influenced by a small amount of effort, or be able to turn on a dime.

What is her legacy going to be? We probably won't know for several years, and we may never really know. Remember, nobody gets credit for what *didn't* happen. Solving small problems is a non-event in our reactionary culture. She will always be known as the first woman to run one of the Detroit Three, but she may also go silently into history for making tough decisions and preventing great disasters that never made the headlines. Let's hope so. I wish her all the best.

Good to Great – It's Not About You

One of the best books ever written that talks about leadership is the famous *Good to Great: Why Some Companies Make the Leap...and Others Don't,* by James C. Collins, published in 2001. The author looked for common denominators among some of the great companies at that time, and only 11 companies that made the cut to great. One of the key differentiators was the kind of person who was running each of these 11 companies, what Collins referred to as a Level Five Executive. This leader, who I call an authentic leader, *"builds enduring greatness through a paradoxical blend of personal humility and professional will."*

It is frustrating to me that this information is out there . . . has been out there for years, and yet most companies do not seem to look for this type of leader, and most executives do not seem to aspire to become this type of leader.

"Level Five Leaders channel their ego needs away from themselves and into the larger goal of building a great company. It's not that Level Five Leaders have no ego or self-interest, indeed, they are incredibly ambitious, but their ambition is first and foremost for the institution, not themselves." - Jim Collins

It comes back to the means and the ends. If you were to force-rank these two terms, it is the correct means that generates the best results when you do it right, and it is not instant. Authentic leaders know that it takes time.

When you compare this clear distinction of a Level Five Leader with how CEOs are being chosen, there couldn't be a wider gap in knowledge and understanding of leadership. Boards are choosing larger-than-life "celebrity" CEOs, believing that somehow their fame will translate into some kind of success or profit for their company. The very fact that they have some sort of celebrity attached to them has to make one question the level of humility.

If you had to choose a CEO and you just read the *Good to Great* book and believe in its formula for great leadership, you would spend 90% of your time vetting and assuring yourself that you are getting someone who has a deep sense of humility. If you get that right, you don't risk getting stung by the one common CEO symptom that haunts so many corporations today: *when it becomes about just me,* because it can't.

At Least I'm Consistent

After I left JCI, I had an opportunity to reply to an article in HR Magazine written by contributing editor, Robert Grossman. While I don't believe my response was ever published, I share this to demonstrate that what I contend today in this book is consistent with how I have always felt as a leader. Over a decade later, here I am with the same damn message:

"TO: THE EDITOR OF HR MAGAZINE
March 1, 2005

Your January cover story, "Blind Investment", addresses a legitimate question as to why the strength of a company's management, including how effectively its people (Human Capital) are being motivated and utilized, is some way implied when quarterly projections are met.

It is a valid point; since meeting the immediate bottom line expectations by itself provides no evidence as to whether the people are being managed as a valued asset or overhead expense.

It is, in fact, an extremely important distinction. It's a question of whether a successful quarter was achieved in a large way as a result of the return on investment from a capable and inspired organization or reduction in investment in the people and, even, the elimination of their jobs.

It stands to reason that one would be much more comfortable about the quality of management as well as near- and long-term outlooks if it is apparent that the company's performance was a function of how well the business, and not the results, is being managed.

I can see why Grossman makes a valiant attempt to highlight the value of human capital by creating equations and formulas. However, the level of productivity of a workforce pivots off their morale, perception of their leadership and how they feel about the operating environment, all of which amounts to the company's culture, its "soul", and simply doesn't translate into "accountant-ese."

It's really as complicated as common sense:

A company's most important asset is its people.

The greatest impact on productivity is high morale.

Therefore, focusing on morale by routinely measuring it and driving continuous improvement belongs on any executive leadership's agenda, and must be considered a top priority.

It certainly was important to me while I had the privilege of leading Johnson Controls' multi-billion dollar automotive interiors business and had as much to do with our excellent financial performance as anything that we did.

It is essential that companies respect the market analyst's role and work aggressively to meet their (and the shareholders) expectations. Even though many believe that the present evaluation metrics of a company's performance is far too narrow, they are what they are.

However, regardless of how the market is keeping score, or how bonuses are calculated, it has never influenced my resolve to the following basic beliefs:

1. *Companies that say people are valued and prove it through behaviors and actions...**WIN.***

*Those that say it and don't "walk the talk"...**LOSE.***

2. *Companies that focus on achieving high morale...**WIN.** Those that don't...**LOSE.***

3. *Companies whose leadership believes that trust and respect must be earned and mutual at all levels...**WIN.** Those that don't...**LOSE.***

4. *Companies that motivate the workforce through inspiration and encouragement...**WIN.***

*Those that do so through intimidation...**LOSE.***

5. *Companies who believe that humanization of leadership, sincerely caring about the success and security of their team and believe that trust and respect for leaders is earned, and not an entitlement, is all mutually exclusive from holding people accountable and passionate about world-class execution...**JUST DON'T GET IT.***

If you really want to realize how far off course we've gotten, think of how many times we hear "it's only business." It can NEVER be only business when PEOPLE are the most important asset and whose development and success is an obligation of the company and its leaders.

If it is really only business, then it can't be a very good one.

Rande S. Somma"

CHAPTER 8
FORK IN THE ROAD
ARE WE CIRCLING THE WAGONS OR CIRCLING THE DRAIN?

Work Smarter

Picture in your mind a boat made of the highest quality wood. In its day, the boat's design was state of the art. The oars are the most efficient in the industry. The oarsmen were the best anywhere.

Time went on, and the boat needed to go faster and faster, and carry more and more. In order to accommodate the increased payload, the boat grew longer and longer. It also grew wider and heavier. It became necessary to add more oarsmen, and then more oars. But there came a time when no matter how hard the oarsmen pulled, the boat just couldn't go fast enough. Through growth and over time, the boat had discovered the limitations of its design.

To reach new levels of speed and maneuverability, the boat would have to be reinvented.

Business operating models, the way we organize and run our businesses, are just like that boat. They are specifically designed for certain conditions, payload and speed, and any alterations in those factors need to be considered in the remake of the design in order to maintain efficiency. Just like the boat's design, business operating models need to be remodeled, and ultimately reinvented to avoid becoming obsolete.

I want to talk to you about change – what's going on in the world of business, recent performances and trends, and what changes need to be made with regard to leadership and a new direction. First let's look where we have come from and where we are.

Fed Up

There is an undercurrent of impotent acceptance of lackluster performance by leaders in America. In my opinion, this crosses over into politics and every other aspect of leadership, as well. People say "You know how it is," or "That's just how it is," taking for granted that deception by leadership is a normal experience. Yeah, I know how it is. Let's fix it.

While every viable definition of leadership is being dumbed down and rewritten, we have forgotten that it is our responsibility to choose the right leaders. This is our problem to fix. We have become desensitized to it and negligent in our responsibility to hold leaders to their duties and obligations.

Our job is to find and promote good leaders for ourselves, our society, communities and nation. And our job is to fire the ones who fall short. They work for us. When actual people are the collateral damage as a result of leadership that is indifferent to their circumstances, something is very wrong. People should not be "in the way" of good outcomes. They should be the reason for them.

As we have seen in previous chapters, in the current system that we as a nation have allowed to take root, leaders in general are permitted – and sometimes encouraged – to choose self-interest over duty, responsibilities and obligations, and we reward them handsomely with big monetary payoffs for doing it the wrong way.

America was built on righteous indignation and not putting up with corrupt and greedy leaders. The path of least resistance that we are allowing our leaders to take is a departure from our founding principles. And while there is no need for violent uprising, we certainly need to come together to assess and reform what is not working for the majority of us. We are fast approaching a time where we will be spurred into action. We can be proactive (cause our circumstances) or reactive (react to our circumstances). One is tougher and the other -- while easier -- is a lot uglier.

For the majority of people, things look bad enough. However, because they don't know what they don't know – which is that it is a lot worse than it even appears – perhaps they have not reached the point where they are ready to take action like those of us who know.

If this whole thing is allowed to gather any more momentum without disruption, there could be ugly consequences when this bubble eventually explodes.

Bubble, Bubble, Toil and Trouble

I don't know for an absolute fact, but I am guessing from my seat at many of the conference room tables in the 90's and early 2000s, that the U.S. car market got ripe for the picking when the world market opened up and Detroit Three's foreign competition began capturing more market share. Prior to this, U.S. automakers were getting profitable prices for cars and trucks that started breaking down and rusting out in about two to three years. That was the established standard, and therefore, it was where customer expectations settled. Quality was low, but they were doing okay because the U.S. automotive market was split up three ways and everyone was making a profit.

U. S. automakers had gone into cruise control and were in the habit of making cars that were only good enough to get them off the showroom floor. Remember, as a company or an industry, if you are not going forward, you are going backwards.

Then came the Japanese. And they came to this market prepared to compete. They swooped in and offered the U.S. market cars and trucks with far better quality and durability. I know. I made those parts for all the domestic and foreign companies. The Japanese did all this at a lower price too because they were efficiency and quality driven, *not price and profit driven*! Their standards were much higher.

In the land where we claim that competition keeps our nation's economy healthy, the established American car companies began to whine and call foul when faced with <u>actual</u> competition. Bumper stickers fiercely attacking people who bought foreign cars appeared, and the finger was pointed at the consumer for choosing a better product. It was also pointed at the American autoworkers assembling cars on the line, like they weren't doing it right. Hell, they were just working with the crappy parts and crappy processes they were given.

All along it was the leaders of the American auto industry refusing to make the necessary changes needed to compete on a global scale. I believe the opening of the global market for automakers was the wake-up call that was sorely needed in an American industry that had been resting on its laurels. I thought finally, now they will have to step up to the plate and really compete and create a better product. I was wrong . . . so wrong.

Then came the European automakers to our shores, the Koreans, and still yet to come, the Chinese. And now the door had been kicked wide open. It was like America was rolling out a red carpet to them because the Detroit Three, in response to the flood of new competition, instead of reinventing their business model to adjust to the new industry circumstances, turned their focus instead to mounting a negative campaign against consumers who chose foreign cars. They also focused on cutting costs on operations and siphoning budget money away from strategic planning and away from development of a new more competitive operations model for the future. Sound familiar?

I'm sure that all Americans, including myself, wanted to buy American at that time, but the value wasn't there. The incremental premium to pay more and get less just didn't make sense. A car is usually the second biggest expenditure that most people make next to a home. This wasn't about patriotism. It was about the reality that an American car cost more, yet was an inferior product.

At the same time, unions were shaking down the auto industry, disregarding the fact that they were choking off their own future at the same time. The leaders of the Detroit Three just kept "kicking the can," cutting costs, caving to the union demands and delivering numbers that were acceptable to Wall Street. Detroit Three leaders kept taking their bonuses and passing the snowballing problems down the line to the next leader, even when they knew – and believe me *they knew* – that this was all going to hell in a hand basket.

The leadership at Ford, GM and Chrysler knew in the mid to late '90s that their business models were in trouble. But they didn't act on it because the problem was so big, and the explosion was not so imminent as to personally impact them during their tenure as leaders. In the end, they knew that they would be long gone with their bags of money and career reputation intact by the time the industry crumbled.

It all tumbled down when Ford, GM and Chrysler went to Washington in November of 2008 to ask Congress for a $50 billion bailout.

Cha-Cha-Cha-Changes

When I talk about the challenge of "change," I break it down into three stages: change, changing and changed.

Change: This is the idea that something needs to change. It is the intellectual understanding that to transform to something better or to prevent potentially bad consequences, a change is necessary. This is where someone would say, 'I've got to quit smoking. I smoke two packs a day. This is bad and it will kill me if I keep doing this.' Ford, Chrysler and GM all went through this stage. They realized that they needed to do something because they were going to die.

Changing: This is the process of affecting the change, breaking a habit and creating a new one. Anyone who smokes can appreciate how difficult changing really is. There are many internal bargains and ceremonial transitions made first. They might mark the "quit" date on a calendar, start meditating, limit themselves to only three cigarettes a day and buy a pack of Nicorette gum. There are setbacks too; cold feet, scratch-outs on the calendar, renewed vows, etc. Aborting, rationalizing and kicking the can are powerful temptations. Perseverance and discipline during this time is paramount.

Changed: This is fully instituting the new habit and realizing the benefits that you perceived you were going to get when you first had the change idea; benefits like no shortness of breath and money savings from not buying cigarettes. Transformational change is complete and I am making it stick. This is usually forced by predictable and foreseen circumstances. I have a spot on my lungs. I throw away my five packs of unsmoked cigs, buy six cases of that Nicorette gum, never smoke again and hope I don't die. This is extremely difficult. None of the American automakers made this leap.

When it comes to changing, GM, Ford and Chrysler knew – I guarantee they knew – that transformation of their business model and of their relationship with the UAW was going to be mandatory in order to realize long term success.

But changing long entrenched corporate habits requires time, patience, effort, and the ability to change the fan belt while the engine is running, so to speak. The automakers were unwilling to make such investments in change.

Let's say if I make a big change in my business, I am going to make $10 million more in profit. Okay, what do I need to do in order to get that done? I need to do A, B, and C. That is where the business analysis usually stops. Almost everybody that I have consulted with stops right there, because they now see how difficult that is, and there is *nothing* motivating them to do it, so long as the current system can keep operating without it. Since things could get worse before they get better during transformational changes, they all say, "Why am I going to spend that money today and take that risk when the return on investment is going to be realized when I'm not even here anymore? The scope of change is beyond the threshold of how analysts value the company and my performance today, so I'm not doing that."

The idea of change is easy. It is purely an intellectual exercise. Even knockoff leaders understand that. But really affecting change marks the quality of a real leader – identifying the objectives, and the end game, building an action plan, implementing it with real money, a lot of time, resources, focus and persistence. It rarely happens, and in the auto industry, nobody chose to even begin. Though there was some noise from U.S. automakers about starting down this road in the 90's, at some point the effort evaporated on all three fronts. One way that I heard it explained was that, when the wave of change moved its way down to a certain level of management, it stopped cold. Hence, I have heard it referred to as the "Frozen Middle." That term speaks a hell of a lot about the culture – or lack of it – and if true, I again put it on leadership. This kind of initiative cannot be delegated. It is the responsibility of vigilant leadership to drive the process of change in any organization from the top all the way down to the assembly floor. It is a huge burden, and another reason why kicking the can is a tempting option that is too often the path taken.

Preserve, Then Change

We seem to have lost something important. While it is important to recognize that leaders need to take on change and persevere through "change/changing/changed" phases, the irony is that maybe the most important progressive change that we can make in today's business environment is to reach back and re-establish the expected standards, principles and virtues that were foundational to leadership behavior some decades ago.

Just as critical – if not more – to secure those virtues is to identify and insulate them as things that cannot be compromised or changed in future change processes.

JCI purchased a successful company on the west side of Michigan that was a truly innovative company. We bought them because they made car interior products that JCI didn't make. But they also executed their business in a way that was foreign to JCI. Johnson Controls was top line oriented – growth and sales and then we figured out a way to make money doing it that way. This smaller company that we purchased was bottom line oriented. They didn't make a move unless it was already determined that it would make money. They also invented a lot of products and created the demand around their innovations. Their core was innovation. We were a "fill demand" driven business. Our customers told us what they wanted, and we put that order together with available parts.

On the surface, there were product synergies between JCI and this smaller innovative company. Underneath that, there was not a lot of overlap in thought process or execution. This created a unique challenge for bringing together all that each company had to offer and leveraging it in the industry.

I was assigned to lead the JCI integration team. Few people understand how important proper integration is – which is one of the reasons why there is such a high rate of failed mergers and acquisitions.

We paid $1.3 billion for that company. To make that money matter, we had to find a way to make 1 + 1 equal to something greater than two. If you just buy another company and simply connect it to your existing organization, the best you can hope for is you end up getting bigger. The worst you can hope for – and what will happen unless you do the integration and many other things right – you end up going backwards.

The two different business models and styles of JCI and its new acquisition had to come together in a symbiotic way without one model cannibalizing the other and destroying what makes them unique and what makes them money in the market.

A gentleman named Brian was my counterpart from the other company who assisted with the integration of our two companies. Looking at the challenge in front of us, I said to him, "Brian, we have to make a lot of changes during this integration. The synergy is where the value is, so we have to bring that forward, but there is something in here we cannot change." Once I spent some time visiting the new company, I saw that there were valuable things that made them exquisitely great and stood out as reasons we purchased this company in the first place. Those things had to remain in place and untouched in the integration process.

I went on to tell Brian, "There are special things about your company that we cannot alter during integration…and I don't really know exactly what they are, and that is why I need your help."

I did not want to modify or corrupt *who* they were that made them so special. The first step in our change management with the integration process in this case was about pinpointing and quarantining the great things about the smaller organization that needed to be preserved.

Connecting the Dots

During this critical time in the '90s, auto suppliers -- including JCI – were told by American automakers to bring engineering changes to parts that would reduce the cost of the part for them.

There is a window of acceptable cost reduction that does not affect product performance. But once cost reduction gets outside that window and companies start killing bunnies, without addressing the root cause of the problem, then there is a real issue.

Companies have to maintain margins, so product performance might drop dangerously close to the line of acceptable quality or reliability. To reduce the cost in cars in the early 2000s, American automakers continuously shopped for cheaper parts. So we had "Frankencars" rolling off the lines that were assembled with a menagerie of the cheapest parts able to be produced . . . and the automaker's websites still claimed that their automobiles were "world class." Please.

Leaders at GM, Ford and Chrysler had many opportunities to turn this around, but rather than face dynamic industry changes, their leaders did what they do best. They kept killing bunnies, cutting costs, using cheaper parts, delaying payments to suppliers, financially raping their supply base, laying off good people, bending to the union's demands, until the long history of this type of erosion led to eventual collapse. That meant that, beginning in 2008, $25 billion in taxpayer money (your money) was committed by President George Bush to industry bailout. President Barack Obama added another $55 billion of taxpayer money (your money again)[5]. In all, taxpayers were paid back all but around $9.26 billion of the roughly $80 billion we "loaned" them. And although nobody really asked Joe

---

[5] http://www.carscoops.com/2015/01/gm-chrysler-bail-out-cost-us-government.html

taxpayer if it was ok, I guess our political leaders have forgiven the rest of the debt that was owed, because it was declared that it was all paid back.

Are you beginning to understand how important it is to find and hire authentic leaders in American business? When leaders fail, we pay, while they continue to receive huge bonuses and are given a pass on a government loan.

I sat in those rooms during those meetings in that crisis time. They kept asking us to engineer cheaper parts to lower their costs. American automakers even *encouraged us to buy more components in Asia because they were cheaper*, even net with the additional freight costs. So much for them harping on their customers to buy American! *Even they weren't buying American anymore!* But they didn't tell consumers that.

It was incremental. It wasn't malicious, but they didn't even try to reinvent themselves. They were just gasping for air in this long, slow downward death spiral. Nobody disrupted the trajectory by making difficult but necessary change, and there was no way it wasn't going to end badly. This was the inevitability of how short term gain turns into long term pain.

Connecting More Dots

Leadership or receivership; when it comes to business, either you do it right, or you never come close to full potential...or you die. Knockoff leaders are completely enabled by the system because the timelines we are dealing with in corporate America death spirals can be very protracted. These leaders are long gone by the time the bomb goes off and nobody connects the dots back to them. And even if someone does connect the dots, those leaders are untouchable by then.

I believe that the corporate fraud of Enron, WorldCom and others that caused the Sarbanes-Oxley law (and other such regulations) actually sent the "deception industry" deeper underground to a new level of sophistication. Sarbanes-Oxley management letter was the response to CPA firms surrendering to the belief that no matter how thorough their audits may be, the level of deception had become so proficient and clever that they could not be held accountable if the financial reports that passed their audits were later found to be inaccurate. The SEC wanted a means to specifically hold the company's leaders responsible for the integrity of the report. I can tell you for a fact that this regulation was not the perfect dragnet it was supposed to be. The bigger message here is that regulation doesn't work.

Because many people in the top CEO positions are only there for a handful of years, they can manage to the goal line and take their bonuses and compensation. In the meantime, as I have said, the employees have an entire lifetime of work that they are likely devoting to one of these big companies. They are far more interested in the sustainability and long term health of the organization. They are relying on their leaders to navigate their futures with care and consideration.

People caught in the fallout of leadershit – plant closings, layoffs, corporate fraud – are usually caught blindsided and innocent. They are good people trying to do their job as best they can, and they are simply sacrificial lambs for great quarterly numbers on a spreadsheet and a corresponding bonus for the leader. All this is not stuff that is generally on the public's radar.

Ka-Boom

Nobody wanted to take responsibility for the very, very hard work involved in changing the foundation of the auto industry's business structure in the 1990s and early 2000s. Instead, they leveraged suppliers for unmerited price reductions, dumped more vehicles on fleets and dealers to keep the plants running, and offered more discounts to potential buyers.

There were huge unintended consequences for the automakers. Their disregard for their overarching responsibility was ripping away the fiber of the dependability and reliability of the various parts. Without them intending to cross the safety line, it seems that they may have. GM maybe went too far. Their decisions regarding cost reduction may have compromised the integrity of the product where it became tragic.

Like many, I believe that Mary Barra, CEO of General Motors has been burned. She had to go to Washington to testify on behalf of GM for problems that originated in 2006 and 2007 – eight or nine years before she took the helm at GM. She was sitting in Washington because of the orthodoxy of how the car companies tried to underwrite the fact that they were toast. Previous leadershit took the short-term successes and pushed the big ugly problems down the line, until there was no where left to push them. They got to the point where they were desperate and continued to try to take costs out of the product where safety was compromised. Their customers received poorly designed cars and paid a heavy price as a result of leadershit kicking the can.

Suggestion Box

I would talk with the people at the JCI plants and ask them what is the biggest thing that you think we could do better? Unanimously, they all said to just communicate with them better. They wanted to know that they were in a position to be heard when they had something to say. When nobody is telling workers what is going on, it feels disrespectful to them. One guy said to me, "You don't even have to tell me what I want to hear. Just communicate with me. Let me know what's going on."

So we did that. We had a suggestion box in the plants for the employees. Each time I visited the plants I would have them empty the box, and if there was a suggestion in any of them that was over a week old, we were having a meeting. If a leader tells employees that they want suggestions, and then shows them that they really don't give a shit by not even reading them, they are reinforcing a culture of disassociation between workers and leadership.

That was not acceptable. Ignoring someone is the worst thing you can do to them.

Back in 1998 GM, Ford and Chrysler were starting to shrink. They were maybe just starting their death spiral. This was hard on the UAW leadership, one of whose major objectives was getting more UAW members. Since that wasn't going to happen at the Detroit Three, the UAW leadership quickly found their way to my office at Johnson Controls.

I had never met the particular visitor from the UAW before, but I did not have a very cozy relationship with the organization because we had about 50 plants in the United States, and less than ten of them were union at the time.

At JCI we didn't really need a third party to convince us that what was right for workers was right for us. What was good for the business was to treat people fairly. Now everybody has a different definition of "fair." Fair to me was to pay people well relative to the value they provide to the company, provide benefits, health and safety measures, warm in the winter and cool in the summer, and invest in ergonomics. Respect them, communicate with them, listen to them, open the suggestion box and read what they have to say – because they know stuff about your business that you don't know! Do everything you can to help them and their families fulfill their life's aspirations.

Anti-Losing-My-Ass

Once the UAW leadership representative entered my office, he started getting up in my face and getting loud. His people had gone to a few of our plants to try to get them unionized. The National Labor Relations Laws back then stated that for the union to legally organize a plant, over 50% of the employees would have to sign a card agreeing to it. So the UAW had to try to get enough of the cards signed before they could launch an organization effort. The representative told me they couldn't get enough cards signed in our plants.

My first thoughts were, well, I bet you are pretty pissed, but I am very happy because that means that the majority of my workers are happy with the way they are being treated. Our performance is great and the people are happy, that means they don't need the UAW.

I said, "Ok, so what's your point?"

He said, "You are anti-union."

I replied, "Look, I don't know you. We just kind of met, but I can promise you this: if you were to get to know me, you would know that I am almost never anti-anything or anti-anybody. I am, however, anti-losing-my-ass in business, so I do whatever it takes to avoid that."

"Now, if I understand your agenda, when workers are being mistreated – whether it's pay, benefits, work conditions or health and safety – you step in on behalf of those employees and get the management to fix those issues on behalf of those employees. If that's your agenda, then I am pro-you. But if that's your agenda, then what the hell are you doing in my office?"

Everybody has a different view, but there are not too many companies who don't know that they could get in a lot of trouble if they mistreat workers, and that it is just bad for business to do that. There used to be a real need to have the union as an enforcer when workers were being mistreated. There is more scrutiny on business operations now. Laws are in place to protect them. Mistreatment is more uncommon. But then again, that may be a relative term these days. Maybe unions have become largely symbolic, serving to preserve the status quo and prevent (rather than fight) mistreatment. It seemed to me even then, though, that the original purpose of the UAW in some ways was becoming obsolete, and that their agenda had shifted.

I went on, "Look, there are three ways you are going to get re-elected in the next UAW election: one is through recruitment of more members. You are not going to be able to do that at GM, Ford and Chrysler because they are shrinking, so you have to come to me and every other supplier that is predominantly non-union – even if we don't have an issue that your organization can help with."

"The second thing that is going to get you re-elected is if you achieve your goal and get more members, then you get more dues. And more dues mean you get more clout with the politicians. I don't really know how that makes our business any better, but that is number two."

"The third way that you are going to get re-elected is if you get new contracts with work rules."

Work rules tend to engineer more inefficiency into the business making it less competitive and less profitable. For example, maybe you have material handlers and assemblers in the same plant. In a non-union plant, I can cross-train you because if one person is gone, I can move another person into their position and keep things moving. In a union plant, there is generally a work rule that forbids that type of crossover. Workers are siloed into one skilled job, which means I need to hire more people. For the unions, more workers meant more members, more dues and more power. For businesses, more workers make them bottom-heavy and inefficient.

Work rules also dictate how many vacation days you get, how many unexcused absences you get, and whole lot more. What is quietly engineered into the work rules is inefficiency, and inefficiency drives up the head count, which drives up membership, which drives up dues, which drives up the UAW power in Washington. More members mean more power.

I told him, "Don't listen to me. Listen to the Johnson Controls plants you just went to."

He then said, "In your non-union plants, the workers make more money than the workers in your union plants."

I said, "What's your point?"

He replied, "You are discriminating against union workers."

I said, "No, I'm not. In my non-union plants I don't have your work rules. So I have much more efficiency, and that translates into lower costs, and because I have lower costs, I make more money and I split that money four ways: one goes to the shareholder, one to reinvest into the technology and upgrades to the plant, the third to offset customer price reductions, and the fourth to the people who work there who make it all possible. They get more because of the built in efficiencies of being non-UAW, not because I don't like you or the union. I don't think about the union at all when I am managing this business. I don't need to."

But the bottom line was that it wasn't really up to me. Unfortunately for my visitor, the workers had already decided not to organize in those plants.

"If you keep clamoring for more money and less work, this business will die," I told him. "I know you know that because it's just the math. The only reason I can't convince you is because the reality of that happening is so far removed that you will never personally suffer the consequences of what you are asking me to do here today." This did not lead to any surrender flags going up.

In fact, just the opposite happened.

The Weakest Link is a Goliath

Weeks after that waste-of-my-time meeting, we ended up in the GM offices. GM was a $4 billion customer of ours. What the UAW had done is go back to GM and put the pressure on them to get us in line.

So here is the gist of my conversation with the leadership at GM:

GM leader: "You're doing a great job for us, Rande, but here is the deal: I really don't want to tell you how to run your business, but because of the leverage situation, if you guys don't do more to organize your plants – at least the ones that service GM – I can't promise you that we can continue to give you the amount of business from GM that you have been receiving."

This is clear proof that the system was broken. The UAW demands had nothing to do with JCI's products, service or any other true aspect of business between our organizations. Yet here is the biggest player in the auto industry folding like a cheap lawn chair under union pressure and willing to compromise our business relationship because of a threat. GM was the biggest dog in the ring. They should have been flexing their muscles and making this whole thing right.

Me: "So in other words, you want us to become part of the problem? That's how we are going to resolve all of this? You know this is taking us all down. Why don't we stand up and fix this instead of just trying to ride it out?" We were all collectively driving this industry off a cliff.

Nobody – the unions, GM —is thinking long term. They don't want to. They can't. They are not getting paid for it and they don't have enough sense of responsibility to care about preventing something really bad from happening six or seven years down the line. When all is said and done with the bonus formulas and everything that is put in place to incentivize leaders, there is nothing in place to incentivize them to *prevent* something from happening. What is incentivized is to take the short term "plus" and the long term "minus".

As a leader, if you don't have your sense of obligation and integrity around your duty to incentivize you to do the right thing, then there is nothing at all in place in the system to make you step up to the plate and do the right thing for the long term benefit of the company and its workers. Nothing.

And yet it is this very same system that excludes the breed of leader who wouldn't settle for kicking the can.

What came after that meeting was a lot of back and forth. Ultimately, we had to sign a neutrality agreement with the UAW. At this "damned-if-you-do-damned-if-you-don't" point inside the broken system, we surrendered. I understood it, but I hated it. I didn't hate the UAW. I hated a system that established and supported *wrong* as *right*.

Looking Into My Crystal Ball

I spoke to a writer at the Wall Street Journal in, I believe, 2004. He asked me if I thought that GM could go bankrupt. I immediately replied, "Yes. I don't see how they don't go bankrupt. What I don't know is when. If you are that big and you start falling, I just don't know how long it takes for you to land."

I can give you many examples why I was so rock solid sure that the answer to his question was yes, but let me just pick one.

Apples and Oranges

One of the main products JCI Automotive supplies to the automakers is seats. At one point in 1997 or 1998, GM truck was really upset with their seats in the last prototype phase. I was the president of JCI Automotive North America at the time and they invited me come out to a vehicle development facility in Pontiac to meet with their head of engineering.

When I walked in, I saw he had his two primary competitive vehicles there on display. He had a Toyota SUV and a Honda right in the room. He wanted to show me how much worse his seats were compared to these vehicles. So he did, and he was right. His seats clearly did not look as good as his competitors' seats.

So I stopped him and I said, "Let me first tell you that these other two vehicles, we make those seats." He didn't know that. So it became kind of obvious that whatever was causing the problems with his seats, it was not us.

I explained that the difference in the quality was the result of how GM was interacting with us versus how these other companies – specifically the Japanese – were interacting with us. It was how the Japanese development process worked versus how the GM development process worked (and Ford and Chrysler, as well). The difference was in the system – which was the result of the leadership – and this was the quality that popped out when the system was not optimized.

During the early Product Definition phase and throughout the approximate three year development process for these seats, we constantly battled decisions made by the Detroit Three that would meet their short term objectives, but that we knew would disadvantage them in the dealer showroom when stacked against both consumer expectations and their (Japanese) competition.

I don't remember if we ever won even one of those debates. Those short term decisions were typically driven by cost, not value. And they were SHORT term costs. Whatever cost they avoided short term was exponentially dwarfed by discounts they had to place on their final product to compete with their competitor's superior product.

When I explained all of this to the GM executive that day, he said, with frustration and a small bit of humor, "You knew better, so why did you let us do that to us?"

I didn't need to answer. It was rhetorical. We were both frustrated by a system neither one of us could control, and that was designed to fail . . .

. . . and that would continue to perpetuate lousy outcomes for GM.

Apathy 101

We did a lot of business with Toyota. We were one of the few American suppliers they used because Toyota was very careful about anyone outside of their organization touching their stuff. We also did a lot of business with the Detroit Three.

At the International Auto Show in 2001, I recall that GM was getting lambasted for their interiors (this was publicized in the industry media), including the seats.

A GM executive came up to our exhibit to talk with us. He said, "You know, they say that our interiors suck. You guys make seats for us, but you also make seats for Toyota. And they say that Toyota stuff is the benchmark. So I am guessing that you guys are not really the problem."

He wanted us to discuss with GM executives – without getting into confidentiality – what it was in the process of designing and building these seats that was different from the Toyota system. There were reasons of course, and we were in a position to explain. We set up meetings to talk with them about what they could do to make better seats and interiors and get a better outcome.

What I knew would be the biggest challenge in our communication with GM was that the tactics and methodologies used by Toyota was a function of their culture. Without GM reinventing their culture, those tactics and methodologies implemented at GM (or Ford or Chrysler, for that matter) would be like trying to nail pudding to a wall. It's just not going to stick.

So we scheduled meetings to talk with them about better seats and interiors and a better outcome. Top executives from GM were invited to visit JCI's Plymouth and Holland, Michigan tech centers. We took them on tours showcasing all of our interior capabilities in engineering, development, manufacturing, design, innovation and research. We discussed how all of these resources and competencies could be leveraged to produce better products, but only if the product definition system that GM provided to us was reinvented and shifted from a "price centered" to a "value centered" buying model.

And do you know what they changed? Not a damn thing.

At different times and for different reasons we were asked to share the same information with Ford and Chrysler, so we did the best we could. And do you know what they changed? Not a damn thing.

They all understood that they needed to change. They learned what was needed to do it. Did any of them begin the process of _changing?_ Nope.

In my opinion, resistance to change was a big part of what drove the American automakers to the verge of extinction.

Later, when I was working as a consultant, this same narrative continued and I felt like I was trying to teach a bunch of tomcats to square dance. A big waste of time.

Fiefdoms

There are cultures within a corporation, and an overriding culture within an industry.

For the Japanese, if Toyota made a decision in Japan, then Toyota Europe, Toyota South America and Toyota North America did it. They were unified. Their goal was one team, one company around the world. They really understood that the more they could standardize their operations, the more they could benefit from scalability and increase their margins.

In GM, Ford or Chrysler, if one of their North American divisions made a decision, Europe and South America could decide not to implement it. These were called silos, vacuums and I called them Fiefdoms. That was their culture. Even though they wanted to be global, they were really multi-national and could never really get good traction around leveraging standardization and scalability.

I would sit in these supplier advisory meetings and tell them how they could use a certain design here, and they could then use it all over the world and save a lot of money. They would sit there and tell me that they can't use it all over the world. When I would ask why, they would tell me that, well, North America wants to use it, but Europe or South America doesn't want to.

My jaw would drop.

This is why Toyota's biggest concern was how they can maintain their identity and their standards while operating outside of Japan. They did not want to be westernized. They were concerned that the methods and mindset of the American car companies would infect their systems that were really far and away better than ours at the time.

In America, we would say that Toyota and the Japanese sounded condescending and arrogant, but the reality is that their culture has so much to do with how they ran things that disruption of the culture would affect the performance of their company. They knew that. We didn't.

Be Careful What you Ask For

JCI was the primary seat systems supplier for Toyota in North America in the '90s and early 2000s. I had the opportunity to attend annual supplier meetings during which Toyota would present award to suppliers under various categories. We were fortunate enough to receive a number of those awards during that time.

However, I noticed that there was one company that each year seemed to need a mid-sized cargo van to haul away all of their quality awards from those meetings.

This was a large Japan-based electronics company. The head of their North American Operations was a Japanese national, who I had the privilege to get to know. He was a very cool guy. I contacted him to ask if – since we were not competitors – we could essentially benchmark their quality systems. Although JCI was doing pretty good, they clearly were doing something that set them far apart from the field.

I hoped that he would see that imitation is the most sincere form of flattery, and allow us to see some of their quality systems. When it came to improving our industry standing, sales and revenue, I wanted to learn how to do things the best way. I wanted to send some of our folks to their facilities to learn what we could apply to our systems and processes. He was agreeable to my request.

While we were having that conversation, I asked him, "You have run plants in Japan and now in the U.S. Can you give me one example of what goes on in Japan that doesn't happen here that contributes to the difference in the quality and reliability in Japanese products versus U.S. products?"

After hesitating a bit, he said, "It is the difference in the U.S. culture versus the Japanese culture."

He said, "In Japan, if someone on the production line conducts an operation that results in a defective part, it is a literal and significant personal humiliation."

Indeed, the human consequence of shame in Japan for a production defect is so personal and so severe that it reaches all the way back upstream to the product's design down to that operator's station. Every individual in that line suffers guilt and shame – which are *internal consequences.*

In fact, those consequences are considered so horrible by the Japanese that everything that can be done to minimize the possibility of producing a defective part is done. Workers take an enormous amount of pride in what they do and what they produce. They are held responsible and given credit by their leaders for the company's success and for their devotion to their work.

And then he said, "In the U.S., the culture is such that defects are not just tolerated, but expected."

When I asked him to explain further, he said, "The layout of a typical manufacturing plant in the U.S. has defect repair/rework stations located throughout the facility."

His simple example spoke volumes to me and demonstrated a classic example of the difference between embracing prevention versus reaction in any business model, and the added cost of the reaction model.

When GM, Ford and Chrysler were only competing with each other, they all did business pretty much the same way. If outside competition from other car companies was not allowed into our market, we might never have been given this gift of a chance to do it better. I am as American as anyone, but the truth is that global competitors hit our market with their hugely efficient and sensible production systems and blew us out of the water. And another truth is that we needed that wake up call.

Why do you think it used to cost less money to buy a great Toyota Camry than a shitty Ford? Because Ford (and the other U.S. automakers) had all this waste in their system. They were not getting it right. It was sloppy. Even when they did it the best that they could, it was half-assed. They all rusted out in two years and cost $20,000. The Japanese would sell consumers something that never rusted out and cost $10,000, but you wanted me to buy American? Come on!

This disconnect of consumers with the American automakers was not the fault of the American worker. It was not the fault of the American consumer, or of the American suppliers. It was a leadershit problem.

Containment vs. Correction

The leader of the multi-award winning Japan based electronics company gave the perfect example of a very telling weakness in U.S. corporate culture that is a direct result of leadershit. The repair/rework stations on our lines are part of what is called containment services. Containment services are a big business in the United States. They are supposed to provide "temporary" manpower to organizations in "crisis."

These services provide workers to help sort parts coming off the production line, separating good parts from bad parts, to prevent the bad ones from being shipped to the customer. Necessary in a culture that does not value getting the damn thing right the first time. So necessary, in fact, that there are entire industries depending on these containment services, and on a regular basis.

Note: the term "crisis" implies a short period of painful time when things are going wrong, before things return to "normal." But when crisis becomes normal, time is irrelevant. Containment services are permanent fixtures in some businesses. A company might bring in a containment service company for one job, and five years later, they are still there. They have been absorbed into the system and the cost of their services passed down to the customer. If leaders don't do a root cause analysis, plug the hole in the dike and send the containment service people home, they are settling in for the long haul with poor to mediocre business practices.

Parts Per Million

Here is how we kid ourselves, justifying our sloppy work and the huge cost of containment services.

A typical quality measure of any company is called parts per million (PPMs). For every million parts that a company ships, this is the metric of how many are rejected. Obviously, zero PPM is the best, but if you can do 10 to 20

PPM, that is pretty good. That means that out of one million parts shipped to the customer, only 10 to 20 of them were defective and were rejected. By the way, PPM is supposed to be an indicator of how good your quality systems are. And it is bullshit.

Parts per million is measured in defective parts *shipped.* Internally a manufacturer could be generating a much higher number. Maybe before shipping you those million parts, a manufacturer had to make 10 million to get one million good ones, and even then you found 10 to 20 bad ones. And to make that one million, maybe they had to repair and rework all these parts along the way in an inefficient system that tolerates and expects defects. In other words, there is no reveal about how the PPM number was ultimately achieved.

As an example, what that manufacturer might have is a bunch of people sitting at the end of their production line sorting bad parts because they can't trust their system. If 80 percent of the parts are being rejected before they are put into a box to ship, the PPM is a bullshit number. So while 10 to 20 PPM *shipped* is a good number, it is not a true indication of how good the quality systems are. It is an indication that Joe and Ed – their sorting team from the containment service – are good.

How much is that costing? How is that cost offset? Higher prices to the consumer, for one. Imagine the savings if the speed and efficiency of manufacturing those parts, minus containment services, could be enhanced.

Why should anyone believe that the published numbers of any company, like the PPM in its standards manual, is an indicator of how well a business is run? Numbers, data, can be – for lack of a better term – manipulated. At the very least, a number is simply an outcome of a process or system and does not reveal the efficiency of the system. In fact, a company can hide a lot of ugly behind some cool looking numbers.

When I worked at JCI, we adopted what the Japanese did. If there was a defective part found, we would contain the problem and not let any bad parts go out the door, and simultaneously we went back into the system, uncovered why those bad parts were happening, fixed it, and then resumed shipping.

In addition to PPM – which is really a measurement used by customers to measure quality performance of a supplier – at JCI, we used a measurement called Internal Parts Per Million (IPPM). We measured our own efficiency. We were striving for first-time capability, which is more widely utilized now and has all sorts of financial benefits.

So for JCI, the implication was that, when the financial numbers were good, it truly was a reflection of how effectively the business was being run, how well the people were being motivated and how well the systems were being managed; not just the numbers.

Leadershit is a system that builds a foundation on reaction to a problem rather than prevention of it in the first place. It is a system that builds entire industries and false heroes out of those who solve problems that should not have happened in the first place.

I am concerned because all of the issues that eventually brought down the American auto industry look to be the same issues I propose are currently contaminating corporate America in general. Damn, I hope I am wrong, but if I am not, we are going to get an ugly view of things from the bottom of that very slippery slope.

CHAPTER 9
THE STANDARD IS THE STANDARD

THE ONE THING WE SHOULD NEVER CHANGE

The Sustainable Steelers

Being born and raised in Pittsburgh, of course I have been a Steelers' fan all of my life. Back in the 60's and early 70's, the team was lousy and just added salt to the wound that had been opened up by the collapse of the steel industry.

But in the mid 70's a new coach and top draft picks brought a whole new mind set to the team. Losing wasn't going to be part of the new standard that was being established.

Sure enough, the Steelers won Super Bowls in 1975 and 1976. While the city was still reeling from the vanishing core steel industry and the population was shrinking proportionately to job loss, the Steelers became a ray of hope for the city. It was a positive distraction from the otherwise extremely difficult time for the people of Pittsburgh.

Those two Super Bowl victories – and then again in 1979 and 1980 -- catalyzed a shift in the Steelers and the Pittsburgh community mindset from losers to winners. Today, the city has bounced back economically and appears to be doing great. I will always believe that those Super Bowl championships in the '70's ignited what was to become a 30-year comeback for both the Steelers and their hometown.

I've come to look at the Steelers through a second perspective. It was not a smooth direct escalator ride to the top for the team or the city, but if you are like me, and look at winning as an established process instead of a single victory, they have certainly figured a few things out. They have won a total of six Super Bowls, the most in the NFL. But over that 30-year period, they have been consistent winners and contenders with a few rebuilding years sprinkled in.

Any team can be a contender or win once in a while. Hell, even a broken clock is right twice a day. I wondered what was the critical success factor that made the Steelers' contending/winning consistent? My conclusion: the culture. What established the culture? The *standards*. And who established the standards? Leadership.

A sign on the wall near the Steelers' locker room in Heinz Field says: *"The Standard...is the Standard."*

The "standard" sets the objective each year to win the Super Bowl. Anything less than just getting to the Super Bowl is performing below the standard.

I also believe that the standard has a lot to do with the "how." How people behave; their attitude, how they treat each other from top to bottom, all matters and matters a lot. Consistent compliance with the organization's values has everything to do with reaching its objectives. Those values include respect, unity and team over self. Not just say it, and not just do it. Do it consistently.

During the 2014 season, the team signed a free agent player to be the back-up running back. As far as on-the-field talent, he seemed to be a very good addition. The team didn't have anyone else on the existing roster that could fill the critical position.

Early in the season, the Steelers were playing a game and that new player decided to leave the field before it ended. It turns out, apparently he was dissatisfied with his playing time and decided to just leave. Remember, the team didn't have a legitimate back-up for this guy. He was it. His importance to the team may have been a good enough reason to excuse his diva-like conduct; you know, essentially give him a pass on his behavior. At the same time, that would have sent a message loud and clear to the rest of the organization about its values -- that its standards around one team and one goal didn't hold any water. It would have set a precedent.

The morning after the game, it was announced well before lunch time that the player was released from the team . . . gone.

There have been times where the team has had an extraordinary number of injuries, or maybe a schedule that looks especially tough. During these times, a question is invariably asked of the coach: given the challenges presented at the time, does he still expect the team to go the distance? His answer always is "the standard is the standard." You can't touch the standards. They are fixed. What you can do is to meet them or not. Those exceptional challenges are seen as nothing more than excuses. The organization isn't graded on a curve. The standard is the standard.

With that said, it appears to me that the standards in the system for who gets and retains leadership positions in business, and for how they are permitted to behave and operate have, over time, drifted far too low.

Culture of Sustainable Excellence

The Toyota Camry that is built in the U.S. is also built in three or four other countries. They are all the same. There is no difference. They design it once. They tool it once. Boom. Done.

With the American automakers, I remember that when they had the same vehicle being built in three countries, they were all different. Why? Because each country got to decide how to do their own car. When allowed, engineers and designers for American automakers would go off on their own creative journey with the product. If they didn't invent it, they didn't want to build it. GM, Ford and Chrysler allowed that. They ran their operations regionally, not globally like the Japanese. Hell, in some cases they ran their operations in every building like they were separate businesses.

Designers are very aware of aesthetics. When something is designed, it usually looks cool. Whether that look can be retained, still be cool and be of high quality when it is built repeatedly is an entirely different discussion. Following design, engineering comes in and takes that design and they typically have to make alterations to it so that they can actually engineer it. It goes from drawing board cool to now they have to put it on the blueprint. It's got to stay cool, but it also has to be practical. That's why engineers have issues with designers, and vice versa. It's classic. Then, manufacturing comes in, and they have to actually fit the parts together and make it run consistently with first-time capability.

In the book, *Taken for a Ride*, Published by Four Walls Eight Windows; 1st edition (May 24, 2000), author and Detroit Free Press writer, Jack Doyle, talks about Francois Castaing who was the head of design of Chrysler, at the time of Daimler Chrysler. He describe an instance when the manufacturing VP, who was Castaing's counterpart, brought Francois to one of their plants where they had all these extra people trying to jimmy-fit and jerry-rig his designs into useable inventory, and tried to show him the difficulty and chaos and cost that his designs were causing the company. It was a lesson in the value of understanding long term consequences when making decisions that otherwise look good.

The other lesson here is that the standard must be set for all steps of the process to work toward. In the GM, Ford, Chrysler systems in the 1990s, design, engineering, and manufacturing typically worked separately. Design did their thing in a vacuum and then threw it over the wall to engineering. It looked cool, but it couldn't be built without being reengineered for function.

Engineering was also usually sequestered from manufacturing. So once engineering was finished destroying the designer's vision and making it functional, they threw the whole thing over the wall into manufacturing, where they looked it over and said, "We can't build it."

When a car or a part is designed, that design has to be high quality and withstand the rigors of mass reproduction as well as the pounding use that the driver was going to deliver to the finished product. The design process should include guidelines that transition easily through the chain and allow engineering and manufacturing to make it repetitively and in an automated way. When something isn't transitioning smoothly, when it needs to be reworked, pushed and pulled, then you have to put extra people in there to make that happen. Meaning extra time, resources and money.

At JCI, we had "simultaneous development teams." We put manufacturing, design and engineering all in the same room, so the three of them could collaborate and bring the best product to the party without several iterations. It was a way of leveraging the collective consensus, which made the whole greater than the sum of its parts.

This way, we were able to achieve "Hey, it looks cool. Hey, it's practical. Hey, I can build it" very early on in the process, when we were still putting stuff down on paper . . . and it was much less costly than trying to hash it out on the assembly line where the struggle would only drive up inefficiency and costs.

In contrast, the left hand frequently didn't know what the right hand was doing at GM, and Ford, and Chrysler. Often they were throwing concepts and drafts over the wall to each other, and it was so obvious that the standard had not been set.

The consequences of failing to set the standard in business again falls on the consumer. Back in the '90s I owned three Grand Cherokees consecutively as company cars. My friend at Chrysler asked me, "How do you like your Jeep?" I said, "Steve, it's a cool-looking car, but honest to God, I really don't know if it has spent more time in my garage or getting repaired at one of your dealerships. It's close. It's always in there getting fixed. Something's always broke."

No Asshole Policy

There are companies who have anchored themselves to the right standards. One great example of that is R.W. Baird, a financial services organization that has been listed on Fortune 100's best places to work in 2016 – for the 13th consecutive year. Their consistent success is a reflection of its culture, the standards that are set and held, as well as the engagement, morale and motivation of its people.

Oh, and they have a "No Asshole" policy. Yes, really.

This particular rule is highlighted in the new employee orientation. The "No Asshole Rule" which states 'Don't put yourself or your ego ahead of the clients or the firm.' CEO Paul Purcell clearly points out to new employees, "If you're an asshole, don't come here. We will fire you." It's true. They do.

Reportedly, they have fired approximately two dozen people who have violated the "No Asshole Rule." I am pretty sure that their lasting recognition on the Fortune 100 list has something to do with that "No Asshole" policy and more importantly, its consistent enforcement by leadership.

Those Blipping Trends

Remember the Molinaroli extra-marital affair with the company consultant? The JCI board first said they fully stood behind their philandering CEO, then a few weeks later, spanked him with a $1 million reduction in his $20 million compensation for the year.

Why didn't the stock drop? Who cares? The stock didn't drop because the numbers were okay. It seemed that nobody really cared about the ethical picture here. It was practically a non-event for the board, and for the public.

Character doesn't seem to be on the radar when companies are shopping for leaders. Character doesn't have any direct effect on, or association with today's PE ratio of the company (PE ratio is the current stock price of a company divided by its earnings per share (EPS): P/E **Ratio** = Market Value per Share.) so it doesn't matter. Not today, and in this system, today is all that matters. There is a quiet erosion taking place behind this false belief. I can feel it and I know that others feel it too. We are incrementally selling out our future. Lack of character may be only one of the indicators of a "leadershit is okay" system, but, in the way that garlic breath can be an indicator of rat poisoning, it is potentially lethal and should not be ignored.

We don't seem to react to the real indicators that tell us that we are unraveling. We only react once we are unraveled. Like a person who has been chain-smoking for 20 years who suddenly finds a spot on his lungs; we will be surprised by the unraveling because we are apathetic to the warnings. We will be fine, fine, fine, fine, and then bam, we are terminal.

With numbers, with stocks and with industries, you can have blips and you can have trends. It is in our best interest to become aware of whether something is a blip or is it a trend. Although blips can be one-time benign events, trends can be harbingers of looming trouble ahead. Trends are warnings that it is time for action.

With corporate entities managing their public image with unsustainable numbers and false claims of core values which do not reflect the true health of the organization, how can we detect trends? In a system that continues to lower standards and emphasize immediate results, it is becoming increasingly difficult.

Speaking of trends, I recently learned that JCI will be shedding its automotive division. Once the flagship that commanded around 75 percent of the revenue and almost 80 percent of earnings for JCI, apparently, it has slowly withered away over the last decade. I can tell you from experience that the automotive supply industry can be a profitable and rewarding sector. I can also tell you that it is a very complicated and demanding business that needs constant attention from leadership in order to prosper.

I was recently contacted by a reporter from a local publication. He asked what I thought of the announcement that JCI was going to exit automotive. I told him, "Well, if you had an airplane that you once knew how to fly and now you don't know how to fly it, I guess it makes sense to get rid of the airplane."

By the way, I am pretty sure that is not the way JCI's PR team will explain it.

Changes – Turn and Face the Strange

When JCI put me in charge of North America and my team made the enormous changes necessary for achieving greater levels of success, we didn't engage in "image management" or "information management." We didn't need to. It turned out so well that there was no need to hide our methods from anyone. In fact, we were way above the S&P 500 index, during a recession when no one else was doing well, and they all wanted to know how we did it.

And, by the way, I think it's important to note here that neither my team nor I, as leader of the North American group, were incentivized to take that risk to make all those difficult operational changes to put us in a better position as a company. There was no carrot on that stick, no bonus.

I was invited to sit in on the visits with the Wall Street analysts and explain how my team did what they did.

There were several meetings with those analysts and after each meeting folks on my staff would ask how iI told them I wasn't sure. Since I wasn't describing the usual ways that profits are generated, let alone increased, during a recession, I really wasn't sure the analysts understood or bought what I told them.

I talked to them about culture, morale, character and business efficiency – nothing they were used to hearing and nothing that could be put on a spreadsheet. I explained how we refused to default to usual methods for assuring that quarterly numbers were secured.

Those usual methods include big layoffs, shortcuts, plant shutdowns, selling off business segments or slashing salaried general and administrative costs (SG&A), which is all code for pirating investments allocated for our company's future and redeploying them to subsidize the present margins. My team and I didn't do any of that. Sadly, this confused a lot of people, when it should be how business is done all the time.

(-1 + -1) + 2 = Wait a Minute

In monitoring blips and trends, it is interesting that numbers are frequently the last indicators of something that is going wrong. Sometimes they conceal other factors that if known, might send shareholders running. Things like *how* the numbers were reached.

One day, shortly after I took over North America at JCI, I was talking with my VP of finance about our working capital.

Working capital is calculated as a company's current assets minus current liabilities. The working capital ratio (Current Assets/Current Liabilities) indicates whether a company has enough short term assets to cover its short term debt. In general, the higher the number, the worse it is. A net lower versus higher working capital is an indicator that assets and liabilities are being managed effectively, leading to better cash flow. Working capital is a very important performance measurement of any business and is comprised of three very significant components: accounts receivable, accounts payable, and inventory.

I asked him, "Tom, how is our working capital?" He replied, "Great". Our working capital, according to Tom, was essentially at zero, which meant that we were neutral. Really great working capital numbers can drop well below zero. We weren't negative, but all in all, pretty good.

I asked about the inventory. His response was that inventory performance wasn't very good; we were carrying too much inventory. In a just-in-time manufacturing environment, we needed to be very confident in sustaining the right amount of inventory to satisfy demand from our customers in a timely manner, and at the same time, not have too much inventory getting dusty on a shelf, tying up money that can be redeployed for better use. Financial penalties for shutting down a customer because you ran out of inventory were plenty high. The black mark on your record could influence your company's ability to win future business and made erring on the high side the better option.

So inventory needed to be just right. It took a lot of logistical skill and methods application to do that, but he was telling me that the inventory numbers were going the wrong way. We were on a bad trend with inventory and we needed to work with the appropriate people to reverse that.

I then asked about our accounts receivable, which tracked how quickly – 30, 60, 90, 120 days – we were collecting the money due to us from our customers – which was always a challenge in business, and especially in big business, and especially in the auto industry, and especially from customers who themselves are struggling from a cash flow position. At the time, GM,

Ford and Chrysler spent a great deal of time and energy figuring out reasons not to pay suppliers. Anyone in the automotive industry understands that.

Tom's response was predictably negative. He reported that our receivables were lagging, that we were not collecting money as we should be, and that we needed to get with the appropriate organizations to figure a way to accelerate the collection of those monies that were due us.

Standard = Substandard

It was at this point that I realized that the answer to my original question about the overall working capital status was that it was "great" because we were leveraging the final component in the equation – the accounts payable – against the other two. This meant that in order to offset the bad performance in inventory and receivables, we were not paying our bills on time. By stretching our payables as far as we could, we were able to balance everything into a relatively positive position financially and report that our working capital was in good shape.

This is a powerful example of the importance of the *how* we get the results, not just *what* are the results. When I heard the working capital was "great," that was good news. When I heard *how* we were getting there, it was bad news. Very bad news.

Here we were proclaiming to be a company that has *integrity* and we valued *Suppliers and Partners* as part of our core values. We were violating some of our core values in order to get the numbers right.

Roll Up Our Sleeves

So we had some work to do. I told Tom and the others that somewhere out there is a future deadline – I don't recall if it was 90 days or 120 days – a time by which we have to have our shit together. We needed to get to work putting processes and systems in place to get inventory down while never allowing a customer to be shut down. You have got to rub your belly and pat your head at the same time. It is not an either/or question.

At the same time, sales needed to come up with more effective ways to get our receivables faster. I gave them some time – I'm not sure if it was 90 or 120 days, but there was a line drawn – to figure that stuff out and get it on track. On that chosen day and on every day going forward, we are going to pay our suppliers per terms and on time – every single one of them.

If the calendar eats up the allotted number of days and we don't have inventory under control and we haven't figured out how to get our money from our customers, the working capital number will go through the roof, and we will be in some real deep crap. We committed to this, so it meant we had to get better at it. Used judiciously, that good ole "have-to" factor can be one hell of a motivator.

We went on to address and correct that situation, and the way we did it caused our numbers to follow suit. These are the real numbers of our working capital improvements at JCI Automotive when we were true to our values and closed the door to the path of least resistance:

Fiscal 2001	0
Fiscal 2002	*minus* $136 million
Fiscal 2003	*minus* $224 million

We went from zero to *minus* $224 million dollars; a fantastic number. Now our VP of finance, Tom, could say with confidence and accuracy that our working capital number really was "great." Our inventory and receivables improved because we demonstrated to our supply partners that we would honor our agreements and pay them *on time as contracted*. That simple act of integrity got us, in return, the best they had to offer -- good quality, timely delivery, the best technology and pricing.

The upshot is that our "good" numbers were supported by a solid "how." We started with what we wouldn't do. And in a leadershit system that asks, "What are you willing to do?" – implying how far would you go for the company? Are you willing to sell out? – ***that*** was the right place to start.

It was a valuable lesson for me, and became a standard for our team.

Standard Reboot

As a team, we agreed that we were going to use our time running North American Operations at JCI to really do something special and attempt to set the business up in such a way that the architecture – both organizationally from a process standpoint and from a culture standpoint – reached a higher standard for operations than had ever been reached. We set our goals significantly higher than our historical performance, which was already very good.

We decided to reengineer our operating model. We were going to start by focusing on a culture shift and emphasizing the value of the people we work with. We recognized that a very large component of reaching improvement would involve commitments to each other, mutual respect and trust. We needed this because going forward we were going to ask a lot of our people.

This bears repeating:

"Talent and character emerge not when you decide what you are willing to do. They emerge when you decide what – under any circumstances – you are absolutely not willing to do." – Rande Somma

With the new model came the discussion of what we were NOT going to do (i.e., path of least resistance) and what was not going to be available to us in terms of reaching our new goals. We put in place all the things that we were going to do to reach our goals, but more importantly, we firmly established all the things we were ***not*** going to do to reach them. These included:

Lay off people in order to hit financial targets

Redirect strategic plan investments to the immediate bottom line

Increasing dependency on creative accounting

Treat employee expectations as subordinate to those of customers and shareholders

Behave as if "living our values" is discretionary

Morale is irrelevant because intimidation is used as a motivator

The ends justifies the means mentality

Manipulate and misrepresent actual performance data

Act entitled to (not earn) support, loyalty and compliance

Disregard the company's code of ethics to suit our convenience

We also established that anyone in the room had the authority to stop us from drifting toward reopening those illegitimate options. After all, the business was complicated and our commitments were lofty. We were not willing to sacrifice values, people or commitments we have made to innovations and investments in the future of the business. We disqualified these as options to accomplish our goals.

We made sure that we didn't cross the line with regard to our corporate values by making a list of the shortcuts that we would not allow ourselves to take to reach our goals. Everyone was a watchdog over the list and we appointed one person who was more or less our sergeant at arms.

We did this because I knew we were going to get tempted to fall off and default to the path of least resistance. We got very tempted on several occasions because we would look at our forecasts and scratch our heads. Our forecasts were difficult to reach and our customers were busy treating us like ATM machines; continuously pressing us for more value for less money, and then stretching out payments as often and as far as possible, and we still had to hit our numbers.

While we knew that a head-count reduction would clearly lower costs, it would also have a negative effect on our "walking the walk" value systems. We already established that human capital and valuing our trained and talented workforce was paramount in our core values. Therefore, using them as an expense item that could be discarded to reduce our costs was not an option. As well, the amount of resources applied to the business – people as well as machines, plants, technology and methods – had to be in alignment with our mission statement, which was to achieve and/or exceed our customers' expectations.

I was privileged to be part of a team effort that made the leap to dig in and really commit to seeing this model through. Despite the high hurdles, we did not quit. It worked. It was a very powerful shift of belief systems when we proved that business could improve dramatically by eliminating decisions that allowed shortcuts like layoffs to be the first decisions made to achieve goals and projected numbers.

Cockle-Doodle-Don't

Just before my team made all of those transformational changes in our business model at JCI in 1999/2000, JCI had also just come off of the best year ever in North America in 1998/1999. The company was getting ready to celebrate because we really did well. I sat down with the people on my team and asked them, if we were to create a chart showing the drivers that got us here, what would be on that chart?

We actually went ahead and mapped that out. When I looked at the top things that drove our success, it turned out that none of them were anything that we controlled. The auto industry built more cars than we expected that year, which created the increased demand for our products. They also built more luxury cars than we expected, and that translated directly into more profit for us. The top things that drove our extraordinary results that year had nothing to do with our company's performance. We didn't control any of it. And yet here we were celebrating our great success and congratulating each other. Isn't that like the rooster taking credit for the sunrise?

That is the kind of mode we are in here in business in corporate America: it doesn't matter how we did it, we are just going to take credit for it whether we had anything to do with it or not. We tend to take credit for it even if we had *nothing* to do with it because we can get away with it.

If I just sat back and squinted and looked at the end results, everything was wonderful. Our working capital number was "great" (according to Tom, the VP of Finance and the JCI standards of 1998) and we had the most extraordinary year in sales ever. Wall Street was happy; leadership was happy; workers were happy...everyone was happy.

I was not happy. And I was about to piss in everyone's cornflakes.

The House of Cards

I looked at the forecast going forward and one of the things I could see was that we were growing very rapidly, but so were our operating costs. Not a great position to be in looking at the looming threat of an economic downturn, which some of us could smell coming. And the horrific tragedy of September 11th that would crush our economy even further wasn't even on anyone's radar yet.

Our victory from the previous year and our self-congratulatory attitude was hollow. There was nothing to sustain it, and in fact, it was due to topple any day. Our economic position looked precarious for the future.

This is when we decided that we needed to make a huge business model change. My thought was that any time we were making a change big enough to affect the entire organization I needed to get out there and tell them what was going on. The worst thing you can do is have people notice a change and leave them in the dark. It is scary and uncomfortable to work in a changing environment and not know why things are changing.

In this case, I had to go tell them that we were going to fix something that – as far as they knew – wasn't broken, but it really was, and it was going to be really hard to fix it and we needed to act quickly to set a new standard that shifted our focus from reaction to prevention.

We had done some things right that had made that a record year, but those things that we didn't do right were beginning to show up. Numbers were falling off and lines were trending down. We were just entering the 2000 to 2003 recession. I saw that changes were coming to the volume of business we were going to do. We were not organized well to deal with lower volumes. We were fine tuned to higher volumes by design. We were a house of cards and a big wind storm was coming.

So we made some big changes. We changed a lot of processes. This turned out to be a very interesting experience ... and it turned out awesome...but not everyone was convinced at the outset that the proposed changes made sense.

Avoiding Mutiny During the Bounty

I needed all management on board to embrace and implement the proposed changes. But one of the manufacturing directors openly expressed to me that he hated the changes we were making. He had been there a long time. He was a good leader and performed well. He was a good person, and he was being very friendly, but he was very clear. He hated it.

We went back forth on this topic, and I said to him that obviously I couldn't guarantee anyone that our new operating model was going to work. I was essentially asking him to throw away what seemed like a perfectly good operating model that had just (supposedly) put us in the history books, and to replace it with something completely new and untested and difficult. Of course he hated it. But it was clear that if we did nothing, there would be a disaster down the road. Even if he couldn't see that, I knew it, and for me to look the other way and ignore it was out of the question.

"I am telling you that difficult times are coming and we have an obligation to do something about it from our vantage point now. So, we need to have this conversation – which I am not really comfortable with because I really like you and you have done a great job – but if we have any chance at making this successful, all of us in leadership have to be on board with these changes 100%. So if you can't get on board with this change and help us make it happen – if you don't think you can do that, I'm really going to miss you."

He said, "You would fire me?"

I said, "Yes, I would have to."

He said, "You want to fire me?"

I said, "No, I don't want to fire you, but I would have to. Having management in a change system that hasn't bought into that change won't work."

That was a hard day. He was okay. He stayed and everything went well.

If I had just let him slide and taken the easy way and said, we can get there by kicking the can it would not have worked in the long run.

If you step back and consider the bigger picture here. We have come a hell of a long way from a "gentleman's" handshake in our past, when you could bet the farm that when a leader promised something was going to happen. Leaders rose to the challenge and it actually happened. Now we even have signed legal documents in place to make a leader do what they promised to do; what they are contractually obligated to do under the law. Even those contracts often cannot force leaders to do their job with integrity.

What the hell happened to us?

Although it is easy to see that leaders have lost integrity, I would argue that it is much, much more than that. They have lost their dignity; they have lost our respect; and worst of all, they have lost our trust. The erosion of leadership melts down our economy and civility. Under this system, people are less and less invested in or united under any corporate entity or national flag. People feel betrayed; disposable, and angry. The damage is deep and the toll could be a heavy one.

It is difficult to repair broken trust.

CHAPTER 10
THE VALUE OF INTEGRITY
THE ENORMOUS ROI OF CHARACTER

*"I was born just five blocks from Forbes Field in Oakland to two high school dropouts, a waiter and a waitress at the Pittsburgh Athletic Club. I was raised in the South Hills and pretty much just an average student. So, I am here to tell you that you can achieve things beyond your imagination **without** surrendering your honor and integrity. I am here to tell you this... and I'm not guessing!" – Rande Somma*

Begin First with Integrity

The scholarships sponsored by me and my wife, Georgia, are called "Integrity First." We offer four of these each year to deserving students at Robert Morris University Business School in Pittsburgh, Pennsylvania. Each year we review many essay submissions on a chosen topic that involves case studies where people are put in the difficult situation of choosing between honesty and integrity or the easy way out. We look for how students navigate these challenging situations. It is our belief that before anyone decides how they will accomplish something or process any decisions that they make, they have to make sure they have the guide rails of honor and integrity in place to keep them on the right course.

It may seem like a quiet, inconsequential and intangible aspect of your life and your career. You might believe it won't play a big role in your success, but I am here to tell you that this is the **only** aspect of your career that will mean anything in the end, its power unmatched by anything you can measure on a spreadsheet or in a bank account.

There's no app that you can download to your smart phone or your iPad that will define success for you. It's something you do through a collection of decisions and dealing with the many inevitable moments in your journey when you will be challenged to stay the course, or abort your integrity . . . . in other words, to sell out.

The Corporate Value of Ethics

Ethics has a connotation of compliance or consequences, like it's a speed limit of sorts. There is no reward for compliance, but there are penalties for non-conformance. The reality is that if you are true to your core values and work with integrity, it *adds value to the business*. You can be honest and make more money.

Does it take a whole different kind of philosophy on how to run a business? Yes. Does it take a whole different type of person to lead? Yes, it sure does. Everything is different when you do it morally, because you engage business with an ethical mindset, a different belief system. The way you engage your management, your workers, your customers, your vendors, your board of directors, your problems, your challenges, your successes is all different. This kind of leader sees themselves differently than the type of leader that is focused on a "win-at-any-cost" strategy, and because of that, people experience them differently.

Leaders that value results in numbers or metrics over everything, make everything expendable in order to achieve those results. People working under that value system feel secondary and disposable in the name of winning. Fear drives their behavior and their performance under that type of leadership. More importantly, it is unclear whether methods that are being implemented are held to a standard that match the corporate values. Boundaries are unclear. The company's future is unclear. Their personal future is unclear. This is a breeding ground for speculation and insecurity. Instead of feeling open and able to share, employees feel disassociated with their work in these conditions because they don't know if what they do matters. What is clear is they have no reason to trust their leaders who do not hold themselves to the same rules or standards.

An ethical and inclusive culture has components of transparency and integrity embodied in the leadership that is apparent to employees. They can relax when they know they can trust their leaders. They see what is going on; they are informed, they communicate, and they know they are part of the big picture of the company's efforts. They matter, and when they matter, they care. And when they care, they invest more effort, which in turn generates better results. This is the equation of the value of integrity.

Why is this compelling intellectually but limited in its implementation? Because it completely flies in the face of today's broken system. By following – I mean *really* following – the core values of the company with integrity, finding business solutions without simply chopping away at company assets will produce extraordinary results far beyond what can typically be achieved.

Erosion of the Rock Layer called Ethics

To me it seems there used to be a time in business when right and wrong were pretty clear. Now, because the standards seem to have fallen so low, and because the path of least resistance has been made so attractive and acceptable, simply choosing to do business in a more ethical way has become more difficult than it needs to be.

This inversion of values is confusing and puts good men and women outside the scope of consideration for leadership positions. We live in a time where acceptable business practices can include violation of rules, violation of ethics, and worst of all, selfish greed that is handsomely rewarded by the system. Short of violating the law, business conduct and transactions have become something of the Wild West. As long as a leader doesn't do anything "illegal" – or I should say as long as a leader doesn't get caught – their behavior is deemed acceptable as *"it's just business."* The worst part of this is that it has really given Capitalism a bad rap. No, greed is not good. Not one damn bit.

Pee in This Cup

Leadership quality should first be measured by a person's character. When investors purchase stock it is always recommended that they research the company, but investing also requires us to make assumptions that the reported earnings and revenue figures are honest and accurate, and that the leaders of that company are competent and honest. How is the average American stock purchaser supposed to know whether any of that is true? Enron, WorldCom and Tyco gave us all reasons to stop and consider that we are quite vulnerable when we do not know the truth.

I gave a talk right around the time when controversy over steroid use by baseball players was hot and heavy and there was discussion about going to Congress with it. It was also around the time of those three big companies caught in corporate financial fraud. I postulated, "Look, if the authenticity of home runs is so important that we make baseball players pee in a cup randomly, then when CEOs do their quarterly calls to Wall Street on their earnings, why are they not hooked up to polygraph machines?"

And everybody laughed. And I said, "Why are you laughing? Are the consequences of those home runs being enhanced somehow more important than the consequences of CEOs misrepresenting their business performance and then their bubble bursting? I submit Enron. I submit Tyco. I submit WorldCom. You probably haven't talked to any of those people who lost everything as a result of the corrupt and irresponsible behavior of those leaders."

Those three companies are certainly not the only ones that have swindled shareholders. In 1986, Emanuel Pinez, CEO of Centennial Technologies reported $2 million in revenue from PC memory cards, when it was really *shipping fruit baskets!* They manufactured fake documents to show sales, and Centennial's stock rose a staggering 451% on the New York Stock Exchange. They overstated earnings by $40 million, and once the fraud was discovered by the SEC, the stock plunged to less than $3. Over 20,000 people lost almost all their investment in a company who shipped fruit. From the very beginning, the company was designed to defraud investors, and Wall Street made it a darling.

And the list goes on and on: Barry Minkow, owner/founder of ZZZ Best Inc.; Bre-X Minerals of Canada, Richard Scrushy, CEO of HealthSouth; and who can forget Bernie Madoff, chairman and founder of the NASDAQ and founder of Bernard L. Madoff Investment Securities?

Leaders have been given something of a pass. They are in a position where they stand to personally make or lose a lot of money in stock options and bonus pay by steering their business toward a certain win...and they are not being scrutinized and held accountable enough for the numbers that they are submitting. They hold the fate of thousands of people in the palm of their hands. With that kind of power and responsibility, shouldn't we be more concerned? Shouldn't we demand more scrutiny?

There are some people that see a title, and by its very presence believe it decorates a really good person. Priests, doctors and other community and industry leaders hold a somewhat elevated profile with some folks who believe they must "know more" or are wiser or smarter than the average person. Their titles alone can elicit feelings of trust.

There are also a growing number of people who believe that anyone with a title cannot be trusted at all, that they are all frauds. Unfortunately, mistrust of all leaders seems all too common when you talk with people these days. And even more unfortunately, they have good reason for their mistrust.

Now what?

Is it apathy? Is it surrender? Is it the inability to envision the consequences of where this takes us all? I don't want to change the world entirely. I do want to wake people up. It seems that we are very off track with leadership and gathering traction and steam. I wish that we had corporate America's version of the ghost of Christmas future. It might help us all to see where our diminished value system is taking us.

Baseball is just a game. Compare the consequences of cheating at that game to the consequences of falsified or manufactured numbers reported by a CEO. Outcomes for Enron and others destroyed the lives of human beings. They lost everything; their jobs, their income, their marriages, their credit, their livelihoods, their retirement savings, their homes. There are also the intangible losses generated from stress and anxiety that cannot be quantified like peace of mind, self-esteem, family harmony, security, and a good night's sleep.

The cheating, lying, and stealing with cooked books of publicly traded companies literally impact the future of thousands, perhaps hundreds of thousands, of people and families. Isn't that worth checking to make sure that those numbers are authentic? Isn't that every bit as important as peeing in a cup to make sure a home run is real?

Even if numbers are not falsified, isn't it just as concerning if they are a reflection of the proficiency of the accountants, rather than the proficiency of the business? Shouldn't we verify that good results in the numbers were a direct function of healthy, robust methods and practices, rather than shortcuts and the path of least resistance?

Authentic leadership is becoming a lost skill because it is not needed or valued any more. In some cases it is not wanted any more. Are boards holding leaders accountable? In the context of the day-to-day operations, they don't even know what is going on 90% of the time. They meet a couple times a year, check off their boxes and are satisfied with the spreadsheets. Done. Let's do lunch. They don't ask how results were achieved. Leaders are not always being asked by their boards to create a sustainable process or culture. They are being asked to hit numbers consistently.

We have had so many disappointments from this type of short-sighted leadership. Interventions with regulation have had temporary success, but they are reactions more than preventions. Think of it this way: one guy got on a plane with a bomb in his shoe, and now everyone has to take their shoes off for airport security. While TSA is busy examining all the shoes, terrorists are simply coming up with new ways to circumvent them. It is the same with corporate leaders. There are regulations designed to thwart fraudulent activity, but where there is a will (and millions of dollars to be made) there is a way. What is really preventing us from getting "Enronned" again? Perhaps we already are getting Enronned and don't know it yet.

Make Character Part of the Process

I was having coffee with a long-time acquaintance who is an executive for an international executive search firm. He does a lot of CEO searches. I asked, "You do a lot of interviewing for CEO positions. Do you have a section in your interview where you at least make an attempt through some methodology to vet the candidate for the depth of their character?"

I was asking him if his firm investigates how deeply rooted the character and belief systems of the leadership candidates are to determine if they can withstand the temptations of the position. In other words, would they walk away from the money, power and celebrity rather than conform to an unethical, immoral or corrupt culture?

I said, "I understand that is much more of an intangible than a GPA or an IQ score, or the number of jobs they had as a VP, president or CEO, but don't you think you should at least try to get an idea of the type of person they are?"

He looked at me and said, "I totally agree with you, and a way to fully measure those intangible traits just doesn't exist. It isn't asked or even talked about." He did add that there seems to be an emerging interest in trying to get at those answers and that some search companies are investing more in assessment tools and methodologies that would evaluate a candidate's character.

It is my opinion that in the corporate leadership system, the "bad guys" and "wrong guys" now outnumber the "good guys" and "right guys," and they are getting much smarter about deception. The system has made it easier for them too, as high standards, oversight and assuring compliance have shifted to an agenda of tolerance and even acceptance or just straight-up disregard of bad behavior.

While there are structured interview questions that test a candidate's principles, unfortunately, there isn't a fully comprehensive and full proof test that you can give people to determine whether they are going to do the right thing in any given situation. Even if there was such a test and you could find honest leaders with integrity, you would have to keep giving them the test as a guard against a system so skewed that over time, even the most honest and forthright leaders can be tempted to sell out. I know. I've seen it.

And considering that this is a systemic issue, what good are character screening tests if they are meaningless to those doing the hiring? If leadershit cultures already administer morale surveys that they have no intention of using; if they put out suggestion boxes for suggestions that they have no intention of reading, why would we expect them to hold potential leadership applicants to a character test? You have to wonder if you can fix the leadershit problem this way without first eradicating existing leadership and/or boards and starting with a clean slate.

It is not easy to tell who might be seduced to leadershit. When a leader has had many solid wins and they win all the time (because they rob the company's long term success for short term gains and leave before the shit hits the fan – I'm looking at you, Welch), people come to expect them to always win. But it doesn't work that way in real life. In real life there are ups and downs; wins and losses; victories and defeats. We all experience setbacks. It's called life.

In order to overcome a setback, some leaders are willing to bend the rules and get to the right numbers the wrong way. But you cannot tell who is doing that because they all say the right thing. The terrorist getting on the airplane doesn't strap the dynamite to their forehead either.

The Checks and Imbalances

When you look into things that are supposed to be preventive, like oversight by boards of directors and whistleblowers, those don't always necessarily work either. Nobody wants to suffer the consequences of standing up against the status quo, even if the status quo is corrupt. The stakes are too high.

I spoke to an acquaintance familiar with the SEC. We were discussing SEC regulations that are in place to check publicly traded company numbers. Accounting firms generally do the best they can, however, if a corporation is intent on deceiving their accounting firm, they can sometimes get away with it by burying things in the numbers.

So the SEC is the next line of defense against this sort of corruption. The SEC can do one of two things: check the quality of the numbers before fraud is discovered – which is a detection or preventive component in the accounting – or they have the forensic accounting – which is called the autopsy – that happens after a company is caught with bad accounting. So they either check that it is pure as it is going on, or it blows up and they go in to do the full autopsy to find out why.

What I learned from my acquaintance that was familiar with the SEC processes is that so many resources are sucked up by forensic autopsy accounting that they don't have anyone left to do the prevention/detection. In other words, a lot of people are being deceptive and trying to get away with it. Prevention is being left behind as the SEC devotes time and personnel to reacting to the damage of the leadershits.

It is not difficult to produce clean numbers once you have a system in place. Lying complicates everything. When I was running Johnson Controls North America, I knew that we were running clean financial numbers. While other companies needed weeks to organize and justify expenses and revenue, we were so clean that we were closing our books within only a few days after the end of each month. North America alone was an $8 billion revenue stream. An added bonus to running clean numbers is that we didn't have to keep track of any bullshit. I'm here to tell you that the truth works just fine. The truth has teeth. It is sustainable. And it is easier than lying.

And eliminating bullshit eliminates the desire for corporate leaders to fudge numbers.

Helping Others Careen Down the Mountain

I watch the winter Olympics, and even though I don't ski, I am fascinated by the slalom skiers. They would run the course and once they arrived at the bottom, the skier who just finished would get on a radio with a teammate who was at the top of the course waiting their turn to come down. The skier at the bottom of the course would tell the teammate at the top to watch out for soft snow on certain turns, watch their speed at certain places on the course, and watch for bumps and other hazards. They had made the journey, they knew where the pitfalls were, and they were passing that information along to their teammate in the hopes that they would be able to better navigate the course and avoid the same difficulties.

I left Johnson Controls in 2003. I thankfully was offered opportunities to join other leadership teams. I received calls from former customers, partners and analysts. Other companies invited me to be part of their leadership team. Despite all of these wonderful invitations to come on board with other big corporations, my separation from JCI was difficult and I was not ready to dive back into corporate America.

I thought that maybe my purpose is better served if I double back down the path that I followed for 30+ years and talk to those who are getting ready to set off on their career journeys. I wanted to give students and young leaders some idea of what they may encounter as they grow in their professional world.

After three companies, six cities, being chairman of a corporate board, a vice chair of a corporate board, and a member of three other boards, for-profit, non-profit, really big ones, and not so big ones, I haven't seen everything, but I have seen about as much of business as any one person can pack into a lifetime.

In talking to the students at universities, I encourage them to truly try to understand the bridge from the academic *knowledge* to the on-the-ground *application* of knowledge in the job. There are subtle but compelling dynamics that everyone experiences as they make that transition in the beginning of a career.

A student's readiness and ability to orient and integrate with a company is a big challenge. My ambition in working with the universities has been to prepare students for the reality of the workplace by showing them how to apply their learned skills and giving them a glimpse of the world that they are about to enter.

Perhaps there isn't a lot of information that I can convey with respect to leadership and business that students haven't heard in some context before. What I think I can help clarify is what bits of information are theories, which are myths, and which need their close attention. Here is what really matters:

Integrity matters. Pay close attention to integrity.

Integrity is a characteristic that will buoy a person's reputation and deliver them through the most difficult of professional situations. People only want to work with people they know they can trust. If professionals lose that trust, they lose their reputation, and they lose the ability to convince people that they are trustworthy. And if they lose that, they may eventually lose everything.

The Parable of the Seed - Plant Today, Reap Tomorrow

A successful business man was growing old and knew it was time to choose a successor to take over the business. Instead of choosing one of his directors or his children, he decided to do something different.

He called all his young executives in his company together and said, "It is time for me to step down and choose the next CEO. I have decided to choose one of you." The young executives were shocked. Their leader continued. "I am going to give each one of you a seed today - one very special seed. I want you to plant the seed, water it, and come back here one year from today with what you have grown from the seed I have given you. I will judge the plants that you bring back, and the one I choose will be the next CEO."

One man named Jim was there that day and he, like the others, received a seed. He went home and excitedly told his wife the story. She helped him get a pot, soil and compost and he planted the seed. Every day, he would water his seed and watch to see if it had grown.

After about three weeks, some of the other executives began to talk about their seeds and the plants that were beginning to grow. Jim kept checking his seed, but nothing ever grew. Three weeks, four weeks, five weeks went by, still nothing. By now, all the others were talking about their plants, but Jim didn't have a plant and he felt like a failure.

Six months went by -- still nothing in Jim's pot. He just knew he had killed his seed. Everyone else had trees and tall plants, but he had nothing. Jim didn't say anything to his colleagues, however, he just kept watering and fertilizing the soil - he so wanted the seed to grow.

A year finally went by and all the young executives of the company brought their plants to the CEO for inspection. Jim told his wife that he wasn't going to take an empty pot. But she asked him to be honest about what happened. Jim felt sick to his stomach, it was going to be the most embarrassing moment of his life, but he knew his wife was right, so he took his empty pot to the board room.

When Jim arrived, he was amazed at the variety of plants grown by the other executives. They were beautiful, and in all shapes and sizes. Jim put his empty pot on the floor and many of his colleagues laughed, a few felt sorry for him! When the CEO arrived, he surveyed the room and greeted his young executives. Jim just tried to hide in the back.

"My, what great plants, trees and flowers you have grown," said the CEO. "Today one of you will be appointed the next CEO!" All of a sudden, the CEO spotted Jim at the back of the room with his empty pot. He ordered the Financial Director to bring him to the front. Jim was terrified. He thought, "The CEO knows I'm a failure. Maybe he will have me fired!"

When Jim got to the front, the CEO asked him what had happened to his seed - Jim told him the story. The CEO asked everyone to sit down except Jim. He looked at Jim, and then announced to the young executives, "Behold your next Chief Executive Officer." Jim couldn't believe it. He couldn't even grow his seed. How could he be the new CEO?

Then the CEO said, "One year ago today, I gave everyone in this room a seed. I told you to take the seed, plant it, water it, and bring it back to me today. But I gave you all boiled seeds; they were dead - it was not possible for them to grow. All of you, except Jim, have brought me trees and plants and flowers. When you found that the seed would not grow, you substituted another seed for the one I gave you. Jim was the only one with the courage and honesty to bring me a pot with my seed in it. Therefore, he is the one who is qualified to be the new Chief Executive Officer."

Plant *honesty* and you will reap *trust*.

Integrity is Deeply Personal

I am not asking leaders to do something simple. All leaders are tested, and tempted A LOT. It is hard to consistently and confidently maintain integrity. Leaders who do, who achieve success the right way, will have something that is so deeply valuable that no amount of money can buy; that is a pride and unwavering confidence in *who you are as a leader and as a person.* You will have your self-respect, your dignity......your authentic you.

Leaders leave a legacy and they don't get a do-over. In the end, when all is said and done, a leader's honor, integrity and reputation are all that really matters.

"People will forget what you said. People will forget what you did. But people will never forget how you made them feel." – Maya Angelou

CHAPTER 11
DISMANTLING LEADERSHIT
WHEN APATHY IS NOT AN OPTION

Hitting Below the Belt and Ringing My Liberty Bell

Harry Reid, a senior U.S. Senator serving as Senate Minority Leader, and arguably one of the most powerful people in our country, essentially admitted that he lied on the Senate floor when he stated that Mitt Romney had not paid taxes for a decade. The bogus claim created a media frenzy and earned Reid a "pants on fire" rating from PolitiFact and a "Four Pinocchio" rating from Washington Post Fact Checker, Glenn Kessler. He lied.

Kessler wrote that Reid should "hold himself to a high standard of accuracy when making claims about political opponents."

Reid is probably not the only one on Capitol Hill who has stooped this low. I suspect that most Americans are a little suspicious if not downright jaded about the honesty and integrity of our government leaders on both sides of the aisle.

When confronted with the fact that he lied on the Senate floor, Reid expressed no regret or apology for his lie. End of story. What effect did this have on Reid's position in the Senate? None.

Part of what has silently drifted away is consequences for leaders. There are few consequences for this type of bad behavior. In fact, bad behavior might get you more air time, so in many instances it works in your favor. As a society, we let this happen. We promote it by being spectators to it. Is this apathy? I think it might be that we haven't yet figured out a fix for this. I believe that if people had an off switch, other than the TV remote, or a way that we could stop such bad behavior, many people would make the effort to go throw that switch. I believe that people just don't know what to do in the face of bad leadership, so we fall into apathy, while our resentment and distrust grows.

I use Harry Reid as my example, but this applies to many leaders in our country: If Harry Reid was a CEO who worked for you, in your company, he would likely have been escorted him out of the building by security that day. But not only did that not happen in the Senate, it is not so clear it would happen in business either. How did we get to a place where this is ok?

Surrender

It seems that anyone can get sued for anything now. It also seems that you can find a regulation for just about anything now. So there is all this complexity built into our system to protect us from assholes, and it adds a lot to the cost of business in this country, but you can only legislate or regulate morality to a certain level, and bad people will always find a way to navigate around it. The bad guys are winning.

This is a bigger problem than we are really appreciating. Honest people with integrity are walking away from the fight because they are so far in the minority now that if they stand up for what's right, they risk getting their face kicked in. In other words, consequences are now doled out to the good guys instead of the bad guys.

Robert Morris University has a speaker series and invited Olympia Snowe, the former Senator from Maine who voluntarily stepped down from the Senate in 2013. I was very impressed with her. She was an eloquent speaker who talked about the country's leaders having the wrong agenda for the wrong purpose, and how it's all broken. She said 'I can't just go along with it, and I can't fix it.' So she left the Senate frustrated.

She wrote in an article in the Washington Post: *"I have spoken on the floor of the Senate for years about the dysfunction and political polarization in the institution. Simply put, the Senate is not living up to what the Founding Fathers envisioned."* [March 1, 2012, Olympia Snowe: Why I'm Leaving the Senate]

She feels defeated by a toxic and corrupt leadership system. She is not alone. The whole thing from politicians to corporate America and from top to bottom is messed up in mammoth proportions. One at a time, the good guys who are trying to do the right thing are giving up, surrendering and leaving or being thrown out the back door. What will bring them back?

Back to Basics

If we back up and really look at the scene from a distance, it seems to me that we are trying to force people to be "good" and do the right thing by motivating, incentivizing and punishing them with things that are essentially "external forces." While everyone has probably made some poor choices in their lives, it is not something that most of us will continue to do in the face of consequences. If those consequences are exclusively outside of someone's character, we have to rely on regulations, laws and other external systems to catch and punish them. That is costly, burdensome and exhausting and obviously it is not working. As our principles drop out of the equation, our prisons fill up.

On the other hand, if those consequences are internalized in the form of guilt or shame, the poor choice or bad deed may not even be attempted. When I look up the word integrity, I am struck by the definition and the synonyms: *"The quality of being honest and having strong moral principles; moral uprightness." Synonyms: good character, honesty, decency, trustworthiness, scrupulousness and honor."*

Imagine a world where this type of character could be counted on in all of our leaders.

These principles begin early. The long-term fix is an effort that needs to come from everyone. We all need to take a part of the responsibility to turn the system around. The effort must come from leaders on all fronts, from parents to presidents.

Ethical Dilemma

Some of the biggest mistakes I made in my own career were decisions that I knew deep down inside were wrong, but I wanted them to be right. It would work out best or easiest for me if they could be considered right.

But leaders doing that are not being honest with themselves. They are rationalizing their decisions, but they are really full of crap.

If you are one of these people – and be honest with yourself here – if you are one of these leaders, get yourself a mentor; someone who will keep you in check and keep you honest. And for heaven's sake, don't let your ego screw that up.

Chrysler, like most of the automakers, had an entertainment policy. This is a policy about suppliers and vendors treating their decision-making managers and purchasers to dinners, shows, sporting events and other entertainment venues. Their policy, in a nutshell, was "don't."

One year we sent some Chrysler guys off to the big Final Four playoffs in Seattle and then a side trip to Pebble Beach to play golf. We didn't just ignore the Chrysler entertainment policy; we blew it to shreds to give these guys this trip. I knew all along what their entertainment policy was at the time. I knew that we were abusing that policy and that it was wrong. The Chrysler guys knew it was wrong too, but they took that trip.

To make matters worse, the tragic outcome was that it cost two people at Chrysler their careers. They didn't get fired, but there were sanctions as well as that black mark on their record. They were punished, but in truth, they legitimately had it coming.

I didn't go on the trip, but as the head of sales, I approved it. I had some knowledge that the choice I was making was wrong. It was not an innocent mistake. Next thing you know, I am getting this phone call from the Vice President of Business Affairs from Chrysler. I think I may have involuntarily soiled my underwear a little when I took that phone call. I did not know a VP of Business Affairs even existed before that day. Well, it did and he was *pissed*.

Those guys at Chrysler who went on the trip we paid for got in deep trouble. On the other hand, apart from sitting through that unpleasant phone call, I did not get in deep trouble because in my business, this was one of those things that were expected of us to remain competitive. In this case, unfortunately, it was found out and it hurt people.

Where it gets really complicated – not to excuse anything – is we had customers who asked us to do these things for them. They asked us for favors all the time, and they expected us to go against entertainment policies and do things for them. And these people were decision-makers. They could choke off our revenue stream with one phone call. All of the suppliers were in this same pickle with the Detroit Three. We were all providing entertainment on the side even though it wasn't permitted by the automakers.

The fear of losing millions or billions of dollars kept all of us seducing auto executives with steak dinners and premier seats at events. It was an ethical dilemma. This was the culture, and the culture was flying in the face of rules and values. Boundaries became fuzzy and things were somewhat up for interpretation for all parties, and that is never a good set up.

So even though I approved the trip for the Chrysler execs, and even though I knew it was wrong, I also understood that it was normal, even expected. It was part of our competitive business model to gain and sustain business from the Detroit Three.

This particular event in my history is memorable because people's careers were in jeopardy and their futures were on the line when Chrysler found out about it. That got my attention. I never wanted to be responsible for anyone losing their job or crippling their career. It woke me up. I learned that if bad is normal, then shit happens.

And yes, if everybody is cheating, it is *still cheating*. And it is *still cheating* even if you don't get caught.

Where Do We Turn?

While we would put a lot of attention on the type of "smart" demonstrated by a resume full of credentials and accolades, I contend that this needs to be a lower priority when it comes to choosing a leader because a leader leads people. A CEO with an MBA may or may not have that ability, and none of those lettered credentials reveal whether one has an aptitude for working with people.

Also, getting a 4.0 in a business class is important only after we know they didn't cheat on the exam. Unfortunately, I believe we have reached a point in our collective experiences over the recent past where it might be considered reckless to assume results like grades or quarterly profits are a function of legitimate performance.

Someone who can influence and inspire people is the person we are looking for. Someone who has unshakable integrity and tenacity and purpose is the person we are looking for. Someone who works hard and treats every worker like they matter as much as he/she does—this is who we are looking for. Someone whose people volunteer to walk through walls for them – that is the leader that we are looking for.

So in assessing the candidates, we need to find out what each of them believes, and then we need to figure out if they mean it, because if they are good enough to be on your short list, they are smart enough to know what they should say and how to act. They may or may not be a selfish asshole, but they are not stupid enough to reveal it to you when you evaluate their leadership potential.

CRAZY AND NOT SO CRAZY

I always told my staff that if they spot a problem or need something changed, feel free to come to me to discuss it, but don't arrive without at least a suggestion as to what the solution might be.

I have laid out the problems with our leadershit model in the previous chapters. Following my own advice, I wanted to devote some time to offering up some possible solutions. While I contend that focusing on embedding virtues in our children is a good long term solution to the leadershit problem, I believe we need some more short term and direct solutions, as well.

I have an ability to tackle and solve pretty complicated problems. I enjoy figuring things out. My bosses were quick to figure this out about me. Back when I was a buyer at what was then an axle plant in Winchester, Kentucky, the Purchasing Manager would send so many assignments to me with the note, "Rande...Handle," that the other buyers gave me the nickname 'Rande Handle'.

Even so, I am not fooling myself that I can stop or even slow the progression of leadershit. What I maybe can do, though, is to spark some conversations and maybe start folks really considering what we can do going forward to turn this around and point us all in the direction of higher expectations for ourselves and for our leaders. We need to uninstall the low character leadershit model and implant one that values humility, empathy, honesty and integrity.

Some of the ideas that I offer here that can be done to correct our course may not be completely practical and may be a bit (only a bit) facetious, or even radical. The point of it all is this: my ideas for solutions to leadershit problems are really a reflection of how broken I know the system is.

Check List for Flight

Whether an airplane pilot is on the job for one day or for 20 years, they have a flight check list that they go through every single time they prepare for takeoff. Every time. Every flight. Without fail. Why? Because human beings have the potential to forget things. They cannot leave anything to chance because the stakes are so high.

Now that we have established how high the stakes are for leadership in this country, we should be willing to adapt similar routine system checks that our "pilots," or leaders, be required to perform. Is it really too much to ask that every morning before a CEO begins work, they be required to click onto their website and read everything in their mission statement, their core values and everything else that describes who you are and how you do business and what values you are committed to practice?

Shouldn't they be required to regularly re-read their full job description, which describes the leader's roles, responsibilities and obligations to the company and its people, vendors, customers and shareholders?

Yes, and then make sure they DO IT!

PED Tests for CEOs

We need to invent a reliable test to measure a person's character. My experience in today's business culture convinces me that it is more important to know what a leader will refuse to do to get metric results than what they will do. It may sound far-fetched, but the business character version of performance enhancing drug (PED) testing would be very helpful. If reliable, objective scientific testing could be developed and done and published for hiring CEOs, chairmen and board members, revealing their character score, we might all sleep better. This could then be repeated annually on a random basis and published with the annual report.

No More BFFs

It would be helpful if we could have a board's nominating committee sign affidavits stating under penalty of perjury that a chairperson or board member being recommended to shareholders for election was not referred to them and/or personally endorsed by the CEO. If the nominated chairperson or board member does not know the CEO, the opportunity for them to work without undue influence under that relationship is more in alignment with protecting shareholder interests.

See No Evil, Hear No Evil

Board members need to stop hiding behind "plausible deniability." They have to stop claiming that any bit of criticism or interference with management by them is impermissible micromanaging. These are mere excuses for avoiding difficult situations that arise. This type of oversight is a bullshit excuse for disregarding their real duty to protect shareholder interests.

The board's job is oversight. There is a fine line for board members between oversight and being too involved in the company's operations. But it is wrong to pull the "micromanaging card" when a board member wants more information about the very things they are required to oversee. That is not micromanaging, it is due diligence.

No Trails of Fails

If a person was on the executive leadership team of a company that filed for bankruptcy during his/her tenure, or within a five-year period after their departure, they are not qualified to serve on the board of directors of any public company board. This may be very unfair to some, but why would shareholders trust that person to know when a company's operations are being run well? How could shareholders be sure that person would even know what well-run operations looked like?

Your Time is Up. Get Out.

As I mentioned earlier, limiting board terms is a good idea to preserve objectivity of the board members, and to keep them working for the shareholders, not for the chairman. Maximum should be two terms or six years.

Also ensure their pay does not exceed the value of the time, effort and skill required for this part-time job. Issuing stock could still be allowed, but only if the vesting period triggers five years after the board member leaves the board. This might incentivize more attention be paid to the long term health of the culture, leadership succession planning and managing the business and not the results, and maybe, just maybe, the future would hold some relevance.

Pants on Fire

Doesn't it make sense to verify the numbers represented by a CEO to shareholders and to Wall Street every quarter? Shouldn't we strive for the truth of how the business is being run? Wouldn't it make sense to avoid being "Enronned" and having the lives of so many human beings destroyed in the wake of corporate incompetence or corruption? If it is important enough to take urine samples to verify homeruns, and if it is important enough to make everyone disrobe before getting on an airplane to ensure everyone's safety, isn't it also important to validate the authenticity of a CEOs and CFOs by hooking them to a polygraph machine with every earnings report release?

What I might suggest we do is wire CEO and CFO candidates to polygraph machines during the interview process as a way to asses that they are who they say they are. Results might help corporations avoid hiring a smart and experienced leader who is also an irresponsible, self-centered jagoff.

People instinctively chuckled when I proposed that, but I am serious. Without a method of validation that specifically calls them out, we are saying that we trust what every CEO tells us. And I know that is not true for me. And I also know that many of us have developed a very jaded and distrustful viewpoint of leadership. I am sure that I am not the only one who wants to challenge that and change it.

I can understand complacency around this issue in the '80s and '90s, but how can anyone in this day and age not have built up some suspicion around leadership after all the corporate disasters? Only a fool wouldn't believe that there are more that we just haven't caught yet.

The terrorist knows to keep a low profile, blend in and not look like a guy who is going to blow the plane up. He knows how to act and what to say to avoid detection. Don't you think any leader who is looking to simply "ride" the system rather than build a corporate culture of success would know the same thing? When are we going to snap out of this and change our approach to hiring leaders?

20 Questions

Wall Street analysts are generally employed with a brokerage firm and may be assigned to specific clients of the firm. Their purpose is to protect the best interests of their clients, offering advice on investing strategies and advising customers on market conditions and market trends that could impact clients' portfolios. There were several who came around JCI when I was employed there. They would interview us to find out how we were doing and what we were forecasting.

In my experience, it has been far too simple for CEOs of publicly traded companies to slip through the questioning of the Wall Street analysts. Many CEOs are relieved when they finish discussing the corporate financial results in their quarterly earnings teleconference call or webcast and nobody asked them quite the right questions that would reveal the deep dark truth about what is really going on under those numbers. They answer in half-truths and sidestep sticky issues.

This kind of evasive action can be avoided if Wall Street analysts are trained how to approach these quarterly earnings reports and what questions to ask to get the real answers.

When public companies do their quarterly earnings call, Wall Street analysts should ask questions in the following categories while the CEO and CFO are connected to a polygraph machine:

- 20% of their questioning is to focus on the current year financial performance
- 30% of their questioning is to find out the methods of exactly how the numbers were generated. Were they generated consistent with the company's core values? Are they sustainable?
- 20% of their questions should focus on the tangible progress and investment in the company's five-year vision plan
- 30% of questioning should focus on status and progress on a plan to improve employee responses to "do you believe in and trust your leadership?"

A CEO's annual performance review should reflect similar categories and weighting. By guiding the analysts toward these questions, CEOs are forced to address foundational issues within the business that can reveal the true health and vibrancy of a company. As a side note, corporate valuation should be made using these same metrics.

Trust Test

CEO performance review is traditionally done by the board of directors. The audit committee of the board that is tied to compliance with the SEC (the government), in addition to their financial auditing, should do a third-party employee morale survey. This would serve to measure the organization's cultural center of gravity, which ultimately impacts the financial health of the company. The audit committee should ask employees the following questions:

1. Do you believe in and trust your leadership?
   A. Yes
   B. No
   C. I don't know
2. Rank the following motivators 1 through 3 for the time and effort you put into your job:
   A. Meet boss's expectations (don't get fired)
   B. Get a good review, get a raise and be promotable
   C. Don't let my team or management down

For question #1, if over 50% answer (B) or (C), and if the highest ranking answer for question #2 is (A), fire the CEO. They are not trusted by those they supposedly lead, and that will end badly if they stay.

Employees are there every day immersed in that system. They are the only ones who know what is going on. They are invaluable resources for determining a CEO's behavior, whether their leader walks the talk, sets the example in adhering to company values, how they treat others and the decisions they make.

Every leader needs their team. Authentic leaders know that and value their team. Don't you think if people are sincerely valued, the better they will feel, and the more productive they would be? So if we can gauge and track the morale of the workers, and we can elevate it, we can make more money. Very few CEOs are connecting those dots. They are more focused on the spreadsheet.

Bonus Block

I recently heard a story about a village that was overrun with rats. So the town's leaders put a bounty on killing rats. People were paid for every rat tail that they brought in. In response to this reward system, some of the folks in the village began breeding rats. More rats meant more rat tails which meant more money. In the end, the village went broke and they were overrun with more rats than when they started out.

This story illustrates the clear problem with a bonus system. People do not always choose the path of integrity to achieve a reward. Attempting to incentivize people to do the right thing usually doesn't work. The best reward systems are embedded within a person's character, where the hardwiring guides the choice between right and wrong.

"As far as I know, nobody's bonus has any component in the calculation based on what you did to prevent something bad from happening. There is no money to be made in preventing something bad from happening, but there is a hell of a lot of money they will pay you to fix it." **– Rande Somma**

I would eliminate all bonuses. Money drives behavior – bad behavior and deception – and most of those bonuses come with a price. They get something done to achieve a bonus and they throw about ten babies out with the bathwater in the process. The collateral damage is worth much more than whatever value is accomplished with a bonus as bait. Nobody is disincentivizing leaders from that collateral damage. They are only incentivizing the target.

Organizations could do a lot to stem the bad behavior by simply paying good wages and benefits; reward quality people/performers through merit and promotional increases. Forget the bonuses.

I don't care whether your numbers are the highest they have ever been during your tenure as CEO. If you set the stage for a collapse by mortgaging the company's future to decorate your tenure, we will know if we wait. Stock shares granted for leaders should vest no sooner than five years after the CEO and chairperson leave the company. If a company does give a bonus or discretionary pay, the CEO should not receive that bonus until five years after they are gone. This would give us an opportunity to find out whether there was a grenade or two that the CEO pulled all the pins for the benefit of short term gain, and then high-tailed it out of there. If the measure of the organization's health is good five years following their departure, they receive their bonus.

That one domino has the power to change every decision that those leaders make.

Another way to force leaders in the auto industry in particular to work for long term sustainable future of their company is to have car companies place all bonus structure on the residual value of their vehicles built during the tenure of that leader; what are they worth in the used car market.

As a guy who used to run a company that made the major interior systems for the Detroit Three as well as other car companies, I believe this is a necessary idea whose time has come, so that consumers are no longer the ones picking up the tab for crappy vehicles. Responsibility for the product's long term value and performance would remains where it belongs if leader compensation is tied to it in this way.

Weighting System for Leadership Selection

It is a very interesting process when boards, advisors, stakeholders and consultants all get together to noodle on the selection process of a leader of an organization. I have been included in on this several times in my career. I am sure I am not the only one who has thought of this, but it is my opinion that a weighting system should be developed and put in place to help with qualifying leaders. Some recruiting companies may have something like this in place already. I also believe there should be a sequential component of qualifying.

For me, number one is the quality of the character of the person – and there would be an entire definition of what "quality" means so that it is not left up to discretion. A "quality" leader means different things to different people. It is very true that one person's treasure is another person's trash. Criteria need to be set in stone for character. This would include the usual suspects that are missing in leadership today, including integrity, honesty and humility, to name a few.

Standards also need to be identified and established as context for a weighting system, as well. What standards are being used to measure against? This would help to define the context of the quality of leader that is being sought and chosen in any particular industry or business, and help to establish the framework for consistency in the weights.

My Bad

We all have that piece of paper that conveys our career history and some relevant and glorious details about the great person that we are, both personally and professionally. Resumes are the first go-to criteria that recruiters look at when selecting leadership candidates. They have to check some boxes to make sure candidates clear the first high hurdle. That's fine.

My issue with resumes is that they paint an unbalanced picture of a person. It tells you everything that they did *right*. I feel that it would be very worthwhile to also know what they did wrong. How did they fail? Failure is part of the learning curve for leadership, so it should be built into the hiring model from the first step.

If you are choosing someone – especially if they are a sitting CEO already – your rationale is that they have already suffered through the learning curve of being a CEO, saving you the trouble. But you don't know if they *really* have or not. Maybe their COO or CFO really ran the show. Or perhaps their secretary made all the big decisions.

I realize that the interview process sometimes asks about past mistakes, but I propose a required section in your resume that lists past mistakes and details about how you handled them and what you learned. I also believe that a viable candidate needs to have three of these solid "Loss Lessons" in order to qualify for leadership. This would tell the recruiter and the board exactly what aspects of leadership you have dealt with, what fires you have put out, and what fires you have walked through to earn your wings as a qualified CEO.

Certify It

With regard to mistakes, of course individual CEOs won't make enough mistakes to learn everything. Things have to go right sometimes. But those painful lessons of failure hold a lot of value. What if all those mistakes and the corrective measures could be aggregated into a course for aspiring leaders to learn about actual mistakes and corrections that others made? Leaders could learn them by proxy without actually doing it themselves. This could be made into an independent certification course.

Many states require lawyers to take continuing education classes, and specifically classes in ethics, in order to maintain their licenses, or just to stay current in the changing landscape. I like this idea for business leaders as well.

Speaking of certification, the qualifications for leadership for many companies are not sufficiently strict, severe, or careful. You have to pass a test to adopt a cat from a shelter these days. I don't think it is unreasonable to ask that our leaders answer a few questions with regard to a required certification process. Many leaders are required to have their MBA in order to qualify for an executive level position. I am not talking about that. I am talking about *required* certification. Ongoing testing; *required* continuing Education Units, like the ones everyone else is required to take on a regular basis in order to remain current in their various industries.

Some companies already require some ongoing education and there are voluntary certifications for CEOs, but I am talking about required regulated certification. Let's raise this bar a little bit.

www.idon'twanttoworkforaliar.com

Corporate websites need to be audited by an independent organization that checks the "walk" against the "talk". There is just too much of a gap between what is said and what actually is going on behind closed doors. If there really is something in place regarding truth in advertising, then let's expose it. A rating system can be put in place with the audit: Walks the Talk = 1, and Full of Shit = 5.

SOME OBSERVATIONS

When our ancestors came to this country, many of them were very simply in search of an opportunity for their family. An opportunity to work hard, earn an honest living and provide their children and grandchildren with a better start than what they had. They were proud and happy to be part of the American workforce. Their focus was not only on themselves. They were committed to providing opportunities for their successors. It was all about their family's future. What's more, they were in a "have-to" situation, arriving with little to rely on other than their wits and various acquired skills.

Americans can disrupt the selfish pattern and trends toward immediate gratification rooting in our culture; however, we need to consciously shift from being reactionary to being preventive and focusing more on the greater good instead of on "what's-in-it-for-me".

With that said, unless we get our collective heads out of our collective, soft, apathetic and self-centered asses, the greater good could well be the greater bad . . . really bad.

Make Me

It doesn't matter whether it is Johnson Controls or a lemonade stand, there are certain fundamentals that need to be established and adhered to if you really want an organization to be good. Making excuses and hiding is a way for leaders to escape the hard work of establishing and adhering to those fundamentals. Excuses are simply code for "I don't want to do it," and "I don't have to do it," and "I don't want to work that hard." What they are really saying, "You can't make me".

I have been a business consultant now for many years, and even though organizations hire me to come in and tell them how they can improve their operations, they can become defensive and rigid when I actually do what I am being paid to do. I think they are all for the positive changes we discuss, until they find out that it takes some risk, some time, and a lot of work to achieve them. And at the same time, nothing is really incentivizing them to change. The status quo is acceptable. Work-arounds are easier. Containment services are available.

You can always hear these escape hatches opening in conversations with leaders when we get around to culture and morale. These are the ones who are not interested in doing things the right way. They say things like, "You don't think results matter. You want me to ignore the results and just manage the means." Just the way they flip the conversation is an indicator that they don't really want to listen or look at a different way.

In leadershit, it is a choice between priorities. Somehow, when standards were lowered, mandates became choices. Authentic leadership does not recognize those as choices. Authentic leaders answer the following questions like this:

- Focus on the business operations or the results? Answer: Yes.
- Focus on the people/culture or shareholder expectations? Answer: Yes.
- Focus on short or long term objectives? Answer: Yes.
- Focus on social responsibility or profitability? Answer: Yes.
- Focus on morale or on the numbers? Answer: Yes.
- Focus on innovation or execution? Answer: Yes.

A leader's center of gravity should always be aligned with managing the business fundamentals instead of the numbers.

Really the only solution is that the system has to be completely reinvented. Higher standards must become a priority again. To flip the critical mass to make that happen involves creating legitimate ways to give leaders a kick in the ass and hold them accountable. Lowering of standards didn't happen overnight, and flipping it back will not be instant or quick either. It could take decades to force leaders to comply and "make them" do the right thing. I don't know if we have that kind of time before the real wrath of what we are doing to our economy, our country and its citizens hits us.

The Cheese Stands Alone

There are a lot of people out there – I have met many of them – who do the right thing because it is all they know how to do. They are hardwired to react in difficult situations with honor and integrity. With business standards and the entire system geared to serve those who don't want the system to change, principled people are soundly punished for their stance. I am referring to leaders who punish whistleblowers, obstruct unwelcome change management, and ostracize others for going against the grain of unethical, immoral and even corrupt corporate cultures.

The net/net of this is upside down.

How do you flip it back when it is so risky to stand alone in these circumstances? How do you push back on it? How do you fix this and shift the critical mass back to where it belongs when so many people are profiting from it being broken? When those profiting in power and money will use it to stop you, to sabotage and retaliate against your efforts?

When people with integrity and principles find out that their employer is doing something bad, wrong or illegal, they sometimes decide to step up and tell someone. Many times they are naïve to the fact that the issue is being perpetuated the "wrong" way on purpose in order for those leaders at the top to profit, and they walk right into a nightmare of persecution.

People who blow the whistle on corporate incompetence and corruption often get destroyed.

Whistleblowers are usually employees – sometimes long time loyal employees – who know how systems and processes are supposed to run, and see that they are not being followed. They know when something is wrong. Within a company under a bad leader, *you could have many potential whistleblowers.* They are terrified to speak up. They feel powerless in the face of a leadership who has the ability to fire them and persecute them. Their livelihood, reputation and safety could be crushed. The risk is too high. If a corrupt or incompetent leadership identifies an individual as a threat, that person is isolated and extinguished and it isn't about right or wrong. It is all about leverage.

I don't blame these people for not blowing the whistle. There are insurmountable pressures that exist to prevent them from acting. Sometimes whistleblowers have to endure legal persecution and death threats. I understand why people do not step up.

So not only is this leadershit problem swelling, but the population of who is willing to take it on is shrinking.

We need to find a way to make it safe for whistleblowers to speak out. We have not been successful with this. We need a platform or an app or a safe zone for whistleblowers to speak out. Something that would firewall them from retribution and at the same time validate their perspective with co-workers to make sure it isn't a disgruntled employee lashing out. Giving the workers on the front line an opportunity to be safely heard is a powerful deterrent to leadershit.

Make the Leap

Everyone can agree at times that change is needed. That doesn't mean that it will happen. Change is hard. It is really the inability to persevere through chang*ing* that is the reason why kicking the can became the default solution in business. None of a leader's bonus is based on making appropriate and timely changes in the business model to avert disaster three to five years down the road, so what is the incentive?

When I was at JCI I spent a lot of time on strategic planning and implementing it and making it real. I did it because it was part of my job description and – call me old school – I guess I thought because I agreed to do it as part of my job, I thought maybe I should do it.

The good news is this: the script is already written. The recipe is on the website in black and white describing our corporate ideals, our corporate values and our corporate culture. Just do that.

I don't understand why this is so hard. We are not only off course; we are still riding along without noticing we've driven into the ditch.

Transparency is the New Black

In 2010 Congress passed a financial overhaul targeting the ever-increasing wage gap that threatens America's economy. The SEC was to require all publicly held companies to disclose the ratio of their CEO's pay to the median pay to all other employees. Why have we not heard of this? Because it took five years to for the SEC to push it through. In August of 2015, the SEC finally adopted the final rule requiring public companies to disclose the ratio of CEO compensation to the median compensation of its employees. There is a lot of flexibility built into the rule, but disclosure of pay ratios will not become mandatory until January 1, 2017.

Corporate executives have vehemently opposed this rule. They claimed it would be too costly to implement. Really? I will come in and do that damn math for free. I am pretty sure it would take me all of maybe 5 to 10 days to gather the numbers and then about 45 minutes to figure out that ratio. I'm pretty sure that the workers would fully cooperate.

That is not the real reason the rule was opposed. The real reason is that corporate executives know that the market is broken. They know that they are not really worth the salaries that they are being given. They will be publicly exposed in an apples-to-apples comparison of their massive income versus the income of their workers, and THAT will reflect negatively on them.

It will also shine the light on them in another way. Folks will start asking why a CEO deserves that kind of pay. What exactly is that CEO doing to deserve that pay? Who in the *WORLD* deserves that kind of pay? And the days of resting on their laurels will come to an end. It is a PR nightmare for any corporate executive. And we need to stop looking to the broken market to set the cadence for compensation. Compensation is not a function of the market. It has become a function of insanity.

Transparency and accountability are the only ways to fully understand what we are dealing with here. CEOs should be eager to reveal their salaries if those salaries are legitimate, but most of them are not. They are pumped up over-inflated balloons that need to be popped, and they know it.

I will be looking for two things between now and January 1, 2017:

1. Who will be early adopters and take it upon themselves to voluntarily expose their CEO compensation ratios.

2. Who will be in a mad rush to scrape off as much money to beat the January 1, 2017 deadline making it mandatory?

Both of those two things will be very telling with regard to corporate culture and leadershit.

Start the Revolution

On April 13, 2015, Dan Price, CEO of Gravity Payments announced that he was surrendering his $1million a year salary and opting to take $70,000 a year. The rest of the $1 million was used to elevate his employees' salaries. Nobody in his company was going to make less than $70,000 a year. This is revolutionary.

The following is an excerpt from the New York Times article of April 15, 2015: *"The market rate for me as a C.E.O. compared to a regular person is ridiculous, it's absurd," said Mr. Price. "As much as I'm a capitalist, there is nothing in the market that is making me do it," he said, referring to paying wages that make it possible for his employees to go after the American dream, buy a house and pay for their children's education.*

Price's idea for his employee pay increase was inspired by an article on happiness written by a pair of men, one of whom is a Nobel Prize-winning psychologist. Essentially, Price took an enormous cut in his salary to avoid having to increase his prices in order to pay his employees more and make them happy. This was totally voluntary on his part.

I consider this newsworthy and a remarkable gesture by a CEO, but this should not be so rare and extraordinary. What would our economy be like if *this was our normal?* I am not for redistribution, but I do believe that leadership pay is out of balance. This is the kind of radical thinking and true character needed to flip this system back and restore balance.

Several weeks after this article was published, the backlash for Price began. Some workers who were highly skilled or who had been there for some time felt that, after the raises were given, they were not sufficiently compensated relative to new or unskilled workers who were given similar paychecks. I might have approached this differently, but frequently the first step to any correction is over-correction. Despite Price's good intentions, there are clearly some bugs to be worked out.

Change comes with pain. Changing this system will be very difficult.

Build a Corporate Culture of Inclusion & Transparency

There are many competencies that seem to be part of the criteria for leadership selection these days that should not be. The ability to make headlines is not a valid competency. Having the right clothes, right hair, great smile are not competencies. An MBA from an Ivy League university is not a competency. Being a regular presenter at rubber chicken dinners is not a competency. Manipulating a spreadsheet is not a competency. Being a jagoff is not a competency.

There are other core competencies that do not seem to be considered when interviewing potential CEO's, but should be. These include: are they any good at learning from their mistakes; do they need to always be right? Do they have humility? How have they demonstrated trust, honesty and integrity? Do they possess a fearless attitude of responsibility for documented losses and failures as well as for victories?

Here is a short list of basic competencies found in any leadership 101 course, but which often seem to be mysteriously missing from the CEO hiring criteria:

1. *Yes, That's What I Said, But Not What I Meant*

The very best CEO's not only communicate effectively, they also follow up on the "trickle down" of their instructions to make sure nothing is lost in the translation down to the hourly wage earner. One team, one goal. If you cannot convey your vision to your team – your entire team – it will feel like you are herding cats, and it is your fault.

2. *Did You Hear About the Cat-Herding CEO?*

Files get lost. Customers leave. Websites crash. Mistakes happen. No company is immune to problems. Heavy-handed leadership, blaming and punishing will only add pressure to the problem and create a culture of fear, and as a leader, you will find yourself herding cats, and it is your fault. Being able to calmly learn from the mistakes and implement a course of correction for your team without panic and blame will go a long way toward morale and productivity. A well-timed sense of humor around certain issues will work wonders to bring about amendment, and make the event memorable enough that the problem probably won't happen again.

3. *I Cannot Tell a Lie*

The honesty and integrity of an authentic leader is contagious. As a CEO, you are responsible *for* and *to* a team of people who are taking a "read" from your leadership and energy. Transparency is important if you want followers to believe in you and see your true motivations. That is the foundation of good business culture. Words are hollow if they are not backed up by a leader's actions and true beliefs. For the right person, compensation is not just financial.

4. Do As I Say, Not As I Do

If you expect your team to be dedicated to the company mission, to work hard and produce quality service and/or products, then you had better be ready to walk your talk and light the way. When they see that you are committed as their leader, there is no greater motivation. If you are just saddling them up and cracking the whip, you are creating a culture of resentment. Be the beacon that shows them the way. Your reputation as a hard worker will go far if there is demonstrable evidence of that.

Boards...There Are Only So Many Advil on the Planet

First of all, it seems obvious, but the chairman of a corporation should not also be the same person as the CEO. I know it sounds cool to have both titles rocking it out on your letterhead simultaneously, but it's not. If someone's criteria for whether they want to come work for your organization is dependent on how many titles they get, move on to the next candidate.

I have never heard a rational argument to defend this arrangement. It flies right in the face of necessary board independence.

Second, there should be mandatory term limits for board members. As suggested before, I would build staggered boards with a maximum of two terms, or six years. Even the most committed to independence and responsibility can become compromised as relationships with corporate management develop over longer terms.

Third, if, God forbid, there is a chairman who is also a CEO, they should have absolutely no input or vote on electing or re-electing board members. That should be handled 100% by a nominating committee who is 100% independent. Period.

Fourth, the CEO should have no input on independent chairman selection and certainly no veto rights. Again, this should be handled 100% by a nominating committee who is 100% independent. Period.

Blow it Up and Start Over

I have never seen an underperforming company that was underperforming because of bad workers. In almost every case, it was fundamentally a result of the company's culture and systems; the very two things that come directly out of the executive suite. Generally, the workers are the ones busting their humps to make lemonade out of the lemons.

I'm from Southside Pittsburgh and I am not wired to punt. I cannot let this go. There is a way to turn this around. Whether it can be done before the whole thing comes crashing down is unclear, but giving up is not an option. This can has been kicked so many times now that what was once a snowball is now the size of a mountain.

Unfortunately, this book can only introduce you to the tip of the iceberg. There are more of these leadershit problems in our country than there are solutions at this point.

We don't need a tweak or a twist to make things all better. I'm calling for a big fix. Blow it up and rebuild it from the ground up. The good news is that we already have the blueprint. Just go do what you are supposed to do. Read your damn job description and your website and just do that.

It bothers me when people misbehave. What bothers me more is when the people who are in charge of them not misbehaving do nothing about it. Whether we like it or not, we are all part of this problem. We all have a responsibility to explore solutions.

We need to find authentic leaders whose personal agendas are secondary to the welfare and future health of their company and its people. As a nation, we need to find those leaders who see the very big picture of America at its best, and who truly comprehend that the only way we get there is through their honorable decisions and steering the huge corporate entities that are our country's economic drivers. Their level of integrity plays out in our success and our legacy as a nation.

Joe Public

Many people own stock and receive lots of prospectuses, notices, invitations to review and participate in quarterly revenue webcasts, etc. I suspect that you throw them in the garbage without reading them.

Today, with this "call to arms" fresh on your mind, pick up one of those notices and review it. You may be surprised to see a familiar name up for election on a board of directors. Then look at the other candidate names, who you don't know, and think how easy it would be to just Google them all and get a clue about what leaders your very own companies are hiring, their experience and what their track records are. It's a start toward educating yourself around the distinction between leadership and leadershit that is out there.

I realize nobody can know everything about every executive and board member on every company. Not many of us have the luxury of time to Google everyone. Another option might be that you vote "No" on proxy statements that recommend the election or re-election of any board member. While there may be legitimate candidates that get caught up in the wash, you can at least have a hand in wiping the slate clean and starting fresh.

If you had 100 bottles of aspirin and you found out that half are tainted, you would not play roulette and guess which ones are bad. You take them all down.

This is not a perfect plan since the people who nominated and voted in the board members in the first place can do it over again with new unknown candidates, but it sends a message.

Maybe...Just Maybe

When I was entering my 60s and my sons were turning 30, I officially told them that when I see you doing something that I think looks stupid, before I react, I will take a minute to first determine if it looks stupid because I'm 60 and they are 30 and my senior citizen prism just cannot process what is normal to them, or it looks stupid because it is stupid.

As a card-carrying member of the AARP, it is my birth right to be a bit critical of the generation that follows mine, as is the case with preceding generations. Just like the Baby Boomers caused quite a stir back in the 1960s and 1970s, the Millennials are now shaking up the nation's perspective on a lot of fronts.

As Millennials inevitably make their way into the workplaces of America, there are some traits that I see in their generation that make me shake my head. While I may not always know what to think of them, it is possible that the Millennials just might usher in a correction to today's leadershit system.

I have many occasions to converse with various Millennials – as a mentor, advisor and as a dad. Each one has shared with me their priorities for their quality of life, and it is different than mine and probably most Baby Boomers. Most in my generation translate the Millennials' interpretation of quality of life as "work less and play more."

But I have come to understand that we could be very wrong in our judgment of Millennials. What they really probably mean is that they do want to be productive and accomplished, but just as importantly, they want to work at a company where the belief system, the culture, the environment is one that they enjoy. First and foremost because the company has a righteous purpose, and as a result of fulfilling that purpose, it is profitable. This is vastly different than focusing on a company whose purpose is to make a profit.

Under the umbrella of their quality of life aspiration is to be part of an organization that operates with sound values and principles, many of which are consistent with those they have adopted to use in guiding their personal lives. When asking what the components would be of such an organization, many of them mentioned that there would be leadership that earned the trust and respect of their team through words and actions.

It seems that Millennials, in general, are doing more research on potential employers to determine if they are a cultural fit for a company. They are interested in knowing which organizations are walking the talk and which ones are just talking.

Consequently, if Millennials put such a high priority on ethical and moral practices when seeking out their employment, companies will be forced to adopt that kind of culture in order to compete for the best and brightest talent in the up-and-coming generation. They will also be more limited in selecting candidates for leaders who will gel with that type of culture.

I can see this type of change being more of an evolution than a revolution as it will happen more organically and take place over a greater period of time. I am rooting for the next generations to clean up the leadershit system that my generation left behind. As they grow into our nation's next workforce and leaders, I urge them to accept nothing less than authentic leadership.

Hope

After we tackled our church's financial crisis and it appeared that the difficult changes that were made turned things around for the parish, I was approached by one of our parishioners. He wanted to thank me for the role I played to help get things in a better place.

He said, "You know, things looked very bleak. Our future was in serious doubt."

While there are no guarantees about the long term plan that is in place for our church, the parishioners now have all that they needed to motivate us all. We have hope.

Hope is huge.

From Patrick to Rande

"This is Patrick from the Ethics Workshop last night. I wanted to email you to thank you. What you do to give back to RMU is motivating. Not only what you teach us as students in business, but the fact that you are giving back says a lot about you. I learned so much last night about the business world, it opened my eyes and in a good way. What you had to say really motivated me to continue away from that path of least resistance; to continue traveling that harder, yet ethical path.

Aside from the workshop and scholarship that you put in place, I must thank you for our conversation. I learned more in that hour and a half than I have in the last two years. I must say you really showed me a different aspect of looking at things and I now take it to heart. I couldn't stop thinking about the things you taught me last night and I can promise you I will hold onto those ideas and principles. . . . When you described certain ways that you think or different aspects of your life, I must admit I saw a lot of myself in you. Without sounding unprofessional, I wanted to tell you that what you stand for and who you are is what I really strive for in my future. You showed me last night that it is in fact possible. So, thank you, sir.

I look to take what I learned to implement not only in SAM or my future career, but just life in general.

Good luck with your book. I look forward to reading it. If there is anything I can do for you or there is anything you need, please feel free to contact me. I sent you a Linkedin invitation. I hope to see you on there.

Thanks you again, Mr. Somma

Best Regards,

Patrick"

Can't Deposit That in Your Checking Account

As long as Patrick was committed to not selling out to the leadershit system, as long as he was determined to hold fast to his honor and integrity regardless of the consequences, the more of an authentic leader he will be, and the more he will likely experience that lonely feeling.

I sent a message to Patrick to encourage him to stay the course. I also told him to always walk the talk.

What I received from Patrick and others like him is much more than he ever got from me, and I am grateful for the opportunity to know him and other good people working hard to improve their circumstances, the circumstances of their families, their communities and this country.

It gives me a glimmer of hope that maybe we don't have to settle for leadershit.

AUTHOR'S BIOGRAPHY

Currently, Rande Somma is President of RANDE SOMMA & ASSOCIATES; a company with a primary focus on leadership coaching and development.

Rande has over 40 years of business experience, primarily in the global automotive industry.

Prior to joining JOHNSON CONTROLS, INC, Rande was employed at ROCKWELL INTERNATIONAL'S AUTOMOTIVE DIVISION, serving in a variety of leadership positions in Purchasing, Sales and Manufacturing.

Rande departed JOHNSON CONTROLS, INC. after a 15-year career in the Fortune 500 Company's Automotive Systems Group. While at JOHNSON CONTROLS, after assuming a number of positions of increasing responsibility in Sales & Marketing, Global Strategic Planning and President of North American Operations, Rande was elected a Corporate Officer. Soon after, he was named President of the Automotive Systems Group's Operations-Worldwide.

In a company with annual revenue of $20 billion, Rande's responsibilities included the leadership of:

- Over 250 manufacturing facilities located in 26 countries
- 5 regional Technical Centers located in the United States, Europe, Japan and China
- 75,000 employees worldwide

During his tenure, the company reported record sales and earnings, as well as receiving over 40 Customer, Industry and Community awards.

While President, Rande was a member of the General Motors, Ford and Daimler-Chrysler Supplier Advisory Councils.

Rande has served as a Chairman, Vice-Chairman and a member of several corporate boards of directors. He is a past Vice- Chairman of the Michigan Minority Business Development Council. Rande has also served on boards of non-profit and charitable organizations.

Rande is a native of Pittsburgh, Pennsylvania where he attended and graduated from Robert Morris University with a Bachelor of Science degree in Business Administration, and was invited back to deliver the commencement speech to the Business School's Master's and Doctorate Graduates, class of 2015.

Today, Rande is a member of the University's Presidents Council and the Business School's Board of Visitors. Additionally, Rande is a recipient of Robert Morris University's Heritage Award, which is the university's most prestigious recognition, honoring a graduate for distinguished service and extraordinary accomplishments.

Rande is also an honorary member of The National Society of Collegiate Scholars and an honorary inductee in Beta Gamma Sigma's International Honors Society for collegiate business schools.

With a focus on giving back, Rande and his wife Georgia are the founders and underwriters of Robert Morris University's Business School's "Integrity First" Scholarships. Established in 2008, scholarships are awarded annually to students based on the demonstration of their understanding of the critical importance of ethical and moral behavior as well as the value of integrity in business.

Rande has devoted a great deal of his time mentoring individual university students and sharing his professional insights in the classroom, school offices, coffee houses, via phone, and at his kitchen table.

Rande continues to make himself available to share his professional experiences and knowledge with students and young professionals in a mentoring role.

Rande and his wife, Georgia, have been awarded the Order of St Sava. Presented by the Patriarch, it is the highest award presented by the Serbian Orthodox Church.

To get in touch with the author, Rande Somma:

dothrtthing@gmail.com

CPSIA information can be obtained
at www.ICGtesting.com
Printed in the USA
LVHW040432130123
737041LV00002B/256